GENDER AND THE DISMAL SCIENCE

GENDER AND THE DISMAL SCIENCE

WOMEN

in the

EARLY YEARS

of the

ECONOMICS PROFESSION

———

ANN MARI MAY

Columbia University Press
New York

Columbia University Press
Publishers Since 1893
New York   Chichester, West Sussex
cup.columbia.edu

Library of Congress Cataloging-in-Publication Data
Names: May, Ann Mari, 1956– author.
Title: Gender and the dismal science : women in the early years of the
economics profession / Ann Mari May.
Description: New York : Columbia University Press, [2022] |
Includes bibliographical references and index.
Identifiers: LCCN 2021058020 (print) | LCCN 2021058021 (ebook) |
ISBN 9780231192903 (hardback) | ISBN 9780231192910 (trade paperback) |
ISBN 9780231550048 (ebook)
Subjects: LCSH: Feminist economics—United States. | Women—Economic
conditions. | Women—Employment—United States. | Equality—United States.
Classification: LCC HQ1381 .M38 2022 (print) | LCC HQ1381 (ebook) |
DDC 330.0820973—dc23/eng/20220103
LC record available at https://lccn.loc.gov/2021058020
LC ebook record available at https://lccn.loc.gov/2021058021

Columbia University Press books are printed on permanent
and durable acid-free paper.
Printed in the United States of America

Cover design: Noah Arlow
Cover image: Getty Images

FOR MY SON, MICHAEL MAY

CONTENTS

PREFACE

The genesis of this book began in the archives of the American Economic Association (AEA). I was visiting the archives in search of information on the organizational structure of the association in the early years when I came across a folder referring to "trouble." Somehow, I knew this would involve a woman, and sure enough—it did.

The file contained communication between the first editor of the *American Economic Review* (*AER*), a female author whose book was reviewed in the inaugural issue, and a male reviewer. Following the threads of these exchanges revealed much about gender and the profession in the early years of the field and about the challenges facing women economists.

As I began to research the topic of women in the early years of the economics profession, it became clear to me that much of the work on the history of women and economics had been primarily biographical rather than empirical. The fact that there were so few women economists, along with the fact that many scholars in this male-dominated profession had little knowledge of or interest in the history of women in the field, limited what we knew about women and about the role of gender in the profession in the early years. Using the AEA archives along with published material in the *AER* and the *Quarterly Journal of*

Economics (QJE), I was drawn to the task of adding an empirical layer to our knowledge about women and the profession and blending what we can garner from data with biographical and historical accounts.

The chapters in this book use novel data sets to offer new information on the proportion of women members in the AEA, their backgrounds, and their limited role in the association's work in its first sixty-three years of existence. At the same time, they provide information on the "old boy network" in publishing—in monographs and in scholarly journals such as the *AER* and the *QJE*. The analysis reveals much about important elements of what we might refer to as networking among economists and the determinants of success in the increasingly pivotal realm of publishing. When examining the likelihood of publishing more than one article in these journals, we can understand how important it would be for authors and editors to share the same institution in their doctoral training. How important would it be that authors and editors share current institutional affiliation? Most interesting, how important would it be for authors who had earned their doctoral degrees from institutions where editors were currently located, and did this bode well or work to the detriment of hopeful authors?

Another overlooked aspect of the history of women in economics concerns differentiating between the institutional barriers facing Black women and white women. Because Black women faced significant barriers to entry as students in higher education, which then resulted in a lack of sufficient numbers for separate empirical analysis, it became important to explicitly examine these institutional barriers and Black women's role in higher education and the labor market. In particular, I examine Black women's lack of access to the Seven Sisters institutions that were so important in carving out a space for white women in economics, as well as their options for education in public institutions.

This research, particularly the archival sources used and the data assembled, would not have been possible without the support of many individuals. I begin by expressing my gratitude to my editor at Columbia University Press, Christian P. Winting. His understanding of the unique nature of this project, expert advice, and encouragement made the process all the more rewarding. I also thank all the members of the Columbia University Press team who generously offered their expertise along the way, including Kathryn Jorge, and Laura Poole for her careful copyediting.

I also acknowledge the kind assistance of the librarians and archivists who generously offered their time and expertise. Most helpful were the staff of the Rare Book and Manuscript Library at Duke University, where the AEA archives are now located. Over many years, Brooke Guthrie has generously provided her time, and I greatly appreciate her kind assistance. Rachel Provost Layher (Duke University 2011) and Juan Carvajalino (postdoc Fellow of the Center for the History of Political Economics at Duke University), provided valuable research assistance in the early stages of this project.

Many other librarians and archivists offered their valuable assistance, including Sarah Hutcheon, research librarian at the Schlesinger Library at Radcliffe College, and Brenden McDermott of the Boston University Library, both of whom provided information on women doctoral graduates, despite the challenges that COVID-19 presented to access. At the University of Nebraska–Lincoln, Signe Bourdreau and Suping Lu offered helpful suggestions and assistance obtaining needed sources along with Josh Caster of the UNL Archives.

Many of the students who took my courses on gender and social provisioning provided research assistance in collecting information on books and articles published by women economists, their doctoral degrees, and the home institutions of economists publishing in the early years. They provided countless hours of tedious but important work, and I am grateful to many undergraduate students. In particular, I relied most on Naomi Atughonu, Clinton Bartek, Allison Black, Taylor Bolam, Darren Brinkerhoff, Jay Byrd, Gabriel Fox, Connor McCoy, Emily Murphy, Giselle Nevarez, Manav Nirmalraj, Emily Noesen, Jennifer Pitsch, Sarah Rakes, Madeline Vavricek, and Rebecca Volten as well as graduate students Kari Eller, Zoe Mays, Joe Sandow, and Andrew Sorensen. Without their assistance populating spreadsheets, the analysis on publishing in the early years would not have been possible. Likewise, I thank my colleague Eric Thompson and the Bureau of Business

Research for providing needed research assistance through their Scholar's Program.

My deepest gratitude goes out to my colleagues throughout the profession who have inspired and enlightened me on the women who came before us as well as the history of the discipline. My occasional coauthor Robert Dimand has been a source of amazement for his depth of knowledge about economists in the early years of the profession. He has been delightful to work with on several projects, and I thank him for his contributions to our work and to the field. Likewise, I thank Mary Ann Dzubeck of Washington University in St. Louis for her careful research on the topic and support over the years. Mary Ann has always provided generously of her time when called on to read a proposal or section of a paper, and I appreciate our continued friendship.

I am also indebted to David Colander for his support, which brought me to Middlebury College as a visiting faculty member. At Middlebury, I found wonderful colleagues and friends, and the college's support of my research helped me in the initial stages to develop the topic through their support of a symposium on the subject of "the woman problem" in economics. Thanks also go to the faculty of Center for the History of Political Economics at Duke University for their kind invitation to give a seminar on women in the early years of the economics profession and what the AEA archives might reveal about their challenges. I offer special thanks to Günseli Berik and the faculty of the University of Utah for their invitation to present my early results on women and membership in the AEA and for helpful comments and suggestions.

I am most grateful to my colleagues Danny Tannenbaum, Brenden Timpe, and Mary McGarvey at the University of Nebraska–Lincoln. Although the data for many of the chapters for this book were collected over several years, this past year offered the solitude to write each chapter. Frequent meetings with Danny and Brenden offered a welcome respite from that solitude and opportunity to discuss our research, and Danny, in particular, willingly reviewed the econometric analysis in several chapters, offering his expertise on how best to explain the model. I am grateful to my new colleagues for their friendship, interest, and generous support.

I am most grateful to my dear friend Mary McGarvey, who has been a longtime coauthor in our examination of gender in the economics profession. We have examined differences in labor market outcomes for women in red versus blue states, gender differences in the views of male and female economists in the United States and the European Union, and the views of editors of economics journals on critiques of the discipline, among other topics. She is an econometrician of exceptional talent who has learned from experience the importance of better understanding the role that gender plays in the profession. For most of our careers, we have been the only two women tenure-track faculty in our department and have learned much from that experience. I am deeply grateful for her friendship and for her contributions to the econometric analysis used in this study.

Finally, I thank my son, Michael May, for his kind encouragement and loving support. He, more than anyone, has understood the challenges that women face working in a STEM field like economics. His no-nonsense clarity on these challenges, as they move from historical analysis to lived experience and back again, provided me with the inspiration to complete this project.

1

CURRENT CHALLENGES, HISTORICAL ORIGINS

The American Economic Association (AEA), and indeed the public at large, is slowly awakening to a problem in the discipline of economics. According to the *New York Times*, "The economics profession is facing a mounting crisis of sexual harassment, discrimination, and bullying that women in the field say has pushed many of them to the sidelines—or out of the field entirely."[1] As writers for *The Economist* put it, "Something is broken within the market for economists, and the profession has moved only belatedly and partially to address it. A lack of inclusivity is not simply a problem in itself, but a contributor to other troubles within the field."[2]

As the premier professional association for economics in the United States, the AEA has seemingly got the message that the gender problem in the dismal science is profound and measurable. As women like Janet Yellen shattered the glass ceiling of public service as the first woman chair of the Federal Reserve Board and first woman to serve as secretary of the Treasury, attention is now turning to the halls of ivy. Among the questions being asked are how can we document the challenges facing a variety of women in the field of economics? What are the costs of this lack of gender balance in the field? What are the institutional barriers preventing women from participating equally and fully in the discipline? What additional racial barriers prevent women of color from participating equally and fully? How deep are the historical roots of the gender problem in economics, and what can we learn about this problem by better understanding this history?

THE GENDER PROBLEM IN ECONOMICS

Although women have made significant progress in certain STEM (science, technology, engineering, and mathematics) fields, evidence suggests that there has been little progress in bringing women into economics since 2000. As of 2018, among the social sciences we find that women earn over 60 percent of doctoral degrees in psychology, anthropology, and sociology. In economics, only 32 percent of doctorates are awarded to women.[3]

Not only are there few women receiving doctorates in economics, studies show underrepresentation of women at all levels of the academic hierarchy. In economics departments with doctoral programs, 28.4 percent of assistant professors were women, 25.8 percent of associate professors were women, and a startlingly low 14.3 percent of full professors were women as of 2018.[4]

Further evidence shows that men are overrepresented in particular disciplines or fields and in elite PhD programs.[5] Looking at a variety of measures, Kim A. Weeden, Sarah Thébaud and Dafna Gelbgiser find extensive gender segregation by field in doctoral programs. Their findings suggest that over a third of male or female doctorates would need to change fields for men and women to earn the same proportions of PhDs in all fields. Importantly, they also found considerable male overrepresentation in top decile programs. In their words, "male overrepresentation in the top decile programs is quite strong in Economics, where men are overrepresented by a factor of 1.27." As status rises in economics programs, women are increasingly absent in those halls of ivy.[6]

As disappointing as the numbers are for women generally in the discipline of economics, the representation of women of color is simply inadequate and unacceptable. Amanda Bayer and Cecilia Rouse indicate that only eleven minority women (African American, Hispanic, and Native American) earned doctorates in economics in 2014. While about 30 percent of the U.S. population is identified as Black or Hispanic, only 6.3 percent of tenured and tenure-track faculty in economics are identified as such.[7]

Today, women faculty in economics are less likely to earn tenure and less likely to be promoted to full professor than their male colleagues are. Evidence suggests that women are half as likely as men to be promoted to full professor within seven years of earning tenure, and controlling for productivity and family status (such as childlessness and being single) does little to change the size of this difference.[8] Explaining at least part of the difficulty is the reality that women-authored papers take an average of six months longer to get published. In her analysis of 9,000 articles in four leading economics journals, Erin Hengel argues that women authors in economics are held to higher standards by reviewers, perhaps due to unconscious bias during the peer review process. In Hengel's words, "Spending more time revising old research means spending less time conducting new research. Fewer papers results in fewer promotions, possibly driving women into fairer fields."[9]

With continuing pressure to publish, coauthorship is an increasingly important aspect of scholarship. Evidence suggests that women tend to write single-author articles significantly more than men in economics and that coauthorship in economics is more likely to occur in same-sex groupings—men are more likely to coauthor with other men and women are more likely to coauthor with other women.[10] With fewer women in the discipline than men, the result is that coauthorship is made more difficult for women. Moreover, women who coauthor research with a male colleague find that their contributions are diminished. Examining tenure decisions in academia, Heather Sarsons finds that an additional coauthored paper is correlated with an 8 percentage point increase in tenure probability for men but only a 2 percentage point increase for women—a gap that is less pronounced if the coauthor is a woman rather than a man. As she notes, this suggests that credit attribution is related to the gender mix of coauthors.[11]

Economists have only recently become aware of the lack of women in economics. Yet the position of privilege of most white men in economics is reflected in countless examples in the early years of the twentieth century. While some were at least somewhat sensitive to the challenges that this might present, many others were not.

In the first issue of the *American Economic Review* (*AER*) published in 1911, Davis R. Dewey, then editor, acknowledged that he was in part prompted to allow a woman author the space for a published reply to a negative review because he was aware that there was a suspicion that he was attempting to silence her "on the ground that she was a woman."[12] In the 1920s, Eleanor Lansing Dulles was pursuing a doctorate from Radcliffe College. While revising her dissertation in Paris, she was visited by economists Robert Murray Haig and James Harvey Rogers of Columbia University. In their conversation, reported by Dulles in her memoir, Haig and Rogers suggested that they could do more with her research notes than she could and that she should turn over her notes so they could "carry on your work as part of our comprehensive project." Dulles refused.[13]

Anne P. Carter reminisced over her experiences entering the profession in 1945. She remembers that the chair of her department at Harvard University, H. H. Burbank, welcomed her with the statement, "we get a lot of little girls who come here with good grades, but they don't last." Although he apologized for his comments a few days later, Carter cites many instances of unequal treatment—such as when she was recruited by Wassily Leontief to join his Harvard Economic Research Project only to learn that her "trailing spouse," who was kindly allowed to join as well to make her move possible, was being paid $1,000 more a year than was she. When confronted, Leontief remarked, "I thought you'd like it."[14]

Despite the rather long history of gender imbalance, unequal treatment, and lack of equal access, the AEA did not adopt principles disavowing sex discrimination in the profession until 1971. At that time, they established a committee to collect information on the number of women in economics in colleges and universities in the United States and make recommendations for affirmative action to address the lack of women in the field.[15] Prompted by grassroots efforts of the Women's Caucus, a series of resolutions were brought to an all-male AEA Executive Committee.[16] According to Myra Strober, the opening statement which began, "Resolved that the American Economic Association declares that economics is not a man's field," was amended to insert "not exclusively." The resolutions offered were adopted, and the Committee on the Status of Women in the Economics Profession (CSWEP) was established.[17] Despite the committee's continued existence, the gender problem remains.[18]

WHY SO FEW . . .

Various approaches have been offered to explain the paucity of women as faculty in higher education, particularly in the research university. Human capital theories explaining labor market differences between men and women, such as those offered by Jacob Mincer and Gary Becker, tend to focus on supply-side factors.[19] Specifically, this approach suggests that women invest less in their human capital because of expected interruptions to their work life for child-rearing. Using this framework, Claudia Goldin, Lawrence Katz, and Ilyana Kuziemko studied women and higher education in the twentieth century. They argued that closing the gender gap in enrollment can be attributed to changes in women's expectations of future labor market involvement and rising age at first marriage.[20] According to this view, the lack of women's representation as faculty after World War II is limited by the small proportion of women earning doctoral degrees—a result based in good part on women's calculated decisions.

In contrast, institutional discrimination theorists argue that dominant status groups engage in practices to maintain their privileged positions in the workplace.[21] According to this view, particular production practices are chosen to maximize the rent of individuals—so-called insiders, who are currently involved in the production process. Moreover, the dominant status group may use increasingly elaborate screening mechanisms to control access to the most desirable jobs.[22] In academia, this form of discrimination can be reflected in the standards and rituals of scholarly conduct that affect hiring and promotion.[23]

Although these explanations help us understand the lack of women faculty in higher education in general, they do not explain why some STEM fields have made progress while others have been slower to advance. Evidence from the examination of other STEM fields by Sarah Thébaud and Maria Charles suggests that the interplay of individual traits with the broader sociological environment in which they develop may explain a great deal about why women have been accepted in some fields and not others.[24] According to this view, Western cultural stereotypes about the nature of STEM work and STEM workers and "the intrinsic qualities of men and women" are powerful determinants driving the views of women and men, shaping their aptitudes, aspirations, and affinities.[25] In other words, Thébaud and Charles argue that cultural gender stereotypes associated with people and jobs reproduce occupational segregation.

These stereotypes, however, have important implications for status. For instance, Laurie Rudman, Corinne A. Moss-Racusin, Julie E. Phelan and Sanne Nauts demonstrate that the traits identified as masculine and that men are supposed to possess are high status (for example, competitiveness), whereas the traits that women are supposed to possess are neutral in status (for example, friendliness). At the other end of the spectrum, the traits that men are not supposed to have (such as being emotional) are low in status, and the traits that women are not supposed to possess (such as aggression) are high in status. According to Rudman and colleagues, gender conformity translates into a status advantage for men, but not for women.[26]

These gender stereotypes vary from discipline to discipline and may be reinforced by disciplinary dogma as well as expressed in rituals and practice. It seems quite possible that a discipline such as economics, which has put perfect competition at the pinnacle of economic thought, might be most likely to value competition as a personal attribute. In other words, in this situation, gender stereotypes validate masculinist academic cultures that express themselves in the assumptions embedded in a theoretical framework.

In such a culture, practices, norms, and academic rituals will reflect these stereotypes and may influence the scope of what is acceptable in terms of research and overall perspectives. As Linda Hutcheon, former president of the Modern Language Association, has pointed out, the mode of professional discourse adopted by what she refers to as the "adepts in the higher learning" most clearly mimics the competitive model of the market.[27] The adopted mode of discourse, she points out, is one of combat and conflict—which is perhaps nowhere as evident as that of the discipline occupied with rationalizing competition: economics. As anyone who has ever attended the AEA annual meetings will observe, individuals present "arguments," which are typically attacked by "discussants," followed by questions that often are not really questions but statements intended to demonstrate the intellectual prowess and status of the questioner. Instead, Hutcheon points out, we could envision an entirely different mode of discourse based on thoughtful exchanges constructively intended to expand discussion, perhaps build consensus, or contribute to the full exposition of a topic.[28]

In the end, masculine cultures send a signal to women, resulting in a lower sense of belonging and attachment to the discipline. What may be unique about economics might be related to the subject matter, and the resulting interactions may reinforce gender differences, making it less likely that women will be found in this discipline.

Is there really a masculinist culture in the discipline of economics that contributes to the gender problem? Growing evidence supports the suggestion that there is. At the encouragement of Janet Yellen, the AEA recently conducted a survey of more than 45,000 economists to better understand the climate for women and minorities in economics.[29] The survey results were nothing less than stunning. When asked about whether women are respected in the field of economics, only 16 percent of women surveyed agreed or strongly agreed, while about half of men agreed. When asked about the overall climate in the field of economics, only 20 percent of women indicated that they were satisfied with the climate while twice as many men indicated that they were satisfied. Perhaps most devastating, when asked if they agreed or disagreed with the statement, "I feel valued within the field of economics," only 25 percent of women agreed or strongly agreed with this statement. A full 75 percent of women did not.[30]

Of course, there is a tendency to believe that there is some inexorable march toward equality that allows those with talent to succeed and those with bias to fade away. According to this view, the problem lies in older male faculty who will (perhaps not soon enough for some) eventually retire and make room for more fair-minded colleagues. However, recent research by Alice Wu cautions us to think otherwise.[31] Wu used content analysis and econometrics to analyze a much-read anonymous job rumor graduate student forum in economics, obtaining data for a six-year period. Her analysis showed an environment where women economists were frequently described in often sexual terms such as " hotter," "hot," "attractive," and "beautiful," along with references to "tits," while male economists were described using terms such as "motivated," "brilliant," and "keen." Obviously, many in the profession were horrified.[32]

Wu's study and views from those experiencing a workplace culture firsthand as documented in the AEA survey prompt most of us to acknowledge the existence of a gender problem in the discipline of economics. At the same time, there are additional concerns that should prompt us further—concerns about promoting better public policy.

. . . AND WHY IT MATTERS

In general, there is growing evidence that diversity in teams is beneficial for problem solving. Katherine W. Phillips, Columbia University psychology professor, and her colleagues examined this issue, and their results were revealing. They found that individuals are, on average, likely to do more preparation for any exercise if they know it will involve working with a diverse, rather than a homogeneous group. The researchers explain that a wider range of alternatives is likely to be debated in a diverse group. They found that diversity encourages people in the majority to think more critically about the issues on which they are working. Not surprisingly, they conclude that a diverse group will more likely generate better results than a homogeneous one will.[33]

Likewise, those advocating for greater gender balance in problem-solving teams often tacitly presume that women need to be included at the table when research is conducted and when policy is debated because they bring a different perspective, perhaps as a result of their unique social location and experiences. The question remains: is this true? Should our concern with gender balance be confined to the not unimportant desire for equality of opportunity or does a lack of gender balance have a deleterious effect on public policy? If women have views on economic policy that are different than those of their male colleagues, how do we evaluate the cost of this exclusion and marginalization?

New research indicates that there are indeed marked differences in the views of similarly trained male and female economists in the United States and other countries in Europe.[34] A wide-ranging survey of economists with doctoral degrees working in the United States finds that although there are shared views on core precepts, methodology, and some areas of economic policy, there are important differences in views between male and female economists as well. Controlling for type of current employment and degree vintage, these similarly trained male and female economists hold different views in three of four policy areas examined—areas that include market solutions versus government intervention; government spending, taxes, and redistribution; and gender and equal opportunity.

Overall, women economists were found to be less supportive of market solutions over government interventions than were their male counterparts. Specifically, women economists were less likely than their male colleagues to support the use of educational vouchers, to support drilling for oil in the Arctic National Wildlife Refuge, and to believe that the United States has an excessive amount of government regulation of economic activity. In addition to these differences, male and female economists in the United States differ in their views on so-called compassion issues. Women economists were more likely to believe that the distribution of income should be made more equal and that employers should be required to provide health insurance for their full-time employees. The survey also showed that male economists were more likely to see the harmful effects of increases in the minimum wage on unemployment.[35] A similar survey of European economists in academic institutions found similar results.[36]

As these studies suggest, if similarly trained male and female economists have different views on economic issues, there is empirical evidence that supports the notion that a lack of women in economics will skew public policy debates that involve economists and fail to provide a full and robust examination of issues of importance to both men and women. When visualizing the average economics department in research institutions, one might legitimately pose the question: is it any wonder we have not yet solved the problem of affordable child care or the gender wage gap when the discipline of economics is so dominated by men? There are significant and perhaps growing public policy issues that remain unresolved and call for robust examination. Yet with so few women directing dissertation research, serving on editorial boards, and having an authoritative voice in public policy, how can a genuinely robust discussion take place?

To better understand the current dilemma facing women in the dismal science, we need to understand the historical roots of this imbalance. What does new evidence suggest about the role of women in the discipline of economics in its formative years? How did growing efforts to professionalize a new discipline limit women's inclusion? To what extent were women active in writing monographs and books in the early years, and how did the emergence of the academic journal affect women's ability to participate in the production of knowledge and influence their career trajectories? What role have institutional factors played in replicating this imbalance, and what can the history of these early years teach us about how women have been excluded in economics?

GENDER AND THE
PROFESSIONALIZATION OF ECONOMICS

Historians and sociologists of the professions have often neglected the degree to which gender and the drive for professional status have played a large role in shaping the actions and priorities of institutions, disciplines, and professional associations.[37] While organized occupations are often acknowledged as acting in their own economic self-interest, as Magali Sarfatti Larson points out, the ethics of disinterestedness claimed by professions has acquitted them of the profit motive.[38] Nonetheless, in her discussion of the rise of professions, Larson sets out to examine how professions organized themselves to gain market power. She sees professionalization as the process by which "producers of special services sought to constitute and control a market for their expertise."[39] In this framework, the conflict and struggle about who shall be included or excluded in the work of a profession is framed and made salient.

What is unique about newly emerging professions, then, is not that they were actually disinterested in financial considerations—they certainly were not and are not—but that they successfully asserted autonomy over their own standards. In another landmark study of the medical profession, Eliot Freidson points out that what is unique about a profession from other occupations is that it is given the right to control its own work. As Freidson sees it, professions are "*deliberately* granted autonomy, including the exclusive right to determine who can legitimately do its work and how the work should be done."[40] Larson sees this autonomy as the source of professional power. In Larson's words, "The singular characteristic of professional power is, however, that the profession has the exclusive privilege of defining both the content of its knowledge and the legitimate conditions of access to it, *while the unequal distribution of knowledge protects and enhances this power.*"[41]

This autonomy has several implications: it insulates members of a profession from criticism, allowing them to "live within ideologies of their own creation, which they present to the outside as the most valid definitions of specific spheres of social reality."[42] At the same time, this autonomy gives members control over who has access to a profession. As a result, this autonomy allowed economists to shape the contours of a discipline in such a manner as to emphasize the virtues of a free market while excluding women from participation in the market for academic labor.[43]

The most important aspect of control over who is allowed to participate as an academic economist revolves around graduate training. As sociologists of the professions have argued, formal training is critical and is what binds professionals together. In other words, "cognitive standardization appears to be one crucial, if not the most crucial, variable in the sequence which, passing through the rise of monopolistic centers of training, leads to credentialized professionalization and market control."[44] This explains why early arguments about the dangers of too much education for women must be viewed less in terms of scientific imperative and more in terms of political economy and self-interest.

Control over "certified knowledge" was perhaps a necessary but not a sufficient condition for professionalization and market control. As Larson points out, knowledge alone was not sufficient to "establish the superiority of trained professionals vis-à-vis their rivals."[45] What was required was the "conquest and assertion of social status"—social status acquired by institutions with their own graduate programs, faculty with doctorates (not just honorary doctorates), and in fact a cadre of full-time academic professionals generating knowledge.[46] Because social status was to be acquired, anything that led to diminished status—such as disagreements on what constitutes knowledge and participation by demographic groups that had reduced social status—was to be avoided.

One of the important factors facilitating social status in the academic professions was the emergence of professional associations such as the AEA, established in 1885. In contrast to other professional associations, such as the American Chemical Society, that were closed to women, the AEA was open to women members from its inception.[47] Yet the AEA served an important role as gatekeeper in many ways, and its leadership had a profound influence, shaping and limiting opportunities for women in the field.

The AEA was an important vehicle for facilitating agreement within the profession on questions where widespread and sometime vehement disagreement existed. Moreover, it provided a forum for settling what Andrew Abbott has called "jurisdictional disputes."[48] In the early years of the AEA, economists were engaged in shaping the contours of their discipline and thus attempting to clarify the difference between economics and sociology and why one was authoritative and based on "hard science" and the other was "soft" and open to interpretation. As news accounts of early annual meetings demonstrated, sociologists and historians report being marginalized in that process.[49]

The annual meetings helped bring professionals together to work at defining these contours and develop a consensus where there was often an embarrassing lack of one. As A. W. Coats argues, the AEA annual meetings provided an opportunity for economists to meet, air their differences, and hopefully come to a reasonable consensus on important issues of the day.[50] Disagreement diminished professional status, thus the annual meeting was an important mechanism for elevating the status of the profession.

The annual meeting also provided an opportunity for those who could travel (which often excluded women) an opportunity for sharing information about jobs and professional opportunities. Professors often paraded their most promising graduate students, bringing them to these meetings in an effort to secure the most advantageous occupational outcomes for them. This not only benefited the students but elevated the status of the advisor.[51]

The AEA further worked to organize knowledge production through its sponsorship of academic journals—another outlet for sharing knowledge and demonstrating the serviceability of an institution. According to Frederick Rudolph, publication had become the guiding interest of the new academician as well as a basis for the informal annual page count in which university presidents indulged.[52] By the end of the nineteenth century, teaching alone would not suffice. As the president of the University of Chicago explained, "The University, I say, will be patient, but it expects from every man honest and persistent effort in the direction of contribution to the world's knowledge."[53]

The academic association provided another layer of potential status elevation in its selection of officers and editorial board members, who were chosen to engage in this "service to the profession." If one had no institutional affiliation, as was often the case for women, or an affiliation without a graduate program and thus less status, one was less useful in this service.

Women faced significant obstacles in obtaining an academic position. Although popular arguments against women's intellectual capacity and fitness for scholarly pursuits had subsided by the turn of the century, more subtle notions of academic identity continued to shape women's careers at the beginning of the twentieth century. Women had worked to gain admittance into institutions of higher learning but were increasingly segmented into disciplines thought to be appropriate for them. Women in the social sciences occupied a particularly ambiguous location. Already involved in charitable and reform activities, in the words of Dorothy Ross, women were "a natural constituency for the social sciences," yet women's presence in the early stages of professionalization threatened the acquisition of status and authority of male professionals in the field.[54] It is little wonder then, that women economists, particularly those whose work crossed the borders of several disciplines, found their professional lives complicated and their ability to gain acceptance limited.

Although several elite universities continued to exclude women from their graduate programs and from serving as faculty, many state universities had, often out of necessity, moved on, accepting women in their graduate programs. However, gaining acceptance as a consumer of knowledge was more easily accomplished than gaining acceptance as a producer of knowledge. Apart from the critically important role that women played as faculty in women's colleges (a role that provided many women their only access to the halls of ivy), women lacked the institutional affiliations necessary for full participation in the burgeoning new profession.

Overall, the drive toward professionalization interacted with gender in ways that often undermined women academics, allowing the profession to overlook a natural constituency and postponing the inclusion of women in this important field of inquiry. The difficulties encountered by women in the early years provide important insights into challenges facing women in the economics profession today. As we examine women's struggle to gain an authoritative voice in economics in the early years and the impediments they faced along the way, we may see current methodological disputes, variations in subjects covered—in terms of research and coursework—in new relief. This examination may, like an M. C. Escher print, allow us to see more clearly not just the history of women in the profession but the current dilemmas facing women in the dismal science.

2

THE POLITICAL ECONOMY OF GENDER IN THE HALLS OF IVY

I n 1895, when women students from Smith College gathered on the day before commencement to celebrate Ivy Day, it was a ceremony rich with symbolism. Students were dressed in white and carrying roses; they led a parade through campus that ended with planting ivy as a symbol of their lifelong connection to the college.[1] This sanguine image masks the lived realities of women's experiences in higher education in the late nineteenth century.

Five years later, Otelia Cromwell, the first Black female student at Smith, graduated. She also participated in Ivy Day and was captured in a photograph honoring the students as they led the parade.[2] Although she graduated, she was not allowed to live on campus. Of the colleges that came to be known as the Seven Sisters, only seven Black students have been identified among the graduating classes as of 1900. These students graduated from Mount Holyoke College, Wellesley College, Vassar College, and Radcliffe College in the nineteenth century.[3] Three of those seven women were enrolled without the college's knowledge that they were Black students. Barnard College and Bryn Mawr College did not have their first Black female graduates until 1928 and 1931, respectively.[4]

After the Civil War, state universities in the South, a region where the majority of the African American population lived, were typically segregated. This practice, along with a long history of educational discrimination, prevented Black students from attending many state colleges and universities.[5] In the North and in border states, separate Black colleges and universities were established; although students were not legally prohibited from attending predominantly white institutions, it was rare.[6] As W. E. B. Du Bois noted, in the period from 1865 to 1900, only 390 Blacks had graduated from predominantly white colleges and universities.[7] In particular, many Black women earning undergraduate degrees before 1900 received them from Oberlin College in Ohio—an institution noteworthy for also being the first coeducational institution in the United States.[8]

COEDUCATION, BACKLASH, AND STATUS MAINTENANCE

In the United States, although women's colleges began in the 1830s, it was the decline in male enrollment during the Civil War along with passage of the first Morrill Act that spurred coeducation in the postwar years and brought renewed controversy about women and higher education. The Morrill Act of 1862 created a system of land-grant colleges and universities, often in sparsely populated states in the West and Midwest. State teachers' associations had been calling for universities to admit female students before the Morrill Act to facilitate teacher training. With the passage of the act, offering separate institutions to train women was simply too costly.[9] Moreover, more girls graduated from high school than did boys in the decades after the Civil War and well into the twentieth century, providing a larger number of potential applicants among girls than boys.[10]

The rise of new coeducational state universities put increasing pressure on existing universities to admit women students, thus raising the eventual specter of women graduate students and faculty.[11] In a very real sense, pressures on state-funded universities to open as coeducational were profound and persuasive, led in part by disappointing early enrollments in land-grant colleges. Women, who were often viewed as unnecessary in established private schools, were increasingly viewed as necessary for fledging colleges in the land-grant system.[12] As a result, their numbers grew significantly. According to Frederick Rudolph, from 1875 to 1900, the number of male students increased threefold in coeducational colleges, while the number of women students increased sixfold.[13]

With the rise of coeducation, women also threatened the status of institutions, and their increasing numbers were often seen as a cause for concern. Male students and faculty from previously all-male institutions often voiced their objection to coeducation.[14] At the University of Michigan, founded in 1817, women were not allowed to enroll until 1870—and then against the will of the faculty. Despite the Board of Regents' earlier belief that admitting women students was a "dangerous experiment" that would ruin the institution, a citizen-led protest resulted in the admittance of the first female student, Madelon Stockwell.[15] Stockwell was welcomed with more difficult entrance exams than her peers and was marginalized and bullied by male students. As another former student, Sara Chase, later described her experience, "It was impressed upon the women of our department that the U of M was a men's school & often we had the feeling that we were trying to rob men of a livelihood. The girls had to study harder & make better records in order to 'pass.' No internships were offered to women or found for them."[16]

Because women were viewed as interlopers, access to coeducational institutions of higher learning was often filled with a variety of challenges. Rosalind Rosenberg describes lecture halls with a "fairly strict pattern of segregation . . . with women seated on one side of the room, men seated on the other."[17] At the University of Wisconsin in 1863, although there were roughly equal numbers of male and female students in the Normal Department (teacher training), the first thirty women students were allowed to take other college courses as well, but "were not allowed to sit down until all male students were seated."[18]

Not only were institutional leaders and their faculty concerned about a loss in status that might be associated with a large number of female students, they also feared the possibility that women educated in Greek and Latin, Kant and Kölliker might shirk the more mundane responsibilities of home and hearth. As a student from Vanderbilt University so artfully framed it, "No man wants to come home at night and find his wife testing some new process for manufacturing oleomargarine, or in the observatory sweeping the heavens for a comet."[19]

There were important differences in the expression of objections to women's education as it pertains to race. As Linda M. Perkins points out, white women were often viewed as being in possible competition for jobs with men, whereas Black women, due to the expectations of a fully segregated labor market, were perceived as less of a threat.[20] This difference in perception influenced views toward Black women's education.

Likewise, the "domestic code" or "cult of womanhood," as historians have labeled it, led many to argue that upper- and middle-class white women should ultimately fulfill their duty as wife and mother, forgoing participation in the paid labor market once they were married. For example, studies of Troy Female Seminary graduates from 1822 to 1872 show that only 6 percent worked during their marriage, and only 26 percent worked at any time during their lives.[21] At the same time, marriage and paid labor were not uncommon for Black women and were not perceived as incompatible. However, as Perkins points out, by the end of the nineteenth century, "sexism had increased significantly among educated blacks."[22] Women were increasingly excluded from organizations promoting education for Blacks and, if not excluded, removed from leadership roles.[23] Nonetheless, the general perception among Black women was that education and marriage were not incompatible.

AS MEN OF ACTION DREW THEIR SWORDS

The most common argument against university education for women after the Civil War centered on questions of innate intellectual ability and physical differences between men and women—arguments that emerged among German scholars as well. Reacting to the publication of John Stuart Mill's *On the Subjection of Women* in 1869, Helene Lange argues that while men "of the higher professions" were unmoved by the women's movement and its support for women's access to higher education, with the publication of Mill's book, these men of action "drew their swords." It was to be expected, perhaps, that women might protest conditions for women, but when one of their own so ably spoke to the inequalities facing women, a response was surely necessary.[24]

In Germany, professor of medicine Theodor von Bischoff articulated his opposition to women students (*Frauenstudium*) one year after Mill's treatise was published and the opposition sprang from perceived differences in physiology. According to Bischoff, women and men had scientifically verifiable differences in bones, muscles, nerves, and perhaps most important, skulls.[25] Offering the promise that controversies such as "the woman question" could be resolved impartially by science, Bischoff was drawn to craniometry and the measurement of brains. In his view, women could not engage equally in the rigors of an education because they were thought to be inferior to men in intellectual capacity.[26]

Much of the effort to scientifically measure brain size took place during autopsies. Nonetheless, a woman student—Alice Lee, who was herself not an advocate of the use of craniometry to infer intelligence—took it upon herself in 1898 to march into the all-male Anatomical Society meeting at Trinity College in Dublin and measure society members' heads. Lee then "ranked their skulls from largest to smallest to find that—lo and behold—some of the most well-regarded intellects in their field turned out to possess rather small, unremarkable skulls." It is not known if this attempt at careful measurement diminished the young men's faith in craniometry. However, Bischoff's attraction to craniometry might have diminished were he to know that, upon his death, his own autopsy showed that his brain weighed substantially less than the average woman's brain.[27]

Other, equally elaborate rationales for limiting educational opportunities for women students also emerged among members of the male medical establishment. In particular, it was increasingly popular to argue that the rigorous education necessary for the study of medicine, and perhaps education in general, would come at a high price since it would harm a woman's reproductive organs.

In his popular book *Sex in Education: A Fair Chance for the Girls* (1873), published one year after Bischoff's *Das Studium und die Ausübung der Medizin durch Frauen*, Harvard medical professor Edward H. Clarke massaged the argument.[28] Whereas Bischoff argued that women were less intelligent than men due to the reduced size of their brain and focused on women and medical education, Clarke emphasized the injurious effect on women's reproductive capacity and focused on education in general. Speaking to the harm that too much education might cause, he offered several examples of young women permanently injured by the stress of higher education. Especially frightening was the fate of Miss G, who entered a western college and later died, Clarke said, "not because she had mastered the wasps of Aristophanes and the Mécanique Céleste ... but because while pursuing these studies, while doing all this work, she steadily ignored her woman's make."[29] Although women might be capable of the mental exertion necessary in the higher learning, this education, he argued, goes against the "laws of nature."

According to Clarke, the special demands nature imposed on a young woman in puberty limited her ability to engage in steady mental effort without incurring undue stress on the reproductive system. He argued that an education for young women similar to that of young men calls for sustained and continuous effort, which is "out of harmony with the rhythmical periodicity of the female organization."[30] While young men develop into manhood through a more gradual or persistent process of maturation, women develop in a relatively short period of time. According to Clarke, "When school makes the same steady demand for force from girls who are approaching puberty, ignoring Nature's periodical demands, that it does from boys, who are not called upon for an equal effort, there must be failure somewhere."[31]

Clarke's theory reflected the "vital forces" notion—a view that the body was a closed energy system in which effort diverted from one activity or function would, if excessive, harm another.[32] According to this view, also known as "conservation of energy," overexertion in one part of the body would deplete the health of some other part. Herbert

Spencer, the British political philosopher and supporter of Charles Darwin, applied the notion of "concentration of energy"—or, as he preferred to call it, the "persistence of force"—to the human body in a way that argued against women's increased education.[33]

Although in *Social Statics* (1851) Herbert Spencer claimed that "Equity knows no difference of sex," his view of women and equity had substantially changed by the 1870s.[34] In "Psychology of the Sexes," published in 1873 in the *Popular Science Monthly* and more fully in *The Study of Sociology* (1873), Spencer argued that men and women are not mentally alike. Invoking the theory of vital forces in the human body along with a Darwinian perspective, he explained how women fall short intellectually and emotionally compared with men. According to Spencer, women's physical development results in a faster and less sustained growth in their mental development, leaving them lagging in "the latest products of human evolution—the power of abstract reasoning and that most abstract of the emotions, the sentiment of justice."[35]

Spencer invoked the "science" of Darwinian evolution to put forth his notion that women are less developed or evolved than men and asserted a masculinist notion of science as detached rational inquiry. Also revealing is his use of concepts from political economy to frame the issue of women's inferiority and develop what could be called a political economy of gender. Preoccupied with "order and scarcity," cognizant of the need to carefully allocate their "scarce" vital energy, and weakened by the "periodicity" of their constitution, women are "taxed" with a special energy demand—a "price" women had to pay for the future preservation of society.[36] Blending metaphors from science into a vision of the political economy of gender, Spencer spoke to the anxieties raised by a market system—a market system seemingly out of control at times.

Although the arguments of physicians like Clarke were influenced more by medical folklore than medical science (some empirical studies did contradict the prevailing wisdom), they were nonetheless taken as "fact" by regents and others seeking to control the social ills that might result from women pursuing the higher learning. In 1877, regents of the University of Wisconsin explained that "at stated times, nature makes a great demand upon the energies of early womanhood and that at these times great caution must be exercised lest injury be done."[37] By 1895, faculty at the University of Virginia pronounced that women students were often "unsexed" by academic strains.[38]

As a result of these views, a variety of actions were taken to address this perceived problem. Physical education classes were added for women students, and other efforts were taken to recruit male students. For example, at Northwestern University, engineering courses were added to stem the dangerous tide. At the University of Nebraska, growing numbers of women students provided an incentive for the regents to create a school of commerce to retain male students, an argument offered by Edward A. Ross.[39] Likewise, when the proportion of women students at Stanford University rose from 25 percent in 1892 to 40 percent in 1899, the university adopted a limit on the number of women students in an effort to "preserve the college from unwanted change in character."[40]

OPPOSITION AND A PARTICULAR
TYPE OF EDUCATION

When Thorstein Veblen published *The Theory of the Leisure Class* in 1899, the University of Chicago (where he taught) was coeducational and retained women on the faculty. Yet schools such as Harvard University were notorious in their refusal to admit women. For Veblen, the reluctance of institutions to embrace women was a "ceremonial vestment"—a demonstration of class-worthiness and status. As Veblen put it:

> And even under the urgent circumstances prevailing in the modern
> industrial communities the highest and most reputable universities
> show an extreme reluctance in making the move. The sense of class
> worthiness, that is to say of status, of a honorific differentiation of
> the sexes according to a distinction between superior and inferior
> intellectual dignity, survives in a vigorous form in these corpora-
> tions of the aristocracy of learning.[41]

Veblen's observation that the preservation of male domination should be viewed as a form of status maintenance was not lost on women activists at the time. Women were often well organized and set about targeting particular institutions such as Harvard University to gain admittance for women, most certainly with the knowledge that if prestigious institutions were to open their doors to women, other universities would emulate them.[42] Moreover, women in the United States traveled to Europe to earn their degrees when they were unable to do so in the United States, often hoping to pressure universities in the United States to open their doors to women.[43]

In addition to noting the concerns of many that the mere presence of women would "be derogatory to the dignity of the learned craft," Veblen points out that, to the extent that women were allowed the privilege of admission to the higher learning, it was felt that they should be constrained to acquire knowledge only in those areas that conduce "immediately to a better performance of domestic service" or to the "quasi-scholarly and quasi-artistic, as plainly come in under the head of a performance of vicarious leisure."[44] In other words, the ultimate purpose of education for women was typically thought to support her ultimate role in life—marriage and family.

In reality, the acceleration in coeducation brought with it "a particular type of education" for women in the last third of the nineteenth century and indeed well into the twentieth century. As the expansion of the so-called elective system was continuing, moving schools away from strict adherence to coursework in Greek, Latin, mathematics, philosophy, science, and English, students were allowed to take elective courses, and female students were encouraged to take music, painting, and ballroom dance. As Andrea Radke-Moss points out, land-grant institutions offered music, especially piano and voice instruction, from the 1860s, and women students made up the majority of students in these classes.[45]

These courses did sometimes provide training for other vocational opportunities as well. In the land-grant setting and some women's colleges, the expansion of domestic studies and what eventually became home economics took hold. Journalism, charities and correction, social work, and, at Wellesley College, economics as fields of study were increasingly available to women students who had previously seen their vocation limited to marriage and school teaching until marriage. Although many land-grants listed in *The Yearbook of Education 1878* proudly announced "tuition free to all" along with "open to both sexes," the examination of fees paints a slightly different picture.[46] For example, at the University of Nebraska, the *Seventh Annual Register and Catalogue*, published in 1878, provides the fine print. Tuition was free in all departments of instruction except music, painting, and drawing. Tuition in these departments is $30 a year—the equivalent of $769.17 in 2020 dollars.[47] At a time when the average annual earnings in the United States was $347 according to the U.S. Census, this sum was not insignificant.[48]

That a particular type of education would be supported for women was true at the University of Chicago and elsewhere in the late nineteenth and early twentieth centuries. In the same year that Veblen published *The Theory of the Leisure Class*, Charles Eliot, noted president of Harvard University, argued that coeducation was "not possible in highly civilized communities," but that women's colleges might be useful in encouraging religion and as schools of manners for young women.[49] Therefore, while Harvard would offer their students "as many years as they wish of liberal culture in studies which have no direct professional value, to be sure, but which enrich and enlarge both intellect and character," the education of women should be different than that of men. As Eliot saw it, "their lives are different and their education should be different . . . Their education should take account of the life which is before them."[50]

NOT A FREE MARKET

While economists Alfred Marshall, Arthur Pigou, and Francis Edgeworth were polishing their prose about the virtues of a free market (while supporting barriers to women's entry into occupations), the reality of life for a woman in the late nineteenth and early twentieth centuries was severely limited and subject to a segregated labor market—segregated by sex and by race.[51] However, the labor market was changing. In 1880, only 15 percent of women ten years of age and over worked in the paid labor market. This figure rose to 18.3 percent by 1900, 20.5 percent by 1920, and 24.4 percent in 1940.[52] The most prevalent job for women at the turn of the century was still domestic servant, although this changed by the 1920s. Married women were seldom (yet increasingly) employed outside the home. From 1890 to 1920, the percent of employed married women grew from 4.6 to 9.0 percent.[53]

Labor force participation rates for Black women were higher than for white women. For example, by 1920 roughly 44 percent of Black women were employed, and the most prevalent occupation was farm laborer; for nonagricultural work, it was domestic servant. Data from the census also reveal that married Black women were more likely to be employed outside the home than were married white women. About 33 percent of Black married women worked in the paid labor market in 1920, compared with 6.3 percent of married white women.[54]

The history of women in higher education before World War II is one of fascinating growth and decline. As Women's Bureau data show, women as a percent of all "college presidents, professors and instructors" grew rapidly before the Great Depression, going from 19 percent in 1910 to 30 percent in 1920 to 32 percent in 1930. By 1940, women's representation as professors and instructors had fallen to 27 percent and 23 percent by 1950.[55]

Equally interesting is the growth in the number of Black women employed as college presidents, professors, and instructors. Although the data were not collected by the U.S. Census for all of the decades of the early twentieth century, we do know that the 1910 census recorded 73 Black women in this category, whereas the 1920 census reported 496 Black women and the 1930 census reported 1,020 Black women employed as college presidents, professors, and instructors.[56] Although there is some concern that the reported numbers for this category include some teachers as well, the expansion in the number of Black women employed in higher education was no doubt facilitated by passage of the Second Morrill Act in 1890, which expanded the number of historically Black colleges and universities.[57]

During the time period 1885 to 1940, the prevalence of women earning a baccalaureate degree also rose sharply. Whereas only 18.3 percent of undergraduate degrees were awarded to women in 1885, by 1940 this had increased to 41 percent. As for advanced degrees, only 6 percent of doctorates were awarded to women in 1900. However, the percent of doctorates awarded to women had increased to 13 percent by 1940.[58]

According to Margaret Rossiter, women earning doctorates in the nineteenth century were to be found primarily in ten schools: Yale University, the University of Chicago, Cornell University, New York University, the University of Pennsylvania, Bryn Mawr College, Syracuse University, the University of Wooster, Boston University, and the University of Michigan. Moreover, the largest number of these women concentrated their academic work in Greek, Latin, and English.[59] By 1940, the largest number of women were concentrated in education.[60]

Those few women who secured advanced degrees in areas not thought to be feminized would find that their career advancement was to be attained largely by abiding by the convention of separate spheres.[61] For example, as Jo Freeman points out, while Veblen was at the University of Chicago, not a single woman in the fields of political science, economics, anthropology, history, psychology, or sociology began her career as a junior faculty member and became promoted to full professor.[62] Sophonisba Breckinridge, who had earned a doctoral degree in 1901 in the Department of Political Science and Economics and earned her JD in 1904, found that she would be hired in neither law nor political economy. Her first appointment was assistant professor in the Department of Household Administration. For her part, Edith Abbott, who taught sociology for six years without promotion, transferred to one of the so-called women's departments, where she later became dean of the school.[63]

The segmentation of academic labor ultimately made women with degrees in the social sciences vulnerable to exclusion and prey to ontological disputes. The significant influence of what Virginia Valian has called "gender schemas" allowed academic economists in the late nineteenth and early twentieth centuries to characterize women with doctorates in economics as sociologists and men with doctorates in sociology and history as economists and raised little cause concern about the discrepancy.[64] Overall, the drive toward "professionalization" interacted with gender in ways that often undermined women academics in fields like economics by excluding women whose degrees were in cognate fields while recognizing and accepting men with degrees in cognate fields.

Women's access to graduate work and the sorting of women who earned their doctorates and were thus equally qualified as their male colleagues, is of great interest. To what extent were women precluded from earning graduate degrees in economics in U.S. universities? Where were they accepted, and where did they find the door closed? To what extent did women receive a similar level of support in finding their first academic job? To what extent did institutions set the rules of the game so as to make academic employment impossible for women? To what extent did women participate in the accoutrements of the academic establishment that would facilitate their success? Were they present in newly emerging professional associations? Did they hold leadership positions in those associations? Were they part of the increasingly important network of editors, associate editors, and editorial board members who wielded power in determining whose work was counted as important and whose work was not?

A FINAL WORD

Veblen viewed the institution of higher learning in a way that later philosophers of science might refer to as the sociology of knowledge tradition.[65] These philosophers view the creation of knowledge as a social process that takes place in communities of scholars who are influenced by personal, social, and political values of the larger community. However, these later philosophers of science often failed to examine the gendered nature of socially situated knowledge. They argued that science is often influenced by the agendas of those who fund research, but they often failed to identify how the metaphors and conceptual frameworks in science were gendered. In other words, they were sensitive to the politics of knowledge claims but not the gender politics of such claims.

Extending a gendered lens to the sociology of knowledge tradition, feminist philosophers of science such as Helen Longino, Sandra Harding, and others have shed light on the gendered nature of these communities and the ways perspective is determined by the location of the scholar.[66] According to these scholars, women are often misrepresented in science because they are underrepresented in science. Moreover, as Harding has pointed out, failure to recognize that observation involves subjective perceptions that are shaped by the community and experience of the knower limits our understanding. According to Harding, "Knowledge claims are always socially situated, and the failure of the dominant groups critically and systematically to interrogate their advantaged social situation and the effect of such advantages on their beliefs leaves their social situation a scientifically and epistemologically disadvantaged one for generating knowledge."[67]

These feminist philosophers of science offer valuable insights on gender and knowledge production which, along with Veblen's insights, provide a useful framework for examining gender and the political economy of knowledge production. Understanding the circumstances facing women in higher education in the late nineteenth and early twentieth centuries requires that we examine how the desire for status maintenance influenced the interpretation and application of the standards and rituals of scholarly conduct.

Ultimately, as "intruders" into the halls of ivy, women were seen as a threat to the status of institutions. Restricted in their use of facilities like libraries, laboratories, and living spaces; constrained in their choice of courses; assumed to be lacking in intelligence and analytical skills; women were told that their desire for equal treatment was a "bid for power" and that they were "never satisfied."[68] Success in that environment would come in small, hard-fought victories when it came at all.

3

A LIMINAL SPACE

Graduate Training in the Dismal Science

The accomplishments of women who earned their doctorates in economics in the early years of the profession were quite unique: from one of the first "human computers," to secretary-general of the International Planned Parenthood Federation, the first female secretary of Commerce, and first female director of the New York Stock Exchange. This list of women included a member of Nixon's enemies list and the only woman involved in the Stanford University free speech resignations following the firing of Edward A. Ross. Also included was the first African American woman to earn a doctorate in economics, the first woman to become a full professor in economics in Canada, and the first woman to earn tenure at the Sloan School of Management at MIT. Among these talented women was one who joined the CIA, became a member of the U.S. Tariff Commission, and served on the staff of the Council of Economic Advisers. These remarkable women earned their degrees in economics in the period from 1890 to 1948 and, despite their talent, drive, and tenacity, often faced closed doors in their academic pursuits.[1]

From the beginning, women encountered challenges not faced by white men in their pursuit of education and challenges not shared by their male colleagues in their subsequent desire to use their education in their chosen vocation. The context for women of color was full of

unique challenges. As a result, women of color faced powerful impediments and pushed for acceptance when doors were closed or moved on
to other pursuits where they could hope to be successful.

Such was the case for the first African American women to earn a
doctorate in economics in the United States—Sadie Tanner Mossell
(later Alexander). Alexander earned her bachelor's degree in education
with senior honors from the University of Pennsylvania in 1918 and
pursued her master's degree in economics from the same institution
the following year. She was awarded the Francis Sergeant Pepper Fellowship in Economics, enabling her to go on for her doctorate.

In spring 1921, at the age of twenty-three, Alexander earned her doctorate in economics—one of three Black women in the United States to
obtain a doctorate by that time, the first Black woman to obtain a doctorate in economics, and the first Black woman to get a doctorate from
the University of Pennsylvania. Alexander was one of three individuals
receiving a doctorate in economics from the University of Pennsylvania
that year and the only woman.[2]

Unlike her male colleagues and despite her outstanding accomplishments, Alexander found it difficult to find employment after completing
her degree. In her own words, "I did all my graduate work in economics
and insurance. I couldn't get work anywhere. In fact, the situation was
such in Philadelphia that I could not even have taught high school after
I had gotten all this training because they didn't employ any colored
teachers."[3]

Alexander applied to many insurance companies in Philadelphia,
without success. She was finally hired by a Black-owned insurance
company in Durham, North Carolina, and worked there for two years
in isolation and "great loneliness," experiencing what she later described
as prejudice from Southern Blacks because she was from the North.[4]

Her inability to find employment after obtaining her doctorate was
certainly not for lack of trying. Alexander reports that she was aware
that her major professors had called "not only all over the city but all
over the country to try and get me placed and they couldn't place me. I
knew I couldn't place myself." As a result, she decided to go to law
school.[5]

Alexander faced numerous challenges as a student at the University of Pennsylvania. She had to "carry lunch" every day because "no restaurant would serve colored students." When faced with this indignity, she and a few other students went to the president of the university (Edgar Fahs Smith), stated their concerns, and expressed hope that he would intervene. His response? Smith said that he "realized what we were suffering but really he could do nothing about it."[6]

In her life as a lawyer in practice with her husband, Alexander went on to represent others facing discrimination. She represented those bringing cases challenging unequal access to, for example, movie theaters, eventually breaking up the segregation in theaters. She went on to serve the cause of justice in her long and active life.

Alexander offered a particularly poignant story toward the end of her interview with Walter M. Phillips in 1977.[7] As she tells it, when her sister-in-law was a physician and looking for an associate, she brought Dr. Helen Dickens into her practice. After observing her for a period of time, Alexander suggested to Dickens that she was too smart to be "carrying a bag" the rest of her life and that she should go back to Penn and get a specialty. Dickens eventually applied to the medical school and was turned down. When Alexander asked how do you know this, Dickens replied, "I got a letter; the letter says they won't take a colored student." Alexander's only response was "what stationary is that on?" Dickens indicated, "it's on University stationary."

Wasting no time, Alexander called Thomas S. Gates, then the president of the university, and communicated the contents of the letter. In a meeting called by Gates with Alexander, the dean of the graduate school, and the vice president in charge of all of the deans, Gates inquired about the situation, asking, "did she [Helen Dickens] graduate from a school that is approved and would warrant her admission to the graduate school of medicine? She did, sir . . . Did she graduate with such distinction as to warrant her admission? She did, sir; she graduated with honors . . ." Gates instructed the dean to "tell Mrs. Alexander when her friend should come to register."[8]

The bravery reflected in the actions of women like Sadie Tanner Mossell Alexander was not without cost. For example, when Dr. Dickens was asked to join the Distinguished Daughters of Pennsylvania, Alexander was made aware that they would not elect her. When Dr. Dickens began attending the meetings, she learned why. The Distinguished Daughters had determined that Alexander "was a troublemaker."

The Distinguished Daughters of Pennsylvania did eventually elect Alexander, and Dr. Dickens became a full professor of gynecology and obstetrics at the Perelman School of Medicine at the University of Pennsylvania. For her part, Alexander knew that her circumstances in life and unwillingness to capitulate in the face of injustice would lead her to make what is now known as "good trouble." As she later said, "I don't think they know all this; these people out there don't know it. But, you see, when you do all these things, you're a troublemaker."[9] As her life demonstrates, that is a good thing.

THE SEVEN SISTERS: PRIVILEGE NOT WITHOUT PREJUDICE

A life of privilege did not preclude women from experiencing discrimination in higher education in the late nineteenth and early twentieth centuries. Nor did it prevent women students from petitioning for equal access when that access was denied.

Just five years after Alexander earned her doctorate in economics, nine female graduate students from Radcliffe College signed a petition addressed to Professor Allyn A. Young of Harvard University, requesting permission to regularly attend the weekly seminars in economics. Young was serving as chair of the Harvard Economics Department and had previously served as the secretary-treasurer of the American Economic Association from 1914 to 1920. In making their case, the Radcliffe students pointed out that they were inclined to feel that "the customary exclusion of Radcliffe students from these meetings puts them at some disadvantage," and as a result they must forgo the "opportunity of hearing both the informal lectures of experts in the various fields of Economics, and the results of the research of their fellow students."

They went on to say that they "also miss an invaluable chance for discussion less formal than that of the classroom."[10]

The Radcliffe students who signed the petition in 1926 were Elizabeth Lane Waterman (Gilboy), Mary Chandler Coit, Emily Harriet Huntington, Margaret Fitz Randolph Gay, Eunice Shipton Coyle, Miriam Keeler, M. Gertrude Brown, Ruth Guppy, and Anne Gilchrist. As one of the Seven Sisters women's colleges, Radcliffe was unique. Although women earned degrees from Radcliffe, they would do their work, take their exams, and work with faculty from Harvard University. While acceptance to one of these elite women's colleges in many ways reflected a life of privilege, it was not privilege without prejudice.

The women's colleges that came to be known as the Seven Sisters played an important role in preparing women students for graduate work in economics. The 302 women identified as earning doctorate degrees in economics and related fields from 1890 to 1948 earned their undergraduate degrees from 102 academic institutions. When we examine the schools where these undergraduates were concentrated, we see that 33 percent of those students were at one of the Seven Sisters colleges.

As one might expect, women who had attended one of the Seven Sisters schools for their undergraduate training often went on to do graduate work at one of these schools when possible.[11] Those who attended Bryn Mawr College as undergraduates often chose Bryn Mawr when they pursued graduate training. Of the twenty-two women from Bryn Mawr who earned a doctorate in economics, seven had attended Bryn Mawr as undergraduate students. The next most popular choice for Bryn Mawr undergraduates to pursue doctorates was Radcliffe College, followed by the Brookings Institution. Likewise, of the fifteen women Radcliffe College doctorates in economics, eleven had attended Radcliffe for their undergraduate work.

A similar relationship emerged between Barnard College and Columbia University. Of the nine undergraduate women students earning degrees from Barnard, seven went on to do graduate work in economics at Columbia. Students from Mount Holyoke College often went to graduate school at Radcliffe College, while Vassar undergraduate students were drawn in highest numbers to Columbia, followed by the Brookings Institution. Wellesley College undergraduate students were drawn equally to Radcliffe, Columbia, and the University of Wisconsin during these years.

Clearly, the women's colleges that came to be known as the Seven Sisters played an important role in encouraging female students to pursue graduate work in economics. However, not all women students were welcome at these important institutions in the late nineteenth and early twentieth centuries—at least not when they were African American. Moreover, when allowed to register, these students were often not allowed to live on campus—an indignity as well as an inconvenience that made it difficult for them to be accepted as a peer and take advantage of the opportunities.

According to Linda M. Perkins, Wellesley College, Radcliffe College, and Smith College had the longest history of having Black women students. These three schools accepted African American students in the nineteenth century, although only Wellesley allowed them to live on campus. Moreover, by the beginning of the twentieth century, Smith and Radcliffe typically began to accept at least one African American student each year.[12]

Wellesley College was the first of the Seven Sisters to have an African American student graduate when Harriet Alleyne Rice graduated in 1887. Radcliffe College enrolled African American women continuously from the 1890s. The first African American student to graduate from Radcliffe, Alberta Scott, entered in 1894, graduated in 1898, and went on to teach at the Tuskegee Institute. By 1920, Radcliffe had a total of four African American students in the same class and was the leader in accepting Black women students. Otelia Cromwell was the first known African American student to graduate from Smith College in 1900. Although she was also not allowed to live on campus, she went on to earn her doctorate from Yale in 1926. After Cromwell, Smith College went on to admit African American students at a rate of about one per year.[13]

Bryn Mawr ranks first in training female undergraduate students who went on earn their doctorate in economics.[14] Yet Bryn Mawr's

President M. Carey Thomas actively worked to bar Jewish faculty and students. When Jessie Redmon Fauset, who had graduated at the top of her class at Philadelphia Girls' High, was set to attend Bryn Mawr with a customary scholarship, Thomas found a way to prevent this. On learning that Fauset was African American, Thomas raised money for her to attend Cornell University instead.[15] Bryn Mawr did not award an African American student an undergraduate degree until 1931, when Enid Cook graduated. Although not allowed to live on campus, Cook completed her work and went on to earn a doctorate in bacteriology from the University of Chicago in 1937.[16] From 1885, when Bryn Mawr opened its doors, to 1948, only three African American students graduated from Bryn Mawr College—two in the 1930s and one in 1948.

Sixteen of the women graduate students who went on to earn doctorates in economics got their undergraduate training from Vassar College. Vassar was the last of the Seven Sisters to knowingly admit African American students. The first known African American student to graduate from Vassar was Anita Florence Hemmings, who graduated in 1897. Like several other African American students at the turn of the century, Hemmings kept her racial identity a secret. When it was discovered that she was African American on the eve of her graduation, she barely avoided being dismissed from school by successfully pleading her case to the president of Vassar, James Monroe Taylor. It was forty-three years until Vassar changed its policy and accept its first openly acknowledged African American student.[17]

Like Vassar, Mount Holyoke College's first two African American students, Hortense Parker (Gilliam) and Martha Ralston, were not known to be African American until after they had been accepted and arrived on campus. According to a letter from Dean Florence Puring-ton of Mount Holyoke to Ada Comstock of Smith, the women's race was a surprise to officials when they first arrived.[18] Parker and Ralston went on to graduate from Mount Holyoke in 1883 and 1898, respectively, but they were the only two known African American students to do so in the nineteenth century.

THE TROUBLE WITH (EARLY) NUMBERS

Scholars interested in the history of women and economics have often posed the question: who was the first woman to earn a doctorate in economics in the United States? As with any good question, the answer is not simple. In reality, there is no consensus on this point, and perhaps this explains why some have avoided the issue altogether. One of the primary factors that has complicated this question is the fact that economics was only emerging as a discipline in the last decades of the nineteenth century. In fact, many departments where doctoral degrees were offered had not yet taken the moniker of "economics" until well into the twentieth century.[19]

One of the earliest articles to proffer a view on this question was written by Walter Crosby Eells.[20] According to Eells, Ethel Muir earned her doctorate in economics from Cornell University in 1896, and Helen Page Bates earned her doctorate in economics from the University of Wisconsin that same year. However, the selection of women we might identify as having earned a doctorate in economics is perhaps more of an art than a science. Muir earned her doctorate in philosophy and went on to teach philosophy at Mount Holyoke College, while two other women may have done so before Bates.[21]

If we use digital sources on dissertations, we find that the first woman to have earned a doctorate in economics was Florence Elizabeth Watson (Blackett).[22] Blackett is listed as having completed her doctorate in economics in 1890 from the Boston University Graduate School—the same institution where Helen Magill completed the first doctorate in in Greek the United States in 1877. Blackett's dissertation was titled "The Relation of Ethics to Economics." She married Charles Wesley Blackett, whom she had met as an undergraduate student, one year after earning her doctorate. Her husband also went on to complete his doctorate from Boston University Graduate School several years later in 1904, becoming a clergyman at the Stanton Avenue Methodist Episcopal Church. As a married woman—even one with a doctorate—the doors of academe were not open to Florence Blackett.

Following Blackett, Mary Graham is known to have completed her doctorate in economics from Yale University in 1895. She is listed as teaching philosophy and economics at Mount Holyoke College prior to earning her doctorate. However, like Blackett, Graham did not have a career after completing her doctorate. The Yale Obituary Index reports that "In 1897, her health having been undermined through overstudy, she became a patient at the Connecticut State Hospital at Middletown, where the remainder of her life was spent."[23] Although she died of tuberculosis, the writers clearly infused her tragic story with the (parochial) medical musings of Edward H. Clarke as a cautionary tale, perhaps, on the hazards of "overstudy" for women.

Examination of the remaining individuals that Eells lists as having received their doctoral degrees in the nineteenth century reveals further evidence of the challenges of identifying women in economics in that he did not include some women who might be included. Three such women were Kate Holladay Claghorn, who earned her doctorate from Yale University in 1896; Mary Roberts Smith, who completed her doctorate from Stanford University in 1896; and Nellie Neilson, who earned her degree from Bryn Mawr College in 1898. While their doctoral disciplines leave room for debate, an examination of their backgrounds before and after their doctorates were completed appear to justify their inclusion as economists.[24] Moreover, all three women were members of the American Economic Association—one more indication of their academic identity.

Identifying women worthy of our count as having received doctorates in economics or political economy is an exercise best approached with caution. It should also be approached with the realization that eminent men whose degrees were in fields such as sociology, history, and political science and even those without doctorates easily took their place in the discipline without objection. Men like Davis Rich Dewey (editor of the *American Economic Review* from 1911 to 1940) earned his doctorate in history from Johns Hopkins University in 1886; Allyn Abbott Young (secretary-treasurer of the AEA from 1914 to 1920) completed his doctorate in sociology from the University of Wisconsin; and Charles F. Dunbar (second president of the AEA and first chair in political economy at Harvard University) did not hold a doctorate. Identifying women with doctorates in economics in the early years is an important but nonetheless challenging endeavor—especially in the nineteenth century.

GENDER DIFFERENCES IN ECONOMICS DOCTORATES

The history of graduate education in the United States reveals that only a small number of doctorates were awarded in political economy in the 1870s and 1880s. According to John B. Parrish, only three doctorates in this field were given in the United States by three institutions in the 1870s, and only eleven were awarded by five institutions in the 1880s. The prevalence of doctoral degrees in the United States only began in the 1890s, when a total of ninety-five degrees in political economy were awarded by twelve institutions.[25]

Women were not allowed into graduate programs at all institutions that were open to men. According to Eells, by 1889 ten colleges and universities had granted doctoral degrees in any field to twenty-five women with Syracuse (seven), Boston University (four), and the College of Wooster (four) leading the way.[26]

Although estimates of how many women earned doctorates in economics in the nineteenth century are somewhat debatable, clearly women were limited in the institutions open to them, and women in economics were particularly limited given the notion that economics was a "man's field." But how limited were women in completing a doctorate in the dismal science, and how did they differ from their male counterparts?

To better understand the characteristics of women earning doctorates in economics and closely related fields from 1890 to 1948, I gathered information on their doctoral institution, undergraduate institution, AEA membership ties, marital status, and whether they worked at the same institution where they earned their doctorate.[27] The data were analyzed by decade for the 1890s, 1900s, 1910s, 1920s, 1930s, and 1940s.[28] A random sample of male doctoral recipients in economics equal to the total number of women was established to compare women doctoral recipients to their male counterparts. The full sample consists of all of the women earning doctorates in economics and closely related fields in the United States along with an equal number of men by year over this period.[29]

The sample contains 302 women. The average number of women doctorates per decade was below one per year from 1890 to 1909. Although the average rose to two per year in from 1910 to 1919, in the 1920s there was a larger increase to 7.3 per year, 9.4 per year in the 1930s, and 10.7 per year in the 1940s, and the highest numbers were concentrated in 1946, 1947, and 1948.

The top institutions awarding these doctoral degrees to women were Columbia University (fifty-seven), Radcliffe College (forty-eight), the University of Chicago (twenty-seven), and the University of Wisconsin (twenty-five). The next tier includes the Brookings Institution (sixteen), Bryn Mawr College (fourteen), University of California–Berkeley (eleven), Cornell University (eleven), and the University of Pennsylvania (ten). We can see that the leading institutions awarding doctorates in economics to women changed over time. In the 1890s, Yale University was the leading institution. Yale's inclusion of women appears to have been ushered forward by Arthur T. Hadley, a political economist who became the first dean of the Graduate School in 1892–1895 and later president of Yale. In the first decade of the twentieth century, the University of Chicago and Bryn Mawr College had the largest numbers; in the period from 1910 to 1919, Columbia University had the largest number; in the 1920s, 1930s, and 1940s, Columbia University, Radcliffe College, and Radcliffe College (respectively) led the pack in granting doctorates in economics to women.

As for undergraduate training for those who went on in their doctoral studies in economics, Bryn Mawr College played a large role, preparing 22 of the 302 women. Bryn Mawr was followed by Vassar College (sixteen), Radcliffe College (fifteen), Wellesley College (fourteen), the University of Chicago (fourteen), and Mount Holyoke (eleven). One cannot ignore the important role that many of the Seven Sisters colleges played in encouraging and preparing women students to continue their education—even in the male-dominated field of economics.

When we examine the sample of 302 randomly selected men earning doctorates in economics from 1890 to 1948, we see that the list of top-tier institutions is the same as that for women with the exception that for men, Harvard University is included, and for women, Radcliffe College is included. The top-tier list of institutions awarding doctoral degrees to men were Columbia University (forty-five), Harvard University (thirty-seven), University of Wisconsin (thirty-five), and the University of Chicago (twenty-three).

The second-tier schools awarding doctoral degrees to men include the University of Pennsylvania (twenty-two), Cornell University (twenty), University of California–Berkeley (eighteen), and University of Michigan (ten). Only the University of Michigan was not included in the second tier for women.

We also see variation in the concentration of institutions awarding doctoral degrees by decade for men. The University of Pennsylvania led in the 1890s while there was no distinguishable leader in the 1900s or 1910s. Columbia University led in the 1920s, Harvard University led in the 1930s, and Columbia University again led in the 1940s.

The results of the sample suggest that there were three primary schools providing undergraduate training to these men who went on to obtain their doctorate in economics led by Harvard University (with sixteen students), University of Wisconsin (with fourteen students), and Cornell University (with ten students). The next tier of schools, each with eight men completing undergraduate degrees, include University of California–Berkeley, University of Iowa, University of Pennsylvania, and the University of Illinois.

When we compare the concentration of women and men in their graduate and undergraduate training, we see that the men in our sample earned their doctorates from a total of forty-one different schools while women received them from thirty-nine schools—a surprisingly similar number. However, when we examine the dispersion of men and women students among these schools, we see that men were slightly more concentrated and women more dispersed.[30]

Turning to the undergraduate degrees of those in our sample, we see that men earned their undergraduate degrees from 132 different schools, while women received them from only 104 schools. When we examine the dispersion of men and women students among these schools, we see that men were more concentrated than were women.[31] Thus, in our sample we see that there is more concentration of men in schools at the graduate and the undergraduate levels. Moreover, we see that there is more concentration in undergraduate training for both men and women students than there is for graduate training.[32]

Not only does academic training provide credentials that can facilitate access to a profession, it also provides a framework for establishing networks among professionals. These networks could have substantial benefits. For example, if, as was common in some schools, there was a practice of hiring one's own graduate students, building strong bonds in graduate school becomes especially important. Likewise, membership and participation in professional societies play an important role in establishing professional relationships important to career development. According to Cynthia Epstein, professional ties can influence committee assignments, board appointments, and access to editorial positions in professional journals.[33]

When we examine women doctoral recipients in economics from 1890 to 1948, we see that women were far less likely to join the AEA than their male counterparts.[34] The results of our sample show that 56 percent of women doctoral recipients joined the AEA at some point, while 69 percent of men joined. When we analyze male and female membership by decade, we see no statistical difference in the likelihood of men and women joining the AEA in the periods 1890–1899 and 1900–1909. However, in the period from 1910 to 1919, there is a statistically significant difference with women less likely to join. This difference went away in the 1920s but reemerged in the 1930s and 1940s.[35] The growing difference in women doctoral recipients' memberships in the AEA in the 1930s and 1940s may reflect economic pressures resulting from labor market outcomes that increasingly began to work against women economists.

MAKING THE CONNECTION

The choice of institution for graduate work is an important decision affecting a multitude of outcomes. This choice sets the parameters for collegial relationships with other graduate students as well as mentoring relationships important to professional development. It also seems to have played a significant role in determining occupational outcomes in a very direct way during the period examined.

When we examine our sample of 604 graduate students receiving doctorates in economics from 1890 to 1948, we find many securing faculty appointments in the same institutions they had completed their graduate training. The proportion of women doctoral recipients in economics who went on to get a job in the same academic institution where they earned their doctorate was 26 percent on average.[36] For men, it was higher: 36 percent of male graduate students went on to hold an academic position at the same institution where they matriculated.[37]

When we examine the likelihood of making this connection by decade, we see that there was no difference in the likelihood of holding an academic position where one went to graduate school for men and women in the first three decades of our study—1890–1899, 1900–1909, and 1910–1919. However, in the 1920s and 1940s, male doctoral recipients were more likely to have made this connection than were women doctorates.[38] With far fewer options available to them, as women increasingly earned their doctoral degrees from institutions outside the Seven Sisters, the likelihood of making this connection for women was greatly reduced.

A TREACHEROUS LIMINAL SPACE

Women graduate students in the late nineteenth and early twentieth centuries faced enormous challenges, and these were particularly stark for students of color. As the first Black woman from Yale University to earn a doctorate in economics, Phyllis Ann Wallace described how racial inequities played a large role in her decision to major in economics as an undergraduate, her experiences in graduate school, and her early professional life. In her biography of Wallace, Julianne Malveaux explains that Wallace wanted to leave Maryland, where she was prevented from attending the University of Maryland because of her race. Black students were offered an education at Morgan State College, unless their chosen major was not offered there. Those students would be provided out-of-state expenses to attend a different school rather than opening the University of Maryland to them. Wallace settled on economics because it was offered at the University of Maryland but not at Morgan State. She packed her bags for New York University, where she graduated magna cum laude with a degree in economics in 1943.[39]

In the graduate school at Yale, departmental regulations prevented Wallace from holding a job as a teaching assistant but did not prevent her work as a research assistant. Hence even when institutions of higher learning opened their doors to students of color, they did not necessarily open all the doors.

After earning her doctorate from Yale University in 1948, Wallace went on to teach at the City College of New York and do research at the National Bureau of Economic Research (NBER) until 1953 when she moved to Atlanta University—the first of the historically black colleges and universities in the Southern United States. In 1958, when she was working as an "economic analyst in intelligence" (what she later referred to as "her Agency years"), Wallace wrote to Solomon Fabricant, director of research at the NBER and a member of the AEA Executive Committee. Wallace indicated that she had difficulty attending the AEA meetings when they were held in cities that restricted African American access to public accommodations. She received a response from Fabricant indicating that "Nobody on the Executive Committee wants to hold the meetings in a city that will make it unpleasant for any of our members. As far as I know, the meetings will therefore not be held in New Orleans." The annual meetings were not held in New Orleans until 1971, long after the 1964 Civil Rights Act provided a clear legal foundation guaranteeing to all persons full and equal enjoyment of public accommodations without discrimination or segregation on the ground of race, color, religion, or national origin.[40]

When lucky enough to have been encouraged to pursue their education, women often received mixed messages of a different sort. As Jo Anne Preston explains, women were encouraged to "strive for equality in educational opportunities but not in career opportunities."[41] One of the challenges women faced was a cultural norm asserting that marriage was incompatible with work as a scholar.

Of the 302 women known to have earned a doctorate in economics from 1890 to 1948, 57 percent were married at some point in their lives.[42] Of the 302 men in the sample, 96 percent were married at some point.[43] These differences reflect the reality of the difficult decisions facing many women as they pursued their doctorates—women like Elizabeth Paschel, who provides a firsthand account of the life that was before her.

In 1933, when Paschel was thirty-two years old, she completed her doctorate in economics from the University of Wisconsin. She had not married and realized that she faced limited prospects in her efforts to provide for herself and her mother. She was teaching at the New Jersey College for Women in a temporary position, but she knew that "women didn't have much of a chance in, what was called, a man's occupation—the teaching of economics." She knew she could have gotten a position in a women's college, but she was struck by the unfairness of the limited options and limited wages she believed she would face.[44]

Speaking to the unfairness she had witnessed, she went on to say, "when you went to conventions, to the meetings in the winter, it was always the men that had the opportunities to make speeches and to give their research. Men had a better chance at getting things published in the magazines. And I just thought that I would like to try something else." Such was her thinking when assessing her prospects in the academy.

Paschel decided to take a one-year appointment as supervisor of the Rocky Mount Region for the Consumer Purchases Survey, sponsored by the Bureau of Labor Statistics. During this time, she was faced with another decision involving her career. She had met a man with whom she had established a relationship—a banker. After a time, he asked her to stop working and marry him. Looking back on the situation, she explained that although she was perfectly happy to continue with things as they were, he was beginning to feel uncomfortable. Almost all of his friends were married and, as she describes it, "in his professional life it was time for him to be getting established." She went on to say that "men who are married get better positions, are paid more, than men who aren't married."[45] In the end, Paschel was not willing to relinquish her job for marriage.

Paschel went on to lead an accomplished professional life. She did research for the American Federation of Labor, became chief of the Program Planning Branch of the Social Security Administration (1942–1951), and eventually became an executive for the Ford Foundation (1952–1967). A recurrent theme in the lives of many women professionals during this time was the incompatibility of marriage and work—especially academic work.

GENDER AND GRADUATE EDUCATION IN PERSPECTIVE

As women began the transition from consumers to producers of knowledge through graduate training, it became clear that they were not welcome as full participants in the process. The top institutions awarding doctorates in economics to women and men during this period were the same, except that those men who attended Harvard received their degrees from Harvard and women who attended Harvard did so in a more limited way and received their degrees from Radcliffe College. As their petition requesting permission to regularly attend the weekly seminars made clear, the exclusion of Radcliffe students from activities put them at a disadvantage by not only missing the formal discussion of research but the "invaluable" chance for less formal interactions with fellow graduate students.

The concerns raised by the Radcliffe students demonstrates their awareness of the importance of graduate school in laying the foundation for networks that would typically prove to be important in many ways. Male students in graduate school could expect to establish the bonds of friendship that could result in coauthorship of various publications in the future. Likewise, graduate students were building strong bonds that often paved the way for students to be hired by the institution where they received their degree. A friend was a treasure, indeed.

Even those women who attended other coeducational institutions were aware that "women didn't have much of a chance in, what was called a man's occupation—the teaching of economics." As Paschel acknowledged, it was always men who had the opportunity to make speeches and give their research at annual meetings. The awareness of these and other unequal opportunities led her to pursue a career in government service instead of academe.[46]

At the same time, prejudice and discrimination provided particularly harsh barriers for women of color. The doors to most educational institutions were not open to women of color as undergraduates. Although the Seven Sisters colleges provided a foundation for many women who went on to pursue their graduate degrees, they also shunned women students of color. In the few cases where they were allowed to matriculate, they typically did so with limited access to the facilities. As Wallace's experience shows, significant challenges were in place for Black students, limiting their choice of institutions for graduate work, their opportunities while pursuing their doctorates, and their occupational choices after their education was complete.

In the end, Paschel's story is instructive in another, quite personal way in that she illuminates the challenges facing women who were forced to choose between a career and a family. While well over 90 percent of men earning a doctorate in economics in this period went on to marry, only 57 percent of women did so. The notion that marriage was incompatible with work in academia was a forceful deterrent to many and a painful reminder of the double standards applied to women and men in their choices. In a discipline that waxed poetic about the virtues of a free market and that took on the moniker of the "study of choice," this must have been a bitter pill to swallow.

4

A MEMBERSHIP BEYOND
THE PROFESSORIATE

n spring 1897, following a four-month lecture tour, Charlotte Perkins Gilman spent a week on a ranch in Eureka, Kansas. The previous several years had brought her to Oakland, California, where she began what was a lifelong association with women's clubs—clubs that she later called "one of the most important sociological phenomena of the century."[1] She organized the Oakland Nationalist Club (renaming it the New Nation Club) and joined the Pacific Coast Women's Press Association, the Women's Congress Association, the Ebell Society, the Ethical Society, the Parents Association, and the Economic Club. Gilman was not alone. By the first decade of the twentieth century, over a million clubwomen were active in voluntary reform associations, calling for change.[2]

Through her role as secretary of the Oakland Economic Club, "Mrs. Charlotte Perkins Stetson" (later Gilman) joined the American Economic Association (AEA) in 1892–93, maintaining a membership until 1895–96 when the hand-written membership rolls in the archives of the AEA simply indicate her status as "resigned." Less than a year after resigning her membership in the AEA, Gilman wrote in her diary from Kansas that she had discovered "a new branch in my theory on above subject—the biggest piece & saw it. Now I can write the book."[3] The book she wrote was published in 1898 and titled simply *Women and*

Economics. Although it is thought by many to be one of the most original works on economic thought, in many ways it was written from the
margins of the discipline.[4]

Examination of the membership lists of organizations such as the
AEA offer a unique window into the role that gender played in economists' struggle to gain status and influence. Overall histories examining the rise of economics as a discipline have paid scant attention to the
role of gender in the rise of professional authority, but there is a growing body of literature that examines early women economists and their
contributions, challenges, and conflicts.[5] Materials in the AEA archives
further expand our understanding of the role of gender in the professionalization of economics.

We begin this chapter by examining the origins of the AEA and the
representation of women as members in its early years along with how
the financial frailty of the organization and efforts to boost its member's status shaped its efforts to increase its membership. Ultimately, we
examine how AEA membership drives worked to exclude what would
seem to be a natural constituency in exchange for the financial support
and status that came from associating with businessmen.

PROFESSIONAL EXPERTISE AND
THE ORIGINS OF THE AEA

The rise of the research-oriented university in the late nineteenth century brought a number of specialized teaching positions in political
economy where professors experienced growing pressure to achieve
social standing in a culture that "had never been strongly deferential to
intellectual authority."[6] In contrast to European scholars, whose status
was well established and grounded in the patronage system, professors
in the United States increasingly relied on the authority of professional
expertise to gain status. As Marion Fourcade points out, the professional association, organized around disciplinary silos, was an important mechanism for organizing and cultivating professional expertise.[7]

Although the AEA was originally conceived of as an organization with a reform orientation for "economists who repudiate *laissez-faire* as a scientific doctrine," these sentiments had been toned down in the first constitution, established in 1885.[8] Only two years later, the constitution had been amended to remove the somewhat radical statement of principles. Nonetheless, significant divisions in the membership remained— disagreements that threatened the status of economists as experts. In fact, the AEA's first seven years were fraught with tension over what A. W. Coats describes as the underlying question of principle: "how far was the Christian impulse to social reform compatible with the scholarly impartiality deemed appropriate to a scientific body?"[9]

Disagreements over policy brought unwelcome external visibility for the fledging organization in the 1890s and early 1900s as economists came under attack for expressing various views on free silver, the labor movement, and public utilities. As Edward Ross soon discovered, holding unpopular views—particularly with those who founded Stanford University—was dangerous territory. Ross was fired by Jane Stanford for his views and for violating her alleged prohibition on partisan political activity. However, he was not alone. Edward W. Bemis was dismissed from the University of Chicago, Henry C. Adams dismissed from Cornell University, and John R. Commons forced to temporarily retire from Indiana University, all because their views on a variety of issues did not comport well with the views of those in authority.[10]

Internal disagreements on economic issues, along with the external assaults on academic freedom, forced a reckoning of sorts that facilitated a particular kind of professionalism in economics. According to Mary Furner, as knowledge production became increasingly accountable to external institutions, such as university boards and state governments, advocacy came to be viewed as incompatible with "scientific professionalism." Safer ground could be found in "hands-off professionalism" channeled through research bodies and expert commissions, thus transforming reformers into technical experts.[11] The AEA did little to address academic freedom directly, but the organization was important in providing opportunities for professors to meet, exchange information, and sign letters of support—in other words, act collectively. For a discipline increasingly devoted to the virtues of the free market, their penchant for collective action in search of status and professional reward was rather impressive.

As Dorothy Ross saw it, the chief casualties to this particular form of professionalization were women. As women increased their presence as students in graduate programs in the last decade of the nineteenth century and early twentieth century, they were steered into social work, reform activities, and women's colleges—"precincts the men were defining as outside the scientific and academic mainstream."[12] As academic professionals, male social scientists interacted primarily with other men in the workplace, expressed their learned views in specialized journals, and gained status and support with their involvement in the professional organization.

WOMEN'S MEMBERSHIP IN THE EARLY YEARS OF THE AEA

From its inception in the 1880s until the mid-1920s, the AEA struggled with securing adequate resources to support its growing list of activities directed toward expanding its influence. The cost of the decision to begin publishing the *American Economic Review* (*AER*) in 1911 along with other initiatives made the slow-growing membership revenues all the more problematic. It was partly this financial stress that brought association leaders to see the business community as a source of needed support. In Coats's words, "In practice, however, at least until the mid-1920's, the organization could not both survive and perform the full range of its self-appointed tasks without the financial aid provided regularly by businessmen's subscriptions or, intermittently, in the form of gifts, life membership payments, and financial aid towards the publication of monographs, the awards of prizes, and the administration of new membership campaigns."[13]

In addition to financial support (which could also be obtained through women philanthropists eager to support prizes for essays on women, for example), leaders of the AEA solicited businessmen in their membership drives as a means of expanding their influence and status.[14] Philanthropic industrialists had established their interest in higher education by founding a number of private universities, such as Johns Hopkins University, Vanderbilt University, the University of Chicago, and Stanford University, along with establishing ties to political elites. Although the progressive era marks a period of significant criticism of business interests, "To all appearances, the age belonged to business."[15] By the 1920s, A. Lawrence Lowell, then president of Harvard University, would close the circle with the founding of the Harvard Business School. In his 1923 *Harvard Business Review* essay, Lowell attributes the "creation of the Harvard Business School to the emergence of business management as a distinct profession" proclaiming that "the great professions have been among the chief agencies of progress."[16]

The reliance on businessmen for AEA activities was evident in all three of its membership drives during this time. These drives, which were concentrated in 1900–1902, 1909–1913, and 1922–1926, revealed not only the financial frailty of the organization but also the desire to improve the status of its members.[17] While the desire to recruit new members and retain existing ones was an ongoing preoccupation, the decisions made on recruitment clearly reflected a desire for financial stability and the status-seeking priorities of those building a new profession with increased influence. This drive toward professionalization had an important effect on women and their participation as members.[18]

Despite the priority on expanding membership, the AEA actively recruited a particular constituency outside of academia in its first two membership drives while ignoring women active in social causes— women who may have represented a more natural constituency. The third membership drive, while not exactly leaving behind its preoccupation with recruitment of businessmen, lawyers, and bankers, expanded recruitment in an effort to bring graduate students and young instructors into the association. It is perhaps not surprising that

the representation of women as members in the AEA expanded somewhat in the 1920s.[19]

A brief survey of the participation of women as members in the early
years of the AEA from 1885 to 1928 is revealing (see table 4.1).[20] The proportion of women among AEA members in the first four decades of
the association peaked in 1888, with 46 women among 430 individual

TABLE 4.1 Membership in the American Economic Association,
1886–1948

Publication year	Total	Institutional	Individual	Men	Women	Percent women
1886	182	0	182	175	7	3.8
1888	455	25	430	384	46	10.7
1889	609	41	568	518	50	8.8
1890	634	61	573	540	33	5.8
1894	781	77	704	672	32	4.5
1895	642	77	565	545	20	3.5
1896	675	86	589	568	21	3.6
1897	678	94	584	565	19	3.3
1898	675	99	576	554	22	3.8
1899	693	117	576	555	21	3.6
1900*	706	125	581	560	21	3.6
1901*	801	133	668	648	20	3.0
1902*	968	131	837	813	24	2.9
1903	1,003	135	868	847	21	2.4
1904	975	138	837	810	27	3.2
1905	1,009	137	872	847	25	2.9
1906	1,006	139	867	841	26	3.0
1907	1,000	146	854	828	26	3.0
1908	1,005	153	852	825	27	3.2
1909**	1,134	153	981	948	33	3.4
1910**	1,509	170	1,339	1,278	61	4.6

(continued)

TABLE 4.1 (continued)

Publication year	Total	Institutional	Individual	Men	Women	Percent women
1911**	2,115	198	1,917	1,841	76	4.0
1913**	2,563	251	2,312	2,227	85	3.7
1914	2,449	301	2,148	2,070	78	3.6
1916	2,392	346	2,046	1,973	74	3.6
1919	2,667	478	2,189	2,125	64	2.9
1922***	2,951	611	2,340	2,257	83	3.5
1924***	3,350	728	2,622	2,511	111	4.2
1926***	3,349	744	2,605	2,480	125	4.8
1928	3,469	803	2,666	2,518	148	5.6
1931	3,821	1008	2,813	2,649	164	5.8
1933	3,496	957	2,539	2,393	145	5.7
1936	2,637	N/A	2,637	2,478	159	6.0
1938	2,697	N/A	2,697	2,536	161	6.0
1940	3,153	N/A	3,151	2,978	173	5.5
1942	3,487	N/A	3,487	3,269	218	6.3
1946	4,408	N/A	4,408	4,038	370	8.4
1948	5,852	N/A	5,851	5,353	498	8.5

Sources: Data derived from numerous individual membership lists found in the American Economic Association Records, Publications of the American Economic Association, *Handbook of the American Economic Association*, supplements to *Economic Studies, Bulletin of the American Economic Association*, and the *American Economic Review*. The sex of the member is determined by first name and when in question by searches of historical documents such as newspapers, obituaries, and census records.

Note: The column "Percent women" shows the percentage of total individual memberships that are held by women.
*First membership drive
**Second membership drive
***Third membership drive

members, or 10.7 percent of the membership. The proportion of women declined to 2.4 percent in 1903 (21 women among 868 individual members), after the AEA's first membership drive (1900–1902). This first drive increased the number of male members in the AEA from 560 in 1900 to 847 in 1903, but not the number of women. There were twenty-one women members in 1903—the same number as in 1900. In absolute numbers, the 50 women belonging to the AEA in 1889 (out of 568 individual members) was not exceeded until 1910, when 61 women were 4.6 percent of 1,339 individual members. This latter level was achieved in the course of the AEA's second membership drive, which increased the membership from 948 men and 33 women in 1909 (3.4 percent women) to 2,070 men and 78 women in 1914 (3.6 percent women). Overall, from 1890 to 1909, the number of women AEA members never exceeded 33, with a low of 19 in 1897. The proportion of women among individual members of the AEA slipped back to 2.9 percent in 1919, thereafter growing slowly but steadily, exceeding 4 percent in 1924 and 5 percent in 1928.

THE DEMISE OF THE BRANCH ASSOCIATION AND THE FIRST MEMBERSHIP DRIVE

At its inception in 1885 and during the years that Gilman was a member, the AEA had embraced the notion of branch associations. In fact, Gilman's interest in the club movement and subsequent membership in the AEA were perhaps facilitated by the existence of branch associations in the early years. The demise of the branch association was no doubt an early factor working against women's participation.

In vol. 1, issue 1 of the *Publications of the American Economic Association* (1886), the names of the officers of the Connecticut Valley Branch were provided, and all were men. As described the following year in his Report on the Connecticut Valley Branch of the Second Annual Meeting of the AEA (1887), Edward W. Bemis (secretary of the Connecticut Valley Branch) brimmed with enthusiasm over the prospects of these branch associations, explaining that the Connecticut Valley branch "has grown steadily in numbers and influence until it now counts upon its rolls sixty-two members, including eleven ladies." He went on to ask, "May it not be one mission, and an important mission, of the American Economic Association to organize such branch associations of men and women?"[21]

The Connecticut Valley Branch was the first, and other branches soon followed including the Orange (NJ), Buffalo (NY), Galesburg (IL), Washington DC, Canton (OH), and Austin (TX) branches. Officer rolls were reported periodically, with all officers being men in 1886 and 1888. In 1889, Annie H. Barus became vice president of the Washington DC Branch, and Miss A. McGregor was vice president of the Canton Branch.[22]

The 1894 handbook reported what appeared to be the first sign of trouble for the branch associations. No names of branch officers were published in the handbook, but it was reported that "It was ordered that the names of all members of branch associations over one year in arrears in their dues be dropped from the rolls."[23]

Concern was clearly emerging about the growing financial pressures brought about by branch associations collecting half the regular dues but providing full access to published monographs. When the appropriate share of the dues was not passed on to the national office, action was swift. In 1895, the association reported,

> Of the branch associations, none remain. All of them had by the beginning of this year ceased active work and had ceased to pay dues some years before, though we still continued to send them monographs. Repeated letters to Secretaries and much diligent work on the part of some of them have succeeded in settling our business with all of them but one, and we hope to get a final settlement with this in due time.[24]

As the Report of the Secretary showed, the loss of branch members was not insignificant for the young association. The Report of the Seventh Annual Meetings showed a decline in branch members from 132 to 0 from January 1, 1894, to December 27, 1894, at a time when regular members totaled a mere 482 that year.[25]

The end of the branch associations is particularly noteworthy in terms of its effect on women's participation in the association. Women were active participations in the club movement, and what little we know about the membership of these branch associations shows a much higher proportion of women than the national rolls. The branch associations allowed women's participation when they were limited by geographic (mobility) constraints. Clearly, the movement toward a national association without the branches worked against women's overall participation.

Along with the end of the branch associations, other changes were underway, including the decline of clergy as members. A careful review of the 1902 AEA membership list reveals a change in the reporting of titles for individual memberships that perhaps reflected more than simply the desire to save space. In that year, remaining clergy were listed by their names alone (only one Rev. remained) and their credentials, where applicable (Doctor of Divinity, D.D.). The transformation of E. Benjamin Andrews from "Rev. Elisha Benjamin Andrews D.D. L.L.D. Chancellor of the University of Nebraska" to "Elisha Benjamin Andrews, Chancellor of the University of Nebraska" speaks to this transformation and the decline in the authority of the clergy. By 1904, the number of members identifiable as clergy stood at one. Thereafter, none are identified as such.[26]

The decline in clergy representation among the AEA's membership has been well recognized as an indication of the changing character of the association's membership.[27] Less well understood is the role of the first membership drive and its effect on women's membership.

In the early years of the association, when Richard T. Ely was secretary, "determined efforts were made to enlist the support of a wide variety of nonacademic persons, and the early membership lists included a high proportion of clergymen."[28] Yet when Ely became AEA president in 1900 and the first membership drive began, a deliberate effort was made to "arouse the support of business and professional men."[29] Charles H. Hull, serving as secretary and treasurer of the AEA, admonished members of the council to "actively interest themselves in adding to the Association's members."[30] Following suit, the council resolved to call on its members to "suggest each at least five candidates for membership in the Association."[31]

That there was not an increase in women members from this solicitation may not be surprising. Although the council consisted of 154 members in 1902, only 1 was a woman—Mary Roberts Smith. In the end, as Coats noted, the first membership campaign was undertaken almost single-handedly by Ely.[32] Pointing to the largest increase in membership in recent history, acting Secretary Frank A. Fetter said, "The secretary may perhaps be permitted to record his opinion, that while this result could not have been reached without the cordial cooperation of the members, it would not have been reached save for the energy of President Ely, who has given much time to advancing the Association's interests."[33] The first membership drive successfully added 279 men to the membership rolls, but it added not a single woman.

A NATURAL CONSTITUENCY?

Efforts to solicit the support and membership of businessmen were particularly pronounced in the second membership drive (1909–1913). This effort reflected desires for an increasing source of membership revenue and status-seeking priorities. This drive toward professionalization had an important effect on women and their participation as members of the AEA.[34]

In the Report of the Secretary dated December 27–31, 1909, T. N. (Thomas Nixon) Carver offered up an extensive review of the association's activities and did so to "show why the finances of the Association will remain in a somewhat unsatisfactory state unless we do one of three things: (1) increase our membership, (2) increase the annual dues, or (3) reduce our publications." Of these possibilities, he went on to say, "the first seems to the Secretary to be the most attractive." The association's leadership concurred, and a second membership drive was launched.[35]

The president was authorized to appoint a committee on membership to work with the secretary to increase the number of members. Appointed to the committee were Roger W. Babson, Frank H. Dixon, and A. W. (Arch Wilkinson) Shaw. Babson was an entrepreneur who had worked for investment firms before founding Babson's Statistical Organization and Babson College; Dixon was professor of economics at

Dartmouth and member of the AEA Executive Committee from 1906 to 1912; and Shaw was the founder of Shaw Company, a publisher. Shaw later returned to Harvard to study economics, thus straddling both milieux. Clearly, the composition of the committee reflected the leadership's desire to increase businessmen among its members while showing little interest in expanding women's membership.[36]

The effort to recruit businessmen extended at various times to most AEA officers and is evident in the activities surrounding recruitment during the second membership drive. In a letter dated October 13, 1913, Davis R. Dewey, editor of the *AER*, wrote to Charles L. Raper of Chapel Hill, NC, to solicit names of potential members. Raper was apparently not the only person from North Carolina to receive such a solicitation. In a letter dated October 20, 1913, William H. Glasson responded to another of Dewey's letters, drawing attention to the "comparatively small number of members of the Economic Association in North Carolina." Glasson responded by suggesting the following names of men who ought to be interested in membership: George Stephens (banker), Joseph G. Brown (banker), J. F. Bruton (banker), J. S. Carr (banker), J. F. Wily (banker), J. A. Long (banker and state senator), Victor Bryant (lawyer and state senator), George Watts (capitalist), and John Sprunt Hill (banker). Noting that they were nearly all bankers, Glasson suggested that Dewey direct their attention to the "great value of our publication to them as a class" as they "are apt to regard our association as a purely academic organization."[37] Dewey responded as directed, including in his solicitations articles that might be of particular interest to the businessmen.

The second membership drive was also accompanied by an increase in annual dues from $3 to $5, which resulted in reductions in members. In the final year of the drive, dues were raised, and the secretary was loath to report that this was "the first year that the present Secretary has had to record in his annual report a loss in membership."[38] In winter 1914, when memberships continued to fall, Secretary Allyn Abbott Young embarked on a campaign sending letters to 5,300 potential members. Measured in terms of association memberships that resulted, these and other solicitations produced seemingly low return. As Young later noted, the returns to this investment appeared to be "disappointingly small."[39]

Nonetheless, officers continued to solicit memberships after the second drive had concluded. In a letter dated May 13, 1918, Dewey directed his secretary to obtain a Boston directory so that addresses might be obtained for "a list of names to use for circulating for members."[40] Although the Boston directory provided few names of women, there is some small evidence that women economists were also solicited for membership in the AEA in this period. In a letter sent in March 1918, Dewey wrote to Young suggesting the following names from the staff of Bryn Mawr for membership in the AEA: Angie L. Kellogg, Anna C. McBride, Clara E. Mortenson, and Anne Bezanson.[41]

The letter soliciting memberships for women from Bryn Mawr College stands out in the AEA Archives as a bit unusual for this time, when almost all of the letters soliciting membership were to businessmen. The archives yield some indication as to the possible origin of this invitation. On January 30, 1918—just a few months before the membership letter, Dewey received a letter from Susan Kingsbury of Bryn Mawr pointing out that the list of doctoral dissertations recently published in the *AER* had not included Bryn Mawr students. While the letter of invitation to members of the Bryn Mawr staff may have been unrelated to the earlier communication, it appears more likely that this was an attempt on Dewey's part to smooth things over.

By focusing attention on wartime funding needs, World War I offered a unique opportunity to secure donations and appeal to the business class for membership. Yet potential problems emerged from this particular solution to the association's financial difficulties. During the war, AEA officers worked to notify members of ongoing war-related activities while raising funds to support the work of committees as seen in a letter by Young to Anne E. Gardner of the AEA sent in May 1918.[42] In this letter, Young informs Gardner of his proposed circular letter to be sent to all association members. He goes on to explain that the "real reason" for sending the circular is that "Professor [Edwin R. A.] Seligman had been offered a fund of $50,000 for the work of his committee and that, while it comes from perfectly good sources, we do not feel that we want to use it except as part of a general fund contributed by members of the Association."[43] Young explained that the "New York business men who will contribute to the Seligman committee expenses, including particularly Mr. Isidor Straus of R. H. Macy and Company and Mr. Thomas Lamont of J.P. Morgan & Company, will join the Association if they are not already members, so that the whole amount will come from members of the Association."[44] This letter demonstrates the sensitivity that AEA officers had over the appearance of nonmembers providing resources and the ethical flexibility they nonetheless mustered to move forward with such donations.

Irving Fisher, then president of the AEA, focused his efforts on recruiting members of the business class and crafted his rhetorical appeal around the war effort. In a letter dated October 30, 1918, Fisher wrote:

> Dear Sir: I am sure that you, as a lawyer, are deeply interested in the great economic problems of the war and of the period after the war. For this reason I venture to call your attention to the work of the American Economic Association. This Association is the representative organization of the professional economists of the country, but its membership includes an increasing number of men in other professions, in business, and in the government service, who are interested in the wider aspects of business and economic problems.[45]

Included in Fisher's letter was a blank application which, along with a "check for one year's dues ($5.00)," would be sufficient for membership. Ivy Ledbetter Lee, publicity expert and a member of the AEA, would have been proud.

The new memberships among the business class were often short-lived, and members often resigned after only one year. More annoying, their resignations were often communicated through letters from disgruntled former members explaining the reasons for their departure. The chief of the Bureau of Foreign and Domestic Commerce was uncharacteristically blunt when he wrote: "There seems to be so little of interest in your periodical and so little of real vital interest in your meetings."[46]

There was, of course, the delicate problem of what the AEA had to offer to the nonacademic business class in an association increasingly focused on academic pursuits. This and the problem of what might be expected of businessmen in return continued to trouble Young. These tensions emerged periodically in letters such as the one received by Young in 1918 from Erastus W. Bulkley, who took it upon himself to investigate the membership of the committees he was being asked to support.[47] Responding to Young's request for contributions to support the "necessary expenses of various special committees appointed to work on the economic problems of the war," Bulkley wrote to express his concerns:

> In looking over these committees, I find that they are composed almost entirely of professors in various institutions. While I do not wish in any way to minimize the work of professors, especially professors of economics, it has always seemed to me that if economics was to make any progress in this country consistent with its general importance, there would have to be close cooperation between the professors and the business men.[48]

Bulkley copied the letter to AEA President Fisher and received a carefully framed response admitting that the suggestion to facilitate close cooperation between professors and businessmen "was a good one in so far as it is consistent with the character of the American Economic Association which is primarily an association of academic economists." Not leaving well enough alone, Fisher added:

> I would suggest that you write to Professor Seligman. His committee is closely in touch with businessmen. When the Committee on the Purchasing Power of Money was formed I suggested having a number of business men as members and the Executive Committee took the

ground that every business man would prefer to have a committee of professional economists.[49]

Fisher's short letter elicited a three-page response from Bulkley, which began with the somewhat acerbic observation that "I was rather under the impression that the membership of the American Economic Association included not only academic economists, but also not a few business men." He went on to entice Fisher with the suggestion of an "institution for economic research, properly endowed." Communicating his strong belief that it would perhaps fall to economists to initiate this delicate relationship, Bulkley referred Fisher to Edward D. Jones, professor of commerce and industry at the University of Michigan, who apparently had the admiration and support of Bulkley and other businessmen in realizing "that he cannot sit in his study and evolve [the] science of economics." After suggesting that "there is no subject before the economic interest of the country today of more importance than this matter of cooperation between academic economists and businessmen and the enlargement of facilities for the scientific study of various business matters," Bulkley closed by indicating, "I am not writing Prof. Seligman, as suggested. I have put this general broad question to you, feeling that it may be a matter to which you, as President of the American Economic Association, may wish to give special and official attention."[50]

A few days later, Young wrote again, perhaps to smooth things over, explaining how it is that many businessmen find little time for the work of committees while professional economists often find that this work comes "so directly in the line of their work vocation that they usually regard it as more or less important."[51] Bulkley responded to indicate that Young's viewpoint "might be open to considerable discussion for and against," insisting again that economists and businessmen would have much to gain by greater cooperation. Apparently not convinced that he had succeeded in influencing Young, Bulkley closed by inviting him to "have luncheon" with him some time now that he was in New York.[52] It is unclear whether Young ever took him up on this offer, but Bulkley clearly had no intention of letting the issue go. In a letter sent a few months later, Bulkley wrote to Young requesting a copy of the AEA constitution and bylaws, list of members, and "any other general information you have regarding the aims, purposes and accomplishments to-date of the Association." This hard-fought battle produced seemingly short-lived results. Bulkley was listed as a member in the 1919 membership rolls, but no record of his membership is found after that date.[53]

EMERGING INDEPENDENCE FOR A PRIMARILY LEARNED SOCIETY

The correspondence between Bulkley and Young illustrates a significant underlying conflict in the AEA—a conflict that was ultimately resolved to a great extent during the 1920s. The second membership drive, with its emphasis on recruiting businessmen, had sparked concerns about just what kind of organization the AEA was to be. For his part, Young expressed growing concerns. Confiding in Dewey, Young admitted in a letter dated November 15, 1915:

I am inclined to think that sooner or later we shall have to face the question of just what kind of an association we want to be. My own efforts, as you know, have been devoted to strengthening our hold upon those persons who might be counted upon to support a strictly professional and scientific association. I do not believe that Babson's efforts among business men have done us any good, for few of his nominees remain members for more than one year. [54]

By 1919, when a deficit again appeared and the association was debating how to address the problem, Young made his views clear and public. In his last report as secretary, he explained:

The apparently obvious way to increase our income is by increasing our membership. But it has been our experience that efforts to extend our membership list meet with rapidly diminishing returns if we go very far beyond the regrettably small group of persons who are definitely interested in the scientific study of economic problems. We cannot go very far in the direction of securing and holding a larger number of members without lowering standards, and it is to be feared, diminishing our influence. Our fundamental purposes must be defined by the fact that we are primarily a learned, or if you prefer, a professional society.[55]

When the third membership drive began in 1922, a shift was underway. A Special Membership Committee was established—the same year that the association's Executive Committee voted to move forward with incorporation. The committee, chaired by F. S. (Frederick Shipp) Deibler, indicated that they had turned their attention toward "graduate and advanced students, to bankers, and lawyers, and to associations of business men where there has been any indication that a library or a research department was maintained."[56] Importantly, the Special Membership Committee's attention to graduate students and young instructors demonstrates a widening of the net that appears to have opened the door for women in this decade. The subtle shift to "associations of business men where a library or research department has been maintained" also reveals a slight shift away from individual businessmen as members.

At the same time, a Special Committee on Finance was established, headed by Seligman. In 1919, the association had a net deficit for the first time since 1911. The net deficit in 1919 was $1,688.48 and to make matters worse, grew to $2,366.60 the next year.[57] This special committee not only called for an increase in membership to address the financial needs, they also called for developing a permanent endowment. The AEA's financial needs were uppermost in the minds of those on the special committees in the years leading up to this final membership campaign, and their recommendations brought financial independence from businessmen and needed long-term financial support for the association.

In their 1922 report, the Special Committee on Finance identified donations totaling $10,000—donations that helped to pay off debt and balance the budget. As Coats reports, "thirty gentlemen" had made substantial progress in starting an endowment, and by January 1923, Seligman suggested, "the committee believes that an attempt should be made to raise a fund of $5,000 for three years."[58] In the end, the outcome was evident in the growth of the association's cash, savings, and investments, which increased from $7,481.54 in 1920 to $39,077.13 by 1929.[59]

The priorities and ultimate success in recruitment during the membership drives is evidenced by the growth in membership broken down by institutional membership and male and female members. The first membership drive from 1900 to 1902 resulted in a decline in institutional memberships as a proportion of total memberships. Institutional memberships went from 17.7 percent of total memberships in 1900 to 13.5 percent in 1903. As previously mentioned, the number of women members from 1900 to 1903 stayed the same, while the number of men rose from 560 to 847. As a result, the percentage of women members declined from 3.6 percent of individual memberships in 1900 to 2.4 percent in 1903.

During the second membership drive, institutional memberships increased from 153 in 1909 to 301 in 1914. Female membership increased from 33 to 78, while the number of male memberships increased from 948 to 2,070. As a percentage of individual memberships, women's memberships grew ever so slightly from 3.4 percent in 1909 to 3.6 percent by 1914. Like the first membership drive, most of the increase in total membership occurred with an increase in individual memberships by men.

Finally, the last membership drive, which took place from 1922 to 1926, reflected a growing interest in graduate students and young instructors, as well as bankers, lawyers, and "associations of business men where there has been any indication that a library or research department was maintained."[60] This widening of the pool of potential members brought about changes in the association's membership. Institutional memberships grew from 611 (20.7 percent of total memberships) in 1922 to 803 (23.1 percent of total memberships) by 1928. More interesting perhaps is the modest but steady growth in women's membership in the 1920s. Women memberships grew from 83 in 1922 to 148 by 1928, or from 3.5 percent of individual memberships to 5.6 percent. By contrast, individual membership for men went from 2,257 in 1922 to 2,518 by 1928 but fell in percentage terms from 96.5 percent of individual membership down to 94.5 percent.

The 1930s began with the possibility that the association officers could turn to the business of overseeing their investments—holding securities in Bell Telephone Company, Northern Pacific Railway, Commonwealth Edison, Illinois Central Railroad Company, and United Biscuit Company, among others.[61]

With a net gain in membership for 1930, despite the tumultuous end to 1929, Secretary Deibler was apparently in good spirits. As he wrote, "Notwithstanding a year of general depression, there has been an increase in membership. This showing has been possible by the splendid co-operation which has been rendered by a large number of the members. The lists of names furnished the Secretary, especially from those connected with institutions conducing graduate work, has yielded fruitful results."[62] By 1932, membership had started to decline—the first time (as Deibler noted) since 1915 that there had been a decrease.[63] The decline continued through 1933.

As overall memberships declined in the early 1930s (as shown in table 4.1), so did women's memberships, falling from 164 in 1931 to 145 by 1933. However, the proportion of women's share of memberships stayed roughly constant at around 6 percent throughout the 1930s and into the early 1940s. It was not until the end of World War II that women's membership levels began to increase, causing the proportion of women members to rise to 8.4 percent in 1946 and 8.5 percent in 1948.

World War II brought women into the AEA in large numbers. Examination of membership lists show that about 11 percent of women listed in the membership rolls in 1933, 1936, and 1938 were women with only a one- or two-year history of membership with the AEA. By contrast, in 1946 this increased, and about 34 percent of women members had only one or two years of membership history in the AEA. By 1948, nearly 50 percent of members had only one or two years of membership in the organization. As women in general were drawn into governmental work, they took the opportunity to build their careers through professional associations.

Who were these women members? Were they philanthropists, activists, academics, and scholars? In the next chapter we examine these members to better understand their backgrounds and how the composition of women members changed over time.

5

A NATURAL CONSTITUENCY

he American Economic Association (AEA) membership lists
from the early years of its existence provide a window into the
characteristics of the men and women drawn to the association
and expand our understanding of what members were like in those early
years and how their backgrounds changed over time. From 1886 to 1948,
in the years for which individual membership data are available, there
were approximately 63,331 total memberships reported—60,017 men
and 3,314 women. Women's memberships were only a small fraction,
about 5.2 percent on average, of the total memberships of the association during its first sixty-three years.

Included among members in the AEA were many well-known people,
including Woodrow Wilson, Learned Hand, Benjamin Strong, Ivy Led-
better Lee, Andrew Carnegie, J. Pierpont Morgan, Seth Low, and Ralph
Easley, and economists such as Alfred Marshall, John N. Keynes, Léon
Walras, F. Y. Edgeworth, Thorstein Veblen, John R. Commons, and John
Maynard Keynes.[1] What is often overlooked are the women reformers,
philanthropists, and academics who were also members of the AEA.
Who were these women members? Did they hold advanced degrees, and
if so, in what fields? Did women hold leadership positions in the AEA and
its flagship journal, the *American Economic Review* (*AER*)? Finally, how
did the nature of women's membership change over time?

SUFFRAGE, ABOLITION, AND PEACE:
SCHOLAR ACTIVISTS IN THE EARLY YEARS

Charlotte Perkins Gilman's membership in the AEA lasted only a few years, but she was in many ways representative of the women who joined the association in the latter part of the nineteenth century. Among the early members of the AEA were many well-known women activists and social reformers—a membership extending well beyond the professoriate. They were not a membership that was, as we saw, sought after or encouraged to join. Moreover, those women scholars who were members often shared the commitment to activism and reform evident in women members from outside the confines of academic halls.

The first organizing meeting of the AEA, held in 1885, had only one woman in attendance, Professor Katharine Coman of Wellesley College.[2] In 1886, the first year memberships were recorded, women were 7 of the 182 members listed and members included two Wellesley scholars—Coman, full professor of history and economics, and Professor Mary Alice Willcox, Department of Zoology. Scholar-activists such as Helen Stuart Campbell, who taught briefly at the University of Wisconsin and at the Kansas State Agricultural College and is considered a pioneer in the home economics movement, and social reformers such as Josephine Shaw Lowell, founder of the New York Consumer's League, were also early members.[3]

From 1886 through 1899, the AEA continued to expand in membership, growing from 182 to 693 total members (including 117 institutional memberships) by 1899. Included among the ninety-three individual women members listed in this time were scholars and reformers. In addition to Coman and Willcox were scholars such as Sophonisba Breckinridge, who graduated from Wellesley College in 1888, became the first woman to be admitted to the Kentucky bar in 1895, and earned a PhD in political science and economics from the University of Chicago in 1901. Jane Marie Bancroft earned her PhD in European history from Syracuse University in 1883, went on to found the Western Association of Collegiate Alumnae, and served as dean of the Women's

College of Northwestern University. Marietta Kies earned her PhD in philosophy from the University of Michigan and had difficulty finding an academic position. Cornelia Maria Clapp, who taught at Mount Holyoke College and earned her doctorate in zoology from the University of Chicago in 1896 along with Jane M. Slocum, who completed a doctorate in social sciences and a law degree and founded the Idaho Industrial Institute.[4] In 1898, Helen Page Bates joined the AEA—the first woman with a PhD in economics to become a member. Bates earned her doctorate from the University of Wisconsin in 1896 and went on to teach at Rockford College before joining Hull House. In all, eight women members of the AEA, or nearly 10 percent of women members during the first fourteen years of its existence, held a doctorate—only one, however, in economics.

Members who were scholar-activists in the nineteenth century include Florence Kelley, who did graduate work in economics and social science at the University of Zurich, earned a law degree from Northwestern University School of Law in 1894, and collaborated with Jane Addams at Hull House. Kelley is well known for helping create the National Association for the Advancement of Colored People. Carrie L. Chapman (Catt), active in the suffrage movement, served as president of the National American Woman Suffrage Association and later founded the League of Women Voters.[5] Perhaps most well known was Emily Greene Balch, who began teaching at Wellesley College in 1896 and won the Nobel Peace Prize in 1946.[6] Balch was only the second woman to receive the Nobel Peace Prize and successfully combined an academic career with social activism on issues such as poverty, child labor, and immigration.

TENACIOUS PERSISTERS

A total of 1,036 individual women were members of the AEA from 1886 to 1948. During that time, about 27 percent of those women held a doctorate and 19 percent held a doctorate in economics. In table 5.1, we see

TABLE 5.1 AEA Women Members, 1886–1948

Decades	Total number of women	All doctorates		Economics doctorates	
		Number	Percent	Number	Percent
1886–1899	92	8	9	1	1
1900–1909	38	12	32	7	18
1910–1919	114	23	20	16	14
1920–1929	161	59	37	42	26
1930–1939	123	43	35	26	21
1940–1948	508	139	27	108	21

Source: Data on AEA memberships are taken from the membership lists found in the *Publications of the American Economic Association, Handbook of the American Economic Association*, supplements to *Economic Studies, Bulletin of the American Economic Association*, and *American Economic Review*. The source used to identify doctoral degrees for women members is ProQuest.

that while only 9 percent of women members held a doctorate during the first thirteen years of the association's history, the twentieth century brought an increase in proportions of women members with doctorates. In the first decade of the twentieth century, about 32 percent of women members held a doctorate. In the period from 1910 to 1919, women with doctorates were about 20 percent of female members. In the 1920s and 1930s, the proportion of women with doctorates went from 37 percent to 35 percent, respectively. Finally, in the 1940s, the proportion of women with doctorates fell to an average of 27 percent, dropping particularly during the war years.

There is often the impression that women members held doctorates in fields other than economics. Although only one woman AEA member had a doctorate in economics in the nineteenth century, in the early decades of the twentieth century, the majority of women members with doctorates earned their degrees in economics. In the first decade of the twentieth century, the proportion of women members with doctorates in economics was 18 percent. From 1910 to 1919, it was 14 percent.

Throughout the 1920s, 26 percent of women members had a doctorate in economics. In the 1930s, this proportion was 21 percent, and in the 1940s, it remained at 21 percent.

Who were these female economists who were members of the AEA in the early decades of the twentieth century, and did they have only a fleeting association with the organization, or were they loyal members whose names appeared year after year on the membership rolls?

The woman with a doctorate in economics with the longest AEA membership was Sarah Scovill Whittelsey (Walden), whose membership spanned twenty-two years. Whittelsey was a graduate of Radcliffe College in 1894, earned her PhD from Yale in 1898, and taught economics at Wellesley College beginning in 1902. Of the 1,036 individual women AEA members from 1886 to 1948, 55 held memberships for over ten years. Roughly half of those longer-term memberships were held by women with a doctorate in economics. Moreover, whereas the average number of years of membership for women in general was three years, for women with a doctorate in economics the average length of a membership was roughly five years.

The woman with the longest AEA membership was Sarah James Eddy. Eddy was active in the abolition and suffragist movements, and she was a philanthropist whose membership lasted thirty-two years. One hundred ninety-six women held AEA memberships for five or more years. Who were these "tenacious persisters?"

Dividing women memberships for these tenacious persisters (women with memberships of five or more years), into five categories and examining the changes by decade allows us to identify the backgrounds of these women members and consider how they changed over time. Some worked in government, academia (including universities, colleges, normal schools, and in libraries), non-profits as diverse as the Hull House, Tax Policy League and Russell Sage Foundation, a small number worked in for-profit organizations, and finally many, especially early on, worked in a category we might call miscellaneous—philanthropists/activists.

In table 5.2, we can see that 48 percent of women AEA members in the period from 1886 to 1899 were primarily activists/philanthropists.

There were no women working in a for-profit organization during this time. About 17 percent of women persisters worked in nonprofit organizations, and 26 percent were academics.

The twentieth century brought change in women's membership. For each decade from 1900 until 1948, a falling proportion of women members with five or more years of membership were activists/philanthropists. This category decreased for each decade in the twentieth century, going from 26 percent in the first decade to 20 percent in the 1910s,

TABLE 5.2 AEA Women Members Classified as Persisters

Decade	Decade total number individual persisters	Employment	Number	Percent of total
1886–1899	23	Government	2	9
		Academic	6	26
		Nonprofit	4	17
		For-profit	0	0
		Philanthropy/miscellaneous	11	48
1900–1909	38	Government	4	11
		Academic	19	50
		Nonprofit	5	13
		For-profit	0	0
		Philanthropy/miscellaneous	10	26
1910–1919	61	Government	6	10
		Academic	35	57
		Nonprofit	6	10
		For-profit	1	2
		Philanthropy/miscellaneous	12	20
1920–1929	103	Government	16	16
		Academic	68	66
		Nonprofit	3	39
		For-profit	2	2
		Philanthropy/miscellaneous	13	13

Decade	Decade total number individual persisters	Employment	Number	Percent of total
1930–1939	154	Government	32	21
		Academic	98	64
		Nonprofit	8	5
		For-profit	4	3
		Philanthropy/miscellaneous	12	8
1940–1948	135	Government	28	21
		Academic	88	65
		Nonprofit	6	4
		For-profit	3	2
		Philanthropy/miscellaneous	10	7

Source: Data on AEA memberships are taken from the membership lists found in the *Publications of the American Economic Association*, *Handbook of the American Economic Association*, supplements to *Economic Studies*, *Bulletin of the American Economic Association*, and *American Economic Review*. Biographical information on employment is determined by examination of historical documents such as newspapers, obituaries, educational institution records, and census records.

Note: Persisters are members with five or more years of membership. One individual in the 1910s and 1920s was uncoded due to lack of information.

13 percent in the 1920s, 8 percent in the 1930s, and 7 percent in the 1940s.

In contrast, the proportion of women with memberships of five or more years classified as primarily "academic" grew from 50 percent in the first decade of the twentieth century to 57 percent in the 1910s, 66 percent in the 1920s, 64 percent in the 1930s, and 65 percent in the 1940s.

As table 5.3 shows, the proportion of the women persisters with a doctorate in economics grew from 18 percent in the first decade of the twentieth century to 30 percent in the 1910s, 47 percent in the 1920s and 1930s, and 51 percent by the 1940s. Clearly, the AEA was becoming a professional organization that appealed to women economists—many of whom held doctoral degrees in economics. Moreover, women with doctorates

TABLE 5.3 Women Persisters with Doctorates in Economics

Decade	Number of doctorates in economics	Total number of individual women members	Percent women members with economics PhD
1900–1909	7	38	18
1910–1919	18	61	30
1920–1929	48	103	47
1930–1939	73	155	47
1940–1948	69	135	51

Source: Data on AEA memberships are taken from the membership lists found in the *Publications of the American Economic Association, Handbook of the American Economic Association*, supplements to *Economic Studies, Bulletin of the American Economic Association*, and *American Economic Review*. The source used to identify doctoral degrees for women members is ProQuest.

in economics were loyal AEA members. The question remains—were these "tenacious persisters" with doctorates in economics able to participate in the activities of the association on a par with their male colleagues? Were they able to attend the annual meetings and serve on the editorial board of *AER*?

PERSISTENCE AND EXCLUSION

When we examine those serving as AEA officers, members of the Executive Committee, and board members, we see a system of overwhelming male dominance and little evidence of women's inclusion. The AEA underwent several changes in its organizational structure from its inception in 1885 to 1948. The Executive Committee originally consisted of the president, vice president, secretary, and treasurer until 1894, when the chair of the Publications Committee was added. In 1903, three members were added, and in 1904, seven past presidents were added. From 1906 to 1919, all past presidents were members of the Executive Committee along with six elected members. In 1920, as a growing number of former presidents made the Executive Committee less like a committee and more like a convention, the past president contingent was reduced to three.

In the 1933, the selection of officers became more democratic when the AEA moved from voting on one-person nominations for each position at the annual meeting to a mail ballot with a choice of candidates brought forward by a nominating committee. From 1934 on, the Executive Committee consisted of the president, two vice presidents, secretary, treasurer, chair of the editorial board, three past presidents, and six elected members. In 1936, the AEA added legal counsel to the board. When the dust had settled in 1948, the Executive Committee consisted of the president, vice president, secretary, treasurer, counsel, editor, the three most recent past presidents, and six elected members.[7]

During the period from 1886 to 1948, 203 men served as AEA officers while only 5 women did so. For the first thirty-three years of the association, there were no women officers.[8] The first woman officer was Edith Abbott, who was appointed for a one-year term as one of three vice presidents in 1918. The following year, Susan Kingsbury of Bryn Mawr College was appointed for a one-year term as a vice president. In 1928, Jessica Peixotto of the University of California at Berkeley was listed as a vice president. She too served only one year. Ten years later, Mabel Newcomer of Vassar College was listed as a vice president, this time serving the first full three-year term (1938–1940). Finally, in the 1940s, Eveline M. Burns was elected to the Executive Committee serving in 1945, 1946, and 1947, and Newcomer served a one-year term as vice president in 1947. Thus, a total of five women served as officers from 1886 through 1948, most for one-year terms. In contrast, the 203 men who served as officers during this time period mostly served three-year terms.

The AEA's ability to recruit officers from its membership within academic circles was, of course, limited but perhaps not quite so much as had been supposed. Secretary-Treasurer Thomas Nixon Carver noted in his communication with Professor Dixon of Dartmouth in a letter dated April 14, 1911, "We have pretty nearly exhausted the academic field, and have practically all teachers of economics in the Association now, though occasionally we find a new one."[9] Yet there were several teachers (many with doctoral degrees) who were not members at the time that Carver wrote: Katharine Bement Davis (PhD in economics, University of Chicago, 1900), Helen Page Bates (PhD in economics, University of Wisconsin, 1896), Florence Elizabeth Watson (PhD in political economy, Boston University, 1890), and Mary Graham (PhD in economics, Yale University, 1895) to name a few.

At the same time, the AEA resisted initiatives that would have potentially appealed to some perhaps more traditionally minded women.[10] For example, in a letter sent in July 1910, Theodora B. Cunningham, who helped found the National Council of American Indians along with Gertrude Bonnin, and Virginia King Frye wrote on behalf of the League of American Pen Women suggesting that a valuable addition to the *AER* might be a "woman's Department of household economics, which would be to the busy but intelligent house-wife what the Economic Review is to her thinking husband." They suggested that this section could describe "what is being done along the line of Household Economics by various State Federations of Women's Clubs."[11]

The League of American Pen Women was a literary club organized in 1897 by journalists in Washington, DC. By 1898, the league reportedly had over fifty members "from Maine to Texas, from New York to California." It is not surprising that its members might have something in common with women in the AEA. Like the AEA in its initial years, the league was a membership organization with local branches—thirty-five local branches across the country by 1921. For women who lacked institutional affiliations but wrote on topics of concern to women and on public policy, these organizations might have been appealing. However, only one group worked to provide a venue for intellectually active women.[12]

It is not clear how widely Dewey consulted on the question raised by Cunningham and Frye. A. W. Coats suggests that there is evidence that "Dewey evidently did not seriously consider Theodora B. Cunningham's suggestion that he should include "a Women's Department of household economics."[13] Regardless, Dewey's brief reply was resolute. "In reply to your inquiry of July 29 in regard to the possibility of establishing a women's department of household economics in the American Economics Review, I am sorry to say that we have not the space."[14]

Of course, primarily through Dewey's decisions (and to a lesser extent those of the board of editors), policies and determinations of what was worthy of inclusion in the valuable space of the *AER* were made. In the nearly three decades of service as editor of the *AER*, Dewey had the opportunity to work with fifty-eight editorial board members who assisted in determining which articles were worthy of publishing and which were not—decisions affecting the professional lives of countless faculty in the process. In his careful documenting of the editors of the *AER*, Dewey reveals what criteria were important as he lists them by name (with men's names only initialized and women's with the full name reported), by institution, and by year of service. The importance given to geographic representation is revealed by a second list, reporting the editors by geographic region.[15] This geographic diversity may have seemed especially important to document given that accusations of an East Coast conspiracy to dominate the association were frequent and somewhat troublesome.[16]

It is noteworthy that over the period Dewey served as editor, only two women economists served on the editorial board of the *AER*—Alzada Comstock of Mount Holyoke College (1937–39) and Mabel Newcomer of Vassar (1940). In other words, women did not serve on the *AER* editorial board until the late 1930s and constituted only 3.5 percent of the editorial board in total. Women served for only 3 of the 125 person-years of service during Dewey's time as editor. When economist and historian Michael A. Bernstein notes that "Time and again, Dewey would canvas his editorial board for suggestions regarding article topics and prospective authors," we must recognize that men's opinions are what he received.[17]

THE SEARCH FOR STATUS AND JURISDICTIONAL DISPUTES

The history of women and membership in the AEA is not a story of simply overlooking the recruitment of women or even the failure of its officers to recognize the importance of women in leadership positions. It is also a story that demonstrates how status-seeking professionals eschewed a natural constituency of individuals beyond the professoriate—people who, given their practical experience with economic issues, in many ways appeared to be more likely candidates for membership than many of the businessmen actively courted by the AEA. Already involved in charitable and reform activities, women would have seemed to be what Dorothy Ross called a "natural constituency" for the social sciences. Yet because they were women, they were not viewed as scientists, social or otherwise.[18] In a profession striving for status as a scientific enterprise, women were viewed as threatening. For this reason, social science was dangerous territory for women academics at the turn of the century.

The discipline of economics was unique in the transformation of higher education in the nineteenth century because, unlike other fields, the "stakes of the game" were particularly high. What economists had to say about monopolies, immigrant labor, and depressions had significant real-world implications. Not surprisingly perhaps, the professionalization of economics was accompanied by jurisdictional disputes—between groups over boundaries that determined who would be allowed to engage in the tasks of the profession and what those tasks would be.[19] The history of women in the early years of the AEA allows us to more clearly understand the role of gender in the process of professionalization in the academic knowledge system.

These jurisdictional disputes began with segmenting academic labor by identifying areas of specialization in doctoral degrees, which set a professional trajectory that was difficult to negotiate—especially for women. Whereas a majority of the founding members of the AEA had doctoral degrees in history, as economics evolved into its own discipline, economists began to argue for a greater separation between economics and other fields such as sociology and a separation between economics and home economics. The disestablishment of religion and advocacy (not to mention criticisms of the soft-headedness of economists such as Ely) would require disciplinary boundaries that made clear the scientific nature of economics.[20] As Thomas Carver put it, "Economists would prefer to stick to the subject of Economists. [One] should especially doubt whether the members of [the] association would easily find a common ground of discussion with Miss [Jane] Addams or Mr. Felix Adler, admirable as these persons are and valuable as their work is. [One] should be afraid that there would be difficulty in trying to think in the same language."[21]

As the press clippings of the "1900–1914 Scrapbook: Annual Meetings Program Clippings" in the AEA archives shows, economists' growing distain for sociology did not go unnoticed. In an article titled "Sociologists Complain of Their Own Standing: Delegates Say They Are Not Regarded as Trained Specialists by Men," those attending the American Sociological Society bemoaned the lack of respect they received as sociologists, considered their role through the tendency of some to talk in language unintelligible to the average person, and suggested that a solution might be to introduce sociology in the early high school years. These jurisdictional disputes reflected the desire for professional status as sociologists complained that they were not regarded with the proper respect.[22]

The growth of these jurisdictional disputes had indisputable consequences for women. Increasing numbers of women were characterized as having doctoral degrees appropriate for placement in labor relations, education and home economics, and sociology. Whereas earlier male scholars were able to transcend such labels and be accepted as professionals in the field of economics—economists such as Davis Rich Dewey, who earned a doctoral degree in history from Johns Hopkins University, and Allyn Abbott Young, who earned his doctoral degree from the University of Wisconsin in sociology—women economists were not so fortunate. There were a very few exceptions: Jessica Blanche Peixotto of the University of California at Berkeley, AEA vice president in 1928, completed her PhD in political science; Susan Kingsbury, AEA vice president in 1919, held a Columbia University PhD in history; and Minnie Throop England of the University of Nebraska had her PhD listed in religion even though her teaching and publications were about business cycles and crises. Dorothy Stahl Brady of the Bureau of Labor Statistics, an analyst of consumption and savings, also held a noneconomics PhD, but this was not a barrier to professional acceptance among economists since it was in mathematics.[23] Of course, the "mathiness" of economics would not be widely criticized for many decades, and those scholars with training in mathematics in the early years were some of the few who found the gates open when they chose to enter.[24]

WOMEN AND THE AEA IN PERSPECTIVE

Historians of professions have neglected the degree to which gender and the drive for professional status played a large role in shaping the actions and priorities of professional associations. Associations such as the AEA neglected and sometimes eschewed initiatives that would have brought increasing numbers of women as members at the same time they were trying to expand their membership. Their actions and priorities demonstrate the complex ways that status-seeking behaviors worked, perhaps unintentionally, to limit women's membership. Although there is evidence that women academic economists were on rare occasions solicited for AEA membership, larger forces were at play that precluded women's participation and membership in the AEA in far more fundamental ways.

The segmentation of academic labor made women with degrees in the social sciences vulnerable to exclusion and prey to ontological disputes. The significant influence of what Virginia Valian has called "gender schemas" allowed academic economists in the early years of the AEA to characterize women with doctorates in economics as sociologists and men with doctorates in sociology and history to stand as economists, and raised little cause for concern about the discrepancy.[25] Overall, the drive toward professionalization interacted with gender in ways that often undermined women academics by excluding those whose degrees were in cognate fields while recognizing and accepting men with degrees in cognate fields.

This examination of women's AEA memberships reveals the unique and talented individuals who joined in the early years. They were activists, many of them quite influential in promoting change, and also scholar activists. Nearly a third of these women held a doctorate, and the majority of these doctorates were in economics.

Many of the 1,036 women members are what we might call tenacious persisters—holding memberships for five or more years. Yet seldom were they allowed to participate in the AEA leadership. They clearly manifested persistence but experienced exclusion.

In the next chapter, we examine these women's ability to participate in the "trade in words"—the book trade—to determine the degree to which any lack of institutional academic affiliation and status influenced their opportunities to publish and express their voices on issues of importance to them.

6

THE TRADE IN WORDS

Gender and the Monograph

he publication of Charlotte Perkins Gilman's *Women in Economics* in 1898 marked a significant transformation, extending her work into nonfiction as well as fiction. *Women in Economics* was an immediate success, which propelled Gilman into the spotlight of lecture tours and resulting in at least some historians praising her as the "Marx and Veblen" of the woman's movement and placing her among the leading critical social thinkers of the early twentieth century.[1]

The success of this publication stands out in several ways, not only because Gilman's education was irregular and limited but because of the situation she found herself in eleven years earlier. In 1887, Gilman (then Stetson) sought the advice of S. Weir Mitchell, a noted physician and pioneer of the "rest cure"—a cure that Virginia Woolf once described as resulting in a patient going in "weighing seven stone six comes out weighing twelve."[2]

Mitchell's advice to Gilman was quite direct. "Have but two hours' intellectual life a day," and he admonished her "never to touch pen, brush, or pencil again" as long as she lived. During her treatment, Gilman took Mitchell's advice. Ultimately she resisted this advice and did so fabulously—becoming well known for her prodigious literary output. She came to see her intellectual life as a central aspect of her existence. As she later remarked, "The one prominent duty is to find one's work and do it."[3]

Gilman embodied many of the transformations underway for women writers in the late nineteenth and early twentieth centuries. Before the 1880s, publishing in the United States was decidedly a "gentlemanly pastime," maintaining what many referred to as a "clubby tone."[4] Yet the period from the 1880s to the 1940s brought significant change in publishing—an opening up to dissident groups and increasingly diverse voices. From the 1910s and 1920s, James L. W. West notes that newer imprints were increasingly headed by men of Jewish background. According to West, "Many prominent publishers, Jewish and gentile, were not products of Princeton, Harvard or Yale, but rather Columbia University."[5] This may have benefited women authors who were seldom seen as faculty in the halls of ivy, but those with a doctorate were more likely to have earned it from Columbia University.[6]

While changes were underway in the publishing industry, higher education in the United States reflected an increased emphasis on production that accompanied a push toward professionalization. As Frederick Rudolph famously put it, "each book, each article, was a notch pegged on the way to promotion."[7] In the 1880s and 1890s, the new university occupied itself with establishing ladders for these new specialists—academic ranks that fed and channeled the competitive drive in the new university. A growing cadre of new academic journals and scholarly presses provided a page count readily available to any administrator with a penchant for numbers and desire for invidious distinctions.

How did women fare with their trade in words in the dismal science when they were often excluded from institutions increasingly involved in the page count? Did women lack advanced degrees relative to their male counterparts publishing at the same time, and did this limit their voice in the book trades? When they did publish, were women limited in their ability to coauthor; when they did coauthor, was it often with a spouse or colleague? Finally, as academic journals expanded, how were their books and monographs publicly reviewed? Were those safely at home in the hallowed halls of academia accepting of the voices of women, even those with advanced degrees? To find some answers to these questions, we turn to evidence from authors with new books listed first in the *Economic Bulletin* from 1908 to 1910 and then the *American Economic Review* (*AER*) from 1911 to 1948 to examine women's role in publishing in the area of economics.

NEW EVIDENCE ON GENDER AND THE BOOK TRADE IN ECONOMICS

The academic journal emerged in the late nineteenth century as a vehicle for communication among members of a discipline and increasingly as a way for professors to demonstrate their serviceability as professionals—as producers and disseminators of knowledge. The *Quarterly Journal of Economics* (*QJE*) (1886) was the first English-language journal in the United States devoted to the discipline of economics and was run by Harvard University faculty. The journal was so steeped in Harvard that 100 percent of its editorial board from its inception to 1948 consisted of Harvard faculty. The *QJE* was followed by the *Journal of Political Economy* (*JPE*) in 1892. The *JPE*, located at the University of Chicago, was also exclusively tied to its home institution. For the entire period from its beginning to 1948, all editors were members of the University of Chicago faculty.

When the American Economic Association (AEA) was established in 1885, it maintained a publication titled *Publications of the American Economic Association* (1886). The *Publications of the AEA* primarily published monographs; association materials, including the constitution, membership lists, minutes and programs of the annual meetings; and lists of doctoral dissertations (completed and in progress). In 1908, it was replaced by the *Economic Bulletin*, which featured book reviews and lists of published doctoral dissertations in political economy, leaving AEA materials and a few monographs to the short-lived *American Economic Association Quarterly* (1908–1910).

One important bridge connecting the publication of a monograph as a sign of professional adequacy to the publication of a journal article was the listing of "New Books" published first by the *Economic Bulletin* and continuing in *AER* along with the reviews of books found in these publications. The lists of new books tell us a great deal about the gender breakdown of publishing books in economics in the early years.

The total number of authors listed in the *Economic Bulletin* and the *AER* from 1908 to 1948 is 36,956. A review of the authors included in these lists shows that women constituted a small but not insignificant proportion of the authors. Roughly 92 percent of books listed were authored by men, and about 8 percent were written by women. Further examination shows that the proportion of women-authored books listed over four decades (1908 to 1948) increased, going from 5.9% in 1908 to 1917, 6.4% in 1918 to 1927, 7.9% in 1928 to 1937, and 9.4% in 1938 to 1948.[8]

Examining the lists of new books published in this time period using all of the women listed and a random sample of male authors offers revealing details.[9] We can examine those with doctorates in fields other than economics, those with doctorates in economics, and various aspects of coauthorship by examining the sex of the coauthor for male and female authors. Also interesting is the type of relationship between coauthors. Were those women with male coauthors married or individuals with a close family relationship, or were they colleagues?

The sample examined consists of 2,809 women authors and 2,809 men. We begin by looking at the overall descriptive features of this sample and examine them over the four decades from 1908 to 1917, 1918 to 1927, 1928 to 1937, and 1938 to 1948 to better identify changes in coauthorship and doctorates. This snapshot provides a fascinating look at evidence on women and publishing in the discipline of economics in the early years.

AN OVERVIEW OF GENDER DIFFERENCES

From our sample, we learn that most authors listed with new books in economics from 1908 to 1948 did not hold a doctorate, and on average, more male authors than women authors held a doctorate in any field. About 34 percent of books written by male authors were by those who held a doctorate during this time period, while about 24 percent of books by women authors were by those who held a doctorate. Moreover, the prevalence of books listed by authors with doctorates grew for both men and women. In the first decade (1908–1917), only 21 percent of books by male authors were written by authors with a doctorate and 13 percent of books by women authors were by women with a doctorate. By the last decade (1938–1948), about 43 percent of books written by men and 27 percent of books written by women were written by authors with a doctorate.

More interesting perhaps is the prevalence of books listed by authors with doctorates in economics. Here, the proportion of books by male authors with a doctorate in economics was quite similar to the that of books by female authors with doctorates in economics. On average, only 15 percent of books by male authors and 14 percent of books by female authors were written by authors with a doctorate in economics over this period. Again, the proportion of books by authors with doctorates in economics grew over this period. In the first decade (1908–1917), nearly 7 percent of books listed by male authors and 6 percent of books by women authors were written by authors with a doctorate in economics. By the fourth decade (1938–1948), 20 percent of books listed by men and 17 percent of books by women were written by an author with a doctorate. This is a striking similarity.[10]

COAUTHORSHIP AND THE BOOK TRADE

There are many interesting questions surrounding book coauthorship during this time. One may wonder if the incidence of coauthorship was similar between men and women authors. When did the pressure to publish began to exert itself and create incentives to coauthor books and journal articles? If one coauthored a book, was it likely to be with a same-sex coauthor or the opposite sex? In other words, did the prevalence of men and scarcity of women in economics influence patterns of coauthorship? When women coauthored with men, were they related to those men through marriage or other family ties?

When we examine the prevalence of coauthorship in the book trade in economics, we see that the majority of authors did not coauthor their books with others. When we examine books listed with male authors, we see that only 22 percent were coauthored during the entire period, while a larger proportion of women (30 percent) published books with a coauthor. Moreover, data reveal that the proportion of male and female authors coauthoring a book increased over time and increased slightly more for male than for female authors. At the beginning of the period, the proportion of books written by men with a coauthor was 10 percent. This rose to 28 percent after four decades. For women, 20 percent of books listed were coauthored in the beginning of the period; at the end of this period, 36 percent of books listed by women authors were coauthors.

Because the increase in coauthorship rose over time, it is useful to examine patterns in coauthorship over time. We learn that the rise in coauthorship for men and women was especially pronounced from 1918 to 1927 through 1928–1937 when, for men, it rose from 15 percent to 24 percent or 9 percentage points and for women authors, coauthorship increased from 21 percent to 34 percent or 13 percentage points.

When we examine the nature of coauthorship in the first four decades of the twentieth century (1908–1948), we learn how segregated coauthorship was by sex. Of the coauthored books written by women, the majority were coauthored with men. Specifically, about 59 percent of coauthored books by women were coauthored with men, and 41 percent were coauthored with other women.

This contrasts sharply with coauthorship patterns for men. Of the books written by men in this sample, about 91 percent of the time they were coauthored with other men. Moreover, men coauthored with other men over 90 percent of the time in every decade except 1938–1948, where it dropped slightly to 88 percent. For women, the incidence of same-sex coauthorship was far less prevalent and fell over time. In the first decade examined, about 56 percent of books listed were by women authors with women coauthors. By the end of these four decades, only about 39 percent of books listed by women authors were coauthored with other women. Clearly, being a minority demographic in a field limits opportunity for coauthorship with one's own sex. Moreover, women's lack of access to academic positions limited their ability to develop working relationships that might result in coauthorship opportunities.

Because there were so few opportunities for women authors to interact with male counterparts in an academic setting, we may wonder about the degree to which women coauthored with a relative. There are several examples of married couples coauthoring during this period, such as Beatrice and Sidney Webb, Mary and Charles Beard, Gladys and Roy Blakey, Ursula and John Hicks, and Caroline Ware and Gardiner Means.

When we examine the prevalence of books written by women who coauthored with men in more detail, we find that of these 499 books, about 126 were written by a female coauthor with a close relative—122 with a husband, 3 with a father, and 1 with a brother. That is, about 25 percent of books written by women with a male coauthor were coauthored with a close relative, typically a husband. Although the majority of women who coauthored their books with men did not do so with a close relative, a not insignificant proportion did. Looking at these women coauthors further, we find that a small minority—about 10 percent—held a doctorate. In contrast, about 46 percent of husbands who coauthored with their wives held a doctorate. Thus, it was much more common in coauthoring couples for the husband to hold a doctorate.

PATTERNS IN COAUTHORSHIP

The analysis that follows provides more detailed information on coauthorship patterns and the sex of coauthors in the four decades from 1908 to 1948.[11] The model allows us to analyze the effect of having no doctoral degree, a doctoral degree in any field, or a doctoral degree in economics on the probability of being a coauthor for men and for women separately using data from "New Books" published in the

Economic Bulletin and the *AER*.[12] The model allows us to examine the effect of having a doctorate in any field or a doctorate in economics on same-sex coauthorship. This will help us understand if women's efforts to earn a doctorate in economics allowed them access to coauthoring with the men in their field. Likewise, testing for a difference between men's and women's outcomes here allows us to examine if there are statistically significant differences between men and women along these lines.[13]

The results show that in the first decade (1908–1917) about 11 percent of male authors without a doctorate in the year of publication or earlier were likely to be coauthors. In contrast, when we examine women authors, we learn that a much larger proportion of female authors without a doctorate (21 percent) were coauthors. These results show that the difference in the probability of being a coauthor without a doctorate is statistically significant for men and women authors.[14]

The results also reveal that male authors with a doctorate in a field other than economics were 7.5 percentage points less likely to be a coauthor than were male authors without a doctorate. At the same time, there was no significant effect of an economics doctorate on coauthorship. That is, male authors with a doctorate in economics were not more or less likely to be a coauthor than male authors without a doctorate or those with a doctorate in a field other than economics.

For women authors, holding a doctorate in a field other than economics makes them 15 percentage points less likely to coauthor than women without a doctorate. In contrast, having a doctorate in economics does affect the likelihood of coauthorship in a positive manner. Women authors with a doctorate in economics were 25 percentage points more likely to be a coauthor than women authors with a doctorate in another field. Likewise, women authors with a doctorate in economics were about 9 percentage points more likely to be a coauthor than were those without a doctorate. For women, in contrast to men, it appears that having a doctorate in economics resulted in more coauthorship or that coauthorship was an important means for women to advance in economics. In the first decade of the twentieth century, while the percentage of women coauthors without a doctorate was almost twice as large as men, having a doctorate in a field other than economics reduced the likelihood of being a coauthor for all authors, while for women, a doctorate in economics increased the likelihood of being a coauthor.

In the second decade (1918–1927), we see that about 16 percent of male authors without a doctorate in the year of publication or earlier were likely to be coauthors. In contrast, about 22 percent of women without a doctorate in any field were likely to be coauthors. Again, the results also show that the difference in the probability of being a coauthor without a doctorate is statistically significant for men and women such that women are about 6 percentage points more likely than men to be a coauthor.

In the first decade, having a doctorate in a field other than economics reduced the likelihood of coauthorship for men, this was no longer the case in the second decade. Having a doctorate in any field, including a doctorate in economics, did not change the likelihood of being a coauthor for women or men authors.

In the decade encompassing a large part of the 1930s (1928–1937), we see that the likelihood of being a coauthor continued to increase for men and women without a doctorate. The results show that 26 percent of male authors without a doctorate in the year of publication or earlier were coauthors. The same pattern continues for women authors. A much larger proportion of women authors without a doctorate, 35 percent, were likely to be coauthors. Once again, the differences between the likelihood of men and women without doctorates being coauthors is statistically significant.

When we examine the effect of having a doctorate on coauthorship, the results of the analysis for the 1930s show that having a doctorate in a field other than economics did not affect the probability of coauthorship for male authors. At the same time, men with a doctorate in economics were 10 percentage points less likely to coauthor compared with male authors without a doctorate. This suggests that having a doctorate in economics brought a degree of independence for men that reduced the likelihood of coauthorship. For women, holding a doctorate did not change the likelihood of coauthorship during this decade.

Finally, in the fourth decade (1938–1948), the data show that about 29 percent of male authors without a doctorate in the year of publication or earlier were likely to be coauthors. For women authors in this decade, we find that an increasingly larger proportion without a doctorate, 39 percent, were likely to be coauthors. We also find that the difference in the probability of being a coauthor for authors without a doctoral degree is statistically different for men and women authors.

In the decade encompassing a large part of the 1940s, the results show that there was no effect of having a doctorate on coauthorship for men. Yet women authors with a doctorate in another field on or before the date of publication decreased the likelihood of coauthorship by 16 percentage points over women authors with no doctorate. However, in the 1940s, having a doctorate in economics for women did not change the likelihood of coauthoring. This contrasts with the first decade of the twentieth century, when having a doctorate in economics increased women's likelihood of coauthoring.

By examining additional differences between men and women authors in decade four, we find that the probability of being a coauthor for authors with a doctorate in a field other than economics is statistically significantly different for men and women authors. The results show that women with a doctorate in a field other than economics were 12 percentage points less likely to coauthor than are men with similar educational credentials. When we examine the sex of coauthors in the next section, we find interesting results that demonstrate the constraints that women face when publishing in a STEM field dominated by men.

WORKING TOGETHER: SAME-SEX COAUTHORSHIP

Contemporary studies of coauthorship patterns in economics have tended to focus on journal articles rather than book authorship.[15] The patterns that have emerged from these contemporary studies suggest that women tend to publish as single authors more frequently than men, and the choice of a coauthor is not gender-neutral. Specifically, women are far more likely to coauthor articles with other women than men are. What does the availability of male and female authors suggest might be a random breakdown of the sex of coauthors, and how does this compare to the actual sex of coauthors for men and women?

If we imagine that all male authors in our sample randomly select coauthors, they will have a 9 percent chance of picking a woman coauthor, given the proportion of all authors who are women. If women are selecting at random, they would also have a 9 percent chance of picking a woman as a coauthor. If we look at the actual percentages of coauthors in our sample, we see that over the period 1908 through 1948, men were coauthoring with women at a rate proportional to their presence as authors (9 percent), while about 41 percent of women coauthors were same-sex coauthors and about 59 percent of coauthored books by women were coauthored with men. From this perspective, it appears that women's lack of access or interaction with men in professional settings may have limited their ability to coauthor with men and encouraged same sex coauthorship. With these overall probabilities in mind as a benchmark, we can examine the effect of holding a doctorate on coauthorship and the degree to which coauthorship produced gender-segregated research teams.

The results for 1908–1917 concerning the sex of a coauthor show that 94 percent of male coauthors without a doctorate coauthored with other men. This contrasts with the likelihood of same-sex coauthorship for women without a doctorate. During the same period, about 55 percent of women without a doctorate coauthored with other women. The results also show that the difference between male and female coauthors without a doctorate and with same-sex coauthors is statistically significant.

During the period 1908–1917, we find that women were about 39 percentage points less likely to coauthor with a woman than with a men. In other words, coauthorship tended to be with others of the same sex but much more so for men. This result shows that the underrepresentation of women in economics limits the number of women available for same-sex coauthorship.[16]

When we examine same-sex coauthorship for men, holding a doctorate in a field other than economics did not have a significant effect on the likelihood of same-sex coauthorship in 1908–1917. For women, holding a doctorate in a field other than economics reduced the likelihood of same sex coauthorship by 55 percentage points over women authors with no doctorate. An examination of the differences in the likelihood of same sex coauthorship for men and women with a doctorate in a different field shows that the probability is statistically significantly different. Women with a doctorate in a field other than economics are 61 percentage points less likely to have a same-sex coauthor than are men with a doctorate in a different field.

Even more interesting is the effect of holding a doctorate in economics on same-sex coauthorship during this first period. We see that women with a doctorate in economics were 83 percentage points more likely to coauthor with another woman relative to a woman author with a doctorate in another field and 29 percentage points more likely to coauthor with another woman compared to women without a doctorate. By examining the differences between the likelihood of men and women with doctorates in economics coauthoring with a same-sex coauthor, we see that the probability is different for men and women authors. Specifically, women authors with a doctorate degree in economics were 17 percentage points more likely to have a same-sex coauthor than were men with a doctorate in economics.

When we examine the second decade in our analysis, 1918–1927, we find that 94 percent of male coauthors without a doctorate in the year of publication or earlier were likely to be coauthors with other men. In contrast, only 51 percent of women coauthors without a doctorate were coauthors with other women. Moreover, the difference in likelihood of same-sex coauthorship between male and female authors is statistically significant.

Although having a doctorate in any field again does not affect the likelihood of same-sex coauthorship for men in this period, women coauthors with a doctorate in a field other than economics were 41 percentage points less likely to coauthor with another woman than women without a doctorate. In contrast to the first decade, holding a doctorate in economics does not influence the sex of coauthors for women in the decade spanning a good part of the 1920s. When we examine differences in the likelihood of same-sex coauthorship for men and women authors with a doctorate in a field other than economics compared with authors without a doctorate, we see that the probability of being a same-sex coauthor was different for men and women. Specifically, the results show that women with a doctoral degree in a different field were 38 percentage points less likely to be a same-sex coauthor than were men with a doctorate in a different field.

Looking at 1928–1937, we find that male authors without a doctorate were again highly likely to coauthor with other men. Once again, 94 percent of male coauthors without a doctorate were coauthors with other men and holding a doctorate did not affect the incidence of same-sex coauthorship. In contrast, only 37 percent of women without a doctorate were likely to coauthor with another woman. This difference between the likelihood having same-sex coauthors is statistically significant. These changes over time show us that the incidence of same-sex coauthorship for women without a doctorate decreased for every decade during the first three decade of the twentieth century. As was the case for men, having a doctorate did not change the likelihood of women's same-sex coauthorship in the decade covering a good part of the 1930s.

Finally, when we examine the period from 1938 to 1948, we find that men were again highly likely to coauthor with other men. Ninety-two percent of men without a doctorate were likely to coauthor with other men, while a growing proportion of women were coauthoring with women. Perhaps a result of World War II, rather than seeing a decline in same-sex coauthorship for women without a doctorate, we find that 40 percent of women without a doctorate were likely to coauthor with other women, up from 37 percent in the previous decade. We also find that the difference in the likelihood of same-sex coauthorship between men and women without a doctorate is statistically significant.

As for the influence of having a doctorate on same-sex coauthorship, the results show that men with a doctorate in a field other than economics were 19 percentage points less likely to have a male coauthor than were men without a doctorate. Similarly, women with a doctorate in a different field were about 20 percentage points less likely to have a same-sex coauthor than were women without a doctorate.

Holding a doctorate in economics had an effect on same-sex coauthorship for men and women in this period. The results show that men with a doctorate in economics were about 5 percentage points less likely to have a same-sex coauthor than were male authors without a doctorate. In contrast, women with a doctorate in economics were 1 percentage point more likely to have a same-sex coauthor compared with women authors without a doctorate. When we compare authors with a doctorate in economics to those with a doctorate in another field, we see that men with an economics doctorate were about 15 percentage points more likely to coauthor with another man than a man with a doctorate in another field. Women with an economics doctorate were 20 percentage points more likely to coauthor with a woman than women with a doctorate in a different field.

THE EFFECTS OF WAR ON COAUTHORSHIP

To conclude our analysis of books listed in the "New Books" sections of the *Economic Bulletin* and the *AER*, we examine the influence of World War I and World War II on our results. What effects did war have (if any) on coauthorship and the sex of coauthors? Did wartime involvement reduce or encourage coauthorship compared with the nonwar years, and did wartime involvement result in a decrease in same-sex coauthorship for men? Were men and women more or less likely to coauthor during wartime?

The results examining the effects of World War I in the second decade shows that the war had no statistically significant effect on the likelihood of coauthorship. The war years resulted in no significant change in coauthorship for those with doctorates in a field other than economics or those with doctorates in economics.[17]

In contrast, the larger U.S. involvement associated with World War II did affect coauthorship for men. The results show that male authors with a doctorate in a field other than economics were 16 percentage points less likely to be a coauthor during the war than during nonwar years from 1938 to 1948 and therefore 16 percentage points more likely to be a sole author. In fact, during nonwar years, the proportion of male authors of new books who were coauthors was about 29 percent for those with and without PhDs alike.

In contrast, for women authors of new books during the 1940s, there is no evidence that the relationship between coauthorship and having a doctorate was different during World War II than during the other years of the decade. According to the estimates, about 43 percent of women authors were coauthors, regardless of whether they have a doctoral degree.

When examining same-sex coauthorship during World War II, for a male coauthor there is about a 90 percent probability that his coauthors were also male. Moreover, male coauthors with a doctorate in a field other than economics were about 17 percentage points less likely to have a same-sex coauthor than men without a doctorate. The results show no evidence that World War II had any effect on the relationship between the sex of the coauthor and the influence of doctoral degrees for men or women.[18]

WOMEN, ECONOMICS, AND THE MONOGRAPH IN PERSPECTIVE

Few previous studies have examined gender and book publishing in economics in the early years of the profession.[19] By examining the lists of "New Books" published in the *Economic Bulletin* and the *AER* from 1908 to 1948, we gain new insights into women and the trade in words in the dismal science. We learn that women authors wrote, on average, about 8 percent of new books during this time compared with 92 percent written by men. Women authors played an increasing role in publishing in economics, going from 5.9 percent of authors in the first decade to 9.4 percent by the 1940s.

In addition, most authors did not have a doctorate. More men than women had a doctorate in any field. Although most authors did not have a doctorate, the proportion of authors with a doctorate increased over time. Most interestingly, we find that the proportion of women authors with a doctorate in economics was very similar to the proportion of male authors who did—on average, about 14 percent of women and about 15 percent of men. This suggests that women who earned a doctorate in economics were not inactive in building knowledge but were actively involved in its construction and dissemination. It may also suggest that men with fewer credentials (no doctorate or one in another field) were nonetheless successful in publishing book manuscripts during this time perhaps because of their institutional affiliations.

What is particularly interesting is that while most authors did not coauthor the books they wrote, more women coauthored their work than men did. This is the opposite of what modern studies have found when examining gender and coauthorship in journal articles.[20] Yet this difference in the gender incidence of coauthorship may reflect the priorities and academic culture of the era. The period examined was when the pressure to publish was just beginning. In this environment, there was still little pressure to coauthor to increase one's publications. Publishing independently was a privilege that men with academic standing could exercise. In contrast, women often lacked an institutional association and thus might well have looked on coauthorship as a mechanism for building academic connections and authority.

To gain more insight into this difference in the rate of coauthorship, it is helpful to know the sex of the coauthor. The results here show that women were more likely to coauthor with men than with other women. In contrast, men were much more likely to coauthor with other men. In fact, they did so over 90 percent of the time, throughout all four decades in this study. As for women, their tendency to coauthor with men increased over time. What does this suggest? The fact that men overwhelmingly coauthored with other men would seem to reflect their monopoly in academic positions at most universities and ease of access to same-sex coauthors. The increasing tendency for men to coauthor (mostly with other men) may reflect a growing pressure to publish.

As for women, the willingness to coauthor does not seem to reflect a pressure to publish due to their lack of long-term institutional affiliations and the character of that affiliation when present. It is also important to note that a fairly large proportion of women authors who coauthored with men did so with a close relative. The results show that 25 percent of women authors with a male coauthor were writing with a close relative— most often a husband. These women typically did not hold a doctorate and, because they were married, would have found the doors of academia closed to them as a general rule.

Instead, coauthorship for women appears to have represented a means of access to a professional network when formal academic ties were impossible. In an environment where women were a small minority of political economists and lacked institutional support and long-term associations, coauthorship may have been one of the few avenues of access to what would be loosely understood as a professional network.

7

TROUBLE IN THE
INAUGURAL ISSUE OF THE
AMERICAN ECONOMIC REVIEW

The Monograph and the Review

I n many ways, Lucile Eaves represents the archetype of a female scholar in the Progressive Era. Like many women who eventually pursued advanced degrees, her father was well educated—a lawyer educated at Yale and in Heidelberg, Germany.[1] She was drawn to higher education as new opportunities for women emerged, enrolling at Stanford University when it opened in 1891 and graduating with its first class in 1894. After teaching high school for several years, she began graduate studies at the recently established University of Chicago in 1898, alongside such future scholars and activists as Sophonisba Breckinridge, Frances Alice Kellor, and Marion Talbot, and taking courses from John Dewey and Albion Small. Eaves returned to Stanford as a history instructor, where she worked with such well-known scholars as Edward A. Ross, George E. Howard, and Mary Roberts Smith.[2]

However, Eaves found herself enmeshed in controversy. She was one of eight Stanford scholars (and the only woman) who were forced out or resigned in protest following the 1901 ouster of Edward A. Ross (a former secretary of the American Economics Association, AEA) from

Stanford University. Ross encountered trouble for expressing views on free silver, Chinese immigration, organized labor, and municipal ownership of public utilities—views that offended Stanford's influential cofounder Mrs. Leland Stanford. The result was an episode that came to be known as one of the most famous free speech tests in American academic life.[3]

After leaving Stanford, Eaves reluctantly turned to social work, becoming head resident of the South Park Settlement in San Francisco.[4] Like many women, the path Eaves "hoped to follow was predominantly male and ensconced in the academy," and the path that welcomed her was "female and rooted in social settlements."[5] Through this work, Eaves developed important connections with labor. She worked closely with the San Francisco Labor Council, where she developed her views on the role of race relations in the labor movement. These connections formed the foundation for her dissertation when she returned to her graduate studies at Columbia University in 1905.

During her graduate work, Eaves applied for and received a Flood Fellowship in Economics at the University of California at Berkeley (1907–8)—a fellowship that came when there was mounting pressure on Berkeley, from philanthropist and university trustee Phoebe Apperson Hearst, to hire and support women.[6] In 1909, Eaves rejoined her former Stanford colleagues Edward Ross and George Howard, who were now at the University of Nebraska. After earning her doctoral degree in labor relations from Columbia University in 1910, she held the position of associate professor in practical sociology at Nebraska until 1915. She continued her connection with the University of California at Berkeley, returning for work in the summer session and for a research lectureship during 1913, where she taught a course on labor organization and a course in elementary economic theory.[7]

Eaves's doctoral dissertation in labor relations was expanded and published by the University of California Press as a monograph titled *A History of California Labor Legislation*, and it was reviewed in the inaugural issue of the *American Economic Review* (*AER*). That is when the trouble began.

THE REVIEWER AND THE REVIEW

Born in 1880, Ira Brown Cross earned his baccalaureate from the University of Wisconsin in 1905 and his master's degree in 1906, taking classes from Richard Ely and John R. Commons. With Commons's help, Cross was recommended to Allyn A. Young, following him from the University of Wisconsin to Stanford University. At Stanford, Young was chair of the Department of Economics and Sociology from 1906 to 1910, and Cross pursued his doctorate on labor issues in San Francisco. In 1908, with the help of Harry Alvin Millis, another member of the department at Stanford, Cross became a special agent for the U.S. Immigration Commission and worked for Millis collecting information on race and labor in California. After completing his doctorate in 1909, Cross remained at Stanford, teaching courses on labor, immigration, charities, and corrections until his departure for the University of California at Berkeley in 1914. At Berkeley, Cross assumed the position vacated when Wesley Clair Mitchell (later the founder of the National Bureau of Economic Research) moved to Columbia University. Cross was promoted to full professor two years later.[8]

The idea of reviewing Eaves's book and the possibility of Cross as a reviewer seems to have originated with Millis and was funneled through E. W. Kemmerer. Kemmerer was editor of the *Economic Bulletin*, the predecessor publication to the *AER*, and acted as a mentor to Dewey when Dewey assumed the editorship of the *AER*. In a letter dated November 14, 1910, Millis wrote to Kemmerer:

> I do not know whether Miss Eaves' History of California Labor Legislation has come to your attention or not. The book is well worth a review in the Economic Bulletin and I would suggest that if the volume has not been assigned to some one else for review, that Dr. I. B. Cross of Stanford would be a good man to review it. Dr. Cross has been working on the History of Trade Unionism on the Pacific Coast and is very familiar with the entire ground. There are a few things in

the volume which ought to be checked up on in order that mistakes should not be accepted as facts.

Kemmerer replied to Millis the next week and agreed to forward the letter to Dewey for consideration.[9] A few days later, Dewey wrote to Allyn Young (a Stanford professor who was then visiting at Harvard), inviting him to MIT for lunch and stating, "I desire to secure a review of Miss Eaves' History of California Labor Legislation, and write to inquire if Dr. I. B. Cross of Stanford University is a competent person to undertake this. I regret that I do not know Dr. Cross sufficiently well to pass a judgment."[10] Young replied on November 28, 1910:

> Dr. I. B. Cross of Stanford is better equipped than anyone else I know to review Miss Eaves' monograph. He has independently traversed most of her sources in connection with his own work (soon to be published) on the History of the Labor Movement in California. From what I know of Cross' attitude toward Miss Eaves' work I suggest that you might do well to guard against an unsympathetic and overly critical review, by telling him that you want an appreciation of the good features of the monograph as well as an account of its errors or limitations. Also you had better set definite limits to the length of the review.

Within a few days, Dewey sent Cross a letter of invitation to provide a review. Although Dewey set a limit of 600 words, he ultimately failed "to guard against an unsympathetic and overly critical review."[11] The review totaled five paragraphs. The first two described the overall need for the work and the topics covered. The third paragraph began with two sentences of praise: "For the most part the work of the author has been admirably done. She has written in full sympathy with her subject, has gathered together a mass of valuable data, and has presented it in a logical and well-ordered manner." In the next sentence, Cross's tone abruptly shifted: "However she has permitted a number of errors to creep into the manuscript which a more careful study of sources would have enabled her to detect." Cross listed six supposed mistakes along with six places where he felt relevant information was omitted. His disagreements with Eaves centered on politicians involved in anti-Chinese agitation in the San Francisco labor movement.[12] Cross went on to state, "These and similar errors, together with frequent statements which are surprisingly general and comprehensive in places where more detailed and exact accounts are desired and would be expected, lead one to question the accuracy of many of her declarations. . . . Numerous other instances of omission, which at times are confusing to the reader, could be cited if space permitted."[13] In the letter dated January 1, 1911, that accompanied the review, Cross added, "I regret that space did not permit a more thorough and complete criticism."

Thirteen days later, Dewey wrote to Cross indicating that Young had suggested that Cross might be invited to contribute an article for the *AER* "of say, 2000 words—that might be made for the Review on the cooperative movement in California," noting that he would need this at once if it were to appear in the first issue. This article was eventually published in the third issue of the *AER* in September 1911.[14]

"THE UNJUST ATTACK"

After the first issue of *AER* appeared in March 1911, Eaves wrote a five-page letter to Dewey dated May 19, 1911, calling attention to Cross's "unjust attack," requesting that she be allowed space in the *AER* for a rejoinder and lamenting that the first issue should give publicity to such prejudiced views.[15] Dewey replied to Eaves three days later:

> I have just received your letter of May 19 and am very sorry indeed that Cross's review has given you any distress or irritation. I read it and judged it as a favorable review. I thought some of the criticisms were rather petty, but that they showed that the reviewer had worked over the field and this gave him some justification for his general judgment which is certainly to your credit . . . I am confident that Dr. Cross did not mean any attack, both from the review and from the correspondence . . . You ought to see some of the reviews I get!

The next day, enclosing an edited version of her complaint, Dewey wrote to Eaves:

> I have reread Mr. Cross's review and my original impression is confirmed. I certainly never thought that I was admitting an attack in the Review. Now your paper is altogether too long, and it seems to me to be far more effective if you can present something like the enclosed. If this is not satisfactory, do not hesitate to change it, but bear in mind that we must be sparing of space.

In the meantime, Eaves contacted George E. Howard, Frank A. Fetter, and Henry Farnam to solicit support in her negotiations with Dewey. Fetter, who later served as president of the AEA in 1912 and had joined Eaves in resigning from Stanford over the Ross affair, wrote to Dewey in May 1911. Fetter stated that he was an old friend of Eaves from Stanford and was "surprised at the nature of the criticisms that the reviewer found it necessary to make," adding that "the person criticized should be given an opportunity to reply" especially on "questions where the economic fraternity is divided in opinion." In contrast, Farnam (who had general oversight over Eaves's dissertation and was a member of the editorial board of the *AER*) told Dewey in a letter around the same time that he found Eaves to be "unduly sensitive."[16]

Within days, Young wrote to Dewey about the "Cross/Eaves controversy," admitting that some of Cross's criticisms are "picayunish" and "the points are relatively small," stating that although Cross has been working in much the same field, he did "not expect him to accomplish so good a piece of work as Miss Eaves." Although he indicated that Cross "lacks balance and a sense of proportion," Young seemed to offer two points to justify Cross's review. According to Young, "The labor movement has been always in the public eye on the Pacific coast, and many of the labor leaders of the past still figure as popular heroes. On this account, strict accuracy as to their activities does not seem to me unimportant—at least in a book so thoroughly documented and apparently so microscopic as Miss Eaves." Besides, Young added in his closing sentence, describing Cross: "He is a boyish, enthusiastic, and very love-able person, and exceedingly sensitive."[17]

In the end, Dewey, with Farnam's support, requested that Eaves withdraw her reply and substitute the reply edited by Dewey.[18] Eaves was not persuaded. In her response, she wrote:

> Your letters have not convinced me that no further attention should be paid to the Ira Cross review. A few lines of general commendation cannot counteract the impression of a page or more of alleged errors & omissions, followed by the assertion that the book contains many more such inaccuracies. While some allowance should be made for the youth and inexperience of the reviewer, such obvious carelessness and misrepresentation cannot pass without correction.

In what Fetter and Dewey hoped would be the end of the matter, Fetter worked to broker a deal with Eaves and Dewey. In June, Fetter wrote to Dewey, "the shortened form of reply as you [Dewey] have revised it is better for both Miss Eaves and for the Review than was the original reply."[19] Not all involved saw it that way. Eaves sent Dewey her revised note from a Cambridge address, and it was published in the September issue. It was a point-by-point refutation of the items in the Cross review, a polite but unyielding demonstration of "the trivial or erroneous character of these charges."[20]

"THE VEXATIONS THAT MUST BESET THE LIFE OF AN EDITOR"

Cross had not been provided with an advance copy of Eaves's response, and he exploded in a letter to Dewey on September 19, 1911:

> I regret very much that for some unknown cause you did not give me an opportunity of replying to Miss Eaves before the publication of her communication in the REVIEW for September. Had this been done,

I am led to believe that there would have been no occasion for its publication. It is a waste of valuable space to print these replies and rejoinders of two unknown individuals. . . . May I ask that you print the enclosed in the REVIEW, for by publishing Miss Eaves's reply you made it possible for the readers of the REVIEW to feel that my criticisms were not justified? My original review of her volume was "mild," as compared with what I could have made it.

Enclosed with the letter was a four-page reply from Cross. Dewey soon wrote to Cross in reply and took it upon himself to explain his situation. He revealed that not only had Eaves written to him to request her published reply, but "friends of hers" had also written. More interesting, Dewey confessed that "I found that there was a suspicion that I was negativing [*sic*] a reply from Miss Eaves on the ground that she was a woman." Speaking "entirely in confidence," Dewey noted that he did not derive this from her attitude but that "as soon as I thought this was the case I hastened to open the review without further delay."[21]

Dewey wrote to Eaves on October 13, 1911, notifying her: "Professor Cross has sent a reply to your communication, and I enclose a copy. This we shall publish, but I do not feel that it is desirable to give further space in the REVIEW to the questions concerned. I shall be very glad indeed, however, to have your comment at once, for we do not wish to be party to any injustice." Dewey received her comment at once, but whether he was very glad indeed may be doubted. Eaves wrote:

I am very emphatically of the opinion that you would be doing me a great injustice if you publish Dr. Cross' reply and refuse to permit me to answer it. In the first place you propose to allow him just about twice the space you permitted me and in the second place his answer in a number of places evades the points at issue, or is not strictly accurate.

Eaves wrote to Dewey four more times in the coming days.

On October 22, 1911, she wrote:

The enclosed will seem a somewhat formidable document, but I know no other way of convincing you of the inaccuracy of this reply of

Mr. Cross. I have felt all along that you were too ready to assume that Mr. Cross must have a more thorough knowledge of the subject than I. As a matter of fact he is a young instructor with no claim on the title of professor which you so kindly bestow upon him. . . . I am at a loss to account for the disregard of historical accuracy in Mr. Cross' reply. . . . I cannot believe that your sense of justice will permit you to publish this very inaccurate reply without permitting me an answer. . . . If you desire to satisfy yourself about the truth of this statement by a personal examination of the legislative Journals, I will send them to you. . . . As you have already permitted Mr. Cross more space in which to spread my errors before the public than you allowed for my reply, you would be doing a still greater injustice if you authorize a repetition and additions to the first false charges. Now, Dr. Dewey, I will gladly accept honest criticism, but intend to fight to the last ditch against such injustice. Fortunately I have a number of good friends among the leading economists of this country, who have read enough of the book to appreciate its real character. . . . I am keeping a copy of my refutation, and in case you publish this reply and refuse me a hearing, I shall find means of fully presenting my side of the case to your readers. I hope that we can drop the matter, as I am overwhelmed with more important work and do not want to worry over this any more. It is probable that you feel the same way about it, but are struggling to do justice. Permit me to close with a word of sympathy for the vexations that must beset the life of an editor.

Dewey replied immediately, suggesting that more discussion might best be pursued through direct correspondence between Eaves and Cross, adding:

I think you misjudge Mr. Cross's motives. His letters certainly do not justify any interpretation that he wishes to lessen the credit which is your due. I still think that the original review was intended to be favorable and from all that I can learn was so considered by our readers. Naturally your reply now puts him on the defensive, giving him claims for consideration.

In a letter to Dewey dated November 1, 1911, Eaves agreed that her notes could be sent to Cross and struck a moderately conciliatory tone, writing of Cross that she was "astonished that a man in his position should be so utterly childish in some of his mental processes." Mentioning her interest in future work on European labor legislation, she concluded, "If it ever comes your way, I want you to pick out a severe old man to review it. Then I will show you how well I can accept a sensible criticism."

The next day, Dewey wrote to Cross: "The board of editors has considered your 'reply' and has come to the decision that it is not wise to publish it in the December issue. I have had further correspondence with Miss Eaves and it appears that there is considerable difference of opinion in regard to the validity of the evidence. I have in my possession a considerable body of material bearing upon this point, and if permission is granted, I see no reason why you should not see it." He added soothingly, "It seems to be the general opinion of the editors that your scholarship has been in no way discredited by Miss Eaves' reply. It is simply a difference of opinion in regard to the evidence." It is not clear whether Dewey had consulted the board of editors or anyone other than Young, to whom he once again wrote plaintively, expressing his desire that the parties "reach some understanding by private correspondence."

In what proved to be a final twist to the Cross/Eaves controversy, Young wrote to Dewey on November 17, 1911:

> I think that so far as Cross's own interests are concerned it would be best for him to drop the matter. At the same time I feel that if he wishes to confine himself to statements of fact (as for the most part he seems inclined to do) the Review could hardly afford to deny him the privilege—if he wishes to insist on it. I agree with Miss Eaves as to the immaturity of his point of view. But the issues seem to [be] mainly ones of fact, on which I am not competent to express an opinion. As things are now Cross would be in a position to claim that by publishing Miss Eaves's communication without submitting it to him and by refusing him a similar privilege the Review had unintentionally placed

him in an unfortunate position. My advice to him (I have written him) is based simply on the point that the points at issue are fairly trivial, and further rejoinder would hurt him more than it would help. This, it would seem, is a matter for his own decision. I hope and expect that he will withdraw his reply.

Apparently prompted by Young, Cross soon wrote to Dewey, withdrawing his previous reply and expressing regret over the trouble that had arisen over the publication of his review. He went on:

Naturally I enjoy a controversy, but I realize the predicament into which it has forced you. I am eager to smoothe [sic] the matter over as easily and as painlessly as possible for all three of the parties concerned, and nothing which has been suggested or which I have thought of, so nicely disposes of the matter as does the enclosed note, an idea which came from a good friend of both you and me,—at least it appears to me to dispose of the matter nicely. The enclosed note does not permit of a reply by Miss Eaves; neither does it leave the readers of the REVIEW with the idea that I wrote a slovenly and grossly inaccurate review of her book. The only objection that I have to it is that it mentions my forthcoming volume.

The enclosed letter to the editor from Cross read:

In the REVIEW for September 1911, Miss Lucile Eaves raises the issue of fact with regard to certain portions of my review of her monograph "The History of California Labor Legislation" which appeared in the REVIEW for June [sic], 1911. As most of the points in question can hardly be supposed to be of interest to the readers of the REVIEW, may I ask the privilege of merely stating that I should not have ventured to point out specific instances of error in the work of Miss Eaves had not my exceptions been based upon a study of the sources of California labor history, including newspapers and documents, supplemented by personal interviews with men who had been prominent in the labor movement of this state? For detailed proof of the statements which I made in the above review I can in this place only refer the reader to my forthcoming monograph on "The History of Labor in California."

Dewey wrote to Cross on December 7, 1911, "to thank you most heartily for the happy solution you [Cross] have provided in your letter of November 29. Would you object to a statement which would include most of what you have said but signed by myself, thus relieving you of any personal statement. If this seems to me advisable I will send you a draft, of course, in advance." Shortly after, Dewey received a letter from Young indicating that he had corresponded with Cross and had suggested that Cross send Dewey a short statement referring the reader to his forthcoming monograph and indicating "I understand that he had done this." The closing salvo in the controversy appeared in the 1912 issue of the *AER*:

> In the REVIEW for September 1911, page 587, Miss Lucile Eaves raised certain issues of fact with regard to portions of the review of her monograph, *A History of California Labor Legislation*, prepared by Mr. Ira B. Cross. It is only fair to Mr. Cross to state that he based his criticism upon a personal study of California labor, including newspapers and documents, supplemented by interviews with men who have been prominent in the labor movement in that state. Readers who are interested in this special field of investigation will have the opportunity to weigh the conflicting evidence as presented in a forthcoming monograph by Mr. Cross on *The History of Labor in California*. California is to be congratulated upon being honored by two exhaustive monographic studies relating to this branch of economic history.—Managing Editor[22]

As an ironic coda to this story, Cross's rival book, *History of the Labor Movement in California*, the work that was part of the reason he was first recommended by Young as a reviewer and that he describes as "soon to be published" in 1911, was not published until 1935. Presumably, Cross put the manuscript aside to write his short book on *The*

Essentials of Socialism published in 1912, but it is not clear why he took so long to complete the larger work. Even twenty-five years later, Cross's criticisms of Eaves continued—this time buried in footnotes. In his *History of the Labor Movement in California*, Cross cites Eaves twelve times: twice in a complimentary manner, one neutral, and the remainder referring to her work as "inaccurate" and the facts she cites as "erroneously," "mistakenly," and "incorrectly" reported. Cross's effort to assert himself as the expert on the subject while maintaining an air of civility emerges most characteristically as he writes in a note to chapter 6 that Eaves's work was "unbiased, and the most satisfactory brief treatment of the subject in print, although it contains a few errors."[23]

"JOCKEYING COMES TO BE THE MAIN FUNCTION OF REVIEWING"

In the years leading up to the inaugural issue of the *AER*, the subject of book reviews published in leading journals was generating impassioned expressions of concern among the learned class in economics. One incident in 1908 sparked a good deal of correspondence when the victim of what he saw as an unjust attack on his recently published book went into action, addressing his concerns to the "the effective forces in the politics of the craft." The result was a flurry of letters between Herbert Joseph Davenport, Frank Fetter, Thorstein Veblen, Irving Fisher, George K. Holmes, and Davis R. Dewey.[24]

Davenport's book, *Value and Distribution*, was published in 1908 and reviewed in the *Journal of Political Economy* in June of that year by Alvin S. Johnson.[25] In his six-page review, Johnson attacked Davenport's point of view, at one point stating, "It is a pertinent question whether a view that is blind to so many distinctions that nevertheless appear to persist will discover any truth that is of practical significance." In the last paragraph, Johnson said, "If space permitted it would now be in order to point out the many excellences of this book." His only kind remark followed: "It appears to the reviewer that very few books that have appeared in recent years are more worthy of careful study than this one."[26]

This well-written but nonetheless brutal book review appears to have prompted Davenport to reach out to several well-known economists. First to reply was Irving Fisher who wrote pointedly about the issue in a letter to Davenport. Fisher opened with "I say Amen to your point."[27] He went on to say the following:

> I think it would be a grand thing if the three of us, or as many as we could get, could do something to influence the custom of reviewing. The trouble usually is that there is the same human nature among professors as among politicians. Each one tries to find out what "there is in it" for himself. The writers of reviews who start out with this standpoint are not so intent on rendering service to the public or doing justice to the author as in magnifying themselves. Consequently their first thought is to show the reader that they know more about the subject than the author—which they usually do not.

Dewey (not yet appointed as editor of the *AER*) wrote to Fetter (secretary-treasurer of the AEA from 1901 to 1906) to express his passionate concern about "the utter badness and hopelessness of our present standard of Economic Reviewing."[28] In his six-page letter on this topic, Dewey asks, "is it not a sample of colossal egotism on the part of the reviewer—and of astounding stupidity on the part of the rest of us—that a scientific publication has come to be made up of this sort of emptiness." Speaking of his desire to minimize personal attacks, Dewey states that "a mere unsupported ipse dixit, whether of approval or disapproval, by some reviewer who takes seriously his own dicta is nothing better than chat and surplusage." Offering his unvarnished view of the dark side of reviewing, Dewey points out that "reviewing of this sort degenerates into the sheer puffery and jockeying appropriate to the level of publishing announcements. . . . Men of assured prestige— particularly such as are heads of leading departments or are effective forces in the politics of the craft—must be accorded all the buttery words in the vocabulary. Enmity comes to stand as the sole result of serious criticism; if one cannot say something genial, he would better say nothing. Jockeying comes to be the main function of reviewing."

That Dewey would himself be caught up in what is described as the Cross/Eaves controversy, where these same issues were raised (yet no attempt was made to stave off Cross's brutal attack) is cause for reflection. In fact, in January 1911, Dewey had communicated with Edwin Kemmerer (then editor of the *Economic Bulletin*), about the issue of troublesome reviews in the matter of Wesley Clair Mitchell's review of Earl Dean Howard's book, also published in the inaugural issue. Kemmerer replied by offering that "my policy was to suggest (and if necessary insist) that personalities be cut out and also criticisms which are clearly either gratuitous or picayunish."[29]

Between 1908 and 1910, Dewey spent some energy devising remedies to address the issues raised by the unjust review of Davenport's book—remedies such as suggesting that important books have multiple reviewers and entertaining Veblen's suggestion that to secure competent reviews, the reviewer should be paid. One cannot help but consider Dewey's own "words of advice" for the new managing editor taking up the reins in 1941. He offered four suggestions—one of which was to "publish at least one review in each issue which will arouse the animosity of the author. There is nothing more stimulating than controversy. Is not controversy the essence of that much debated theme, democracy?"[30]

In his history of the *AER*, Coats reports, "Throughout the Association's history no subjects have been more contentious than book reviews and the refereeing (and rejection!) of articles submitted for publication." He goes on to say, "Generally speaking, reviews gave Dewey more trouble than articles."[31] Indeed, Dewey was twice threatened with legal action in the first five years of his editorship. In a case involving a female author and a female reviewer, Coats describes how Charlotte Molyneux Holloway threatened a lawsuit over what was described as a "mildly critical review" by Emilie Louise Wells—a review in which Wells asserts that the "generalizations, when not based directly on the facts observed, are for the most part worthless, and the whole report is singularly ill-written."[32] Once again, Dewey was urged by editorial board members such as Herbert Millis to enlist Holloway's advisors to intercede with her. Millis suggested enlisting Irving Fisher of Yale because "his word with Miss Holloway's advisers would go far. The Review might well spend some money on his expenses to accomplish the quashing of this attack."[33]

THE CONTROVERSY IN PERSPECTIVE

In the early years of the economics profession, the publication of a monograph, and whether and how it was reviewed, was an especially important milepost signaling one's professional acceptance.[34] The turn of the century was a period of proliferating academic institutions, disciplines, and departments that brought forward a growing list of disciplinary journals. A review of a monograph, appearing in newly emerging journals, represented one of the few available options for women to share their scholarship to a wider audience. How one's work was received was a matter of intense interest for both men and women, but especially to women who held out hope of entering the halls of ivy as a producer of knowledge.

The Cross/Eaves controversy did not involve a woman with a long-established and secure position in the profession. Instead, it involved two relatively unknown academics who had just completed their doctoral work. The editorial correspondence from the AEA archives reveals much about the importance of informal networks, and when it came to informal networks, men had the advantage. Because of her involvement in the Stanford free speech debacle, Eaves had developed friendships with influential members of the AEA—two of whom served as president around the time of the controversy. Nonetheless, the letters reveal more concern for Cross's career and reputation than of Eaves's.

Cross also had what appeared to be professional relationships with several of those involved. He was originally recommended as a reviewer by H. A. Millis, a professor in Cross's department, and Dewey sought confirmation from Allyn Young—Cross's advisor. Behind the scenes,

Young characterized Cross's criticisms as "fairly trivial" and "picayun-ish" and indicated that Cross "lacks balance and a sense of proportion." In private correspondence, Fetter and Dewey referred to Cross's criti-cisms as "petty." Nonetheless, after the *AER* published Cross's original review and Eaves's detailed reply, Dewey initially decided to accept Cross's further reply for publication, giving Cross's nitpicking the last word. Even the final act—the anodyne paragraph signed by Dewey—seems more focused on Cross's interests. After all, the main theme of the paragraph is to demonstrate concern for the fair treatment of the reviewer. In addition, Dewey writes of the importance of Cross's "forthcoming" (in twenty-five years!) volume and thus offers an implicit recommendation for that work while hiding any impression that the review might have been tainted by a desire to promote the reviewer's own work.

Although it seems improbable that the controversy over a single book review strongly shaped the career path of Eaves or Cross, this epi-sode prompts us to consider another common pattern at a time when disciplinary boundaries were being defined: men were more likely to end up in economics while women were more likely to end up in sociol-ogy or social work. After all, Eaves and Cross were professionally simi-lar in many ways, with dissertations on similar topics and completing their doctorates in economics only one year apart.

Eaves and Cross are still recognized as making important contribu-tions to our understanding of the labor movement in California, and both continue to be cited in subsequent work on the topic of labor and immigration.[35] However, it was Eaves, not Cross, who offered the intel-lectual foundation for a labor history that required a more nuanced understanding of the interaction of class and race rather than accounts of organizational elites. While Cross's history relies more on detailed biographical accounts, Eaves's history was unique at the time in offer-ing an examination of social change that integrated race relations and economic relations.[36] Moreover, her study of the evolution of labor leg-islation used a method that later labor historians would embrace as "history from the bottom up."

In the end, Cross assumed the title of economist along with his position at the University of California in 1914, just five years after completing his doctoral thesis. Two years later, he was promoted to full professor. A flamboyant teacher, his career as an economist was eventually recognized with honorary doctorates from the University of Wisconsin and the University of California at Berkeley. In contrast, Eaves's academic appointments at the University of Nebraska and Simmons College were in sociology or social work. Her later journal articles and reviews were more often published in the *American Journal of Sociology, American Labor Legislation Review, Sociology and Social Research,* or *Social Forces* than in economics journals.[37] One of her last publications—a book on women's earnings in business and the professions—was reviewed in the *AER*. By publishing the review, *AER* editor Davis Dewey indicated that he considered Eaves's survey of wage-earning women in Brattleboro, Vermont, to be "part of the literature of economics."[38]

Dorothy Ross noted that women academics in this time, especially those already involved in charitable and reform activities, were a "natural constituency" for the social sciences, but they were also likely to be marginalized in the field where informal mechanisms of control continued to exclude them.[39] It is little wonder then, that women economists like Eaves—particularly those whose work crossed several disciplines—found their professional lives complicated and their ability to gain acceptance limited. Authors with established positions of power in their disciplines were less likely to receive harsh or unfair reviews as power and gender were intertwined to the disadvantage of women.

Dewey came to refer to this episode as the Cross/Eaves controversy— and according to a letter he wrote to Allyn A. Young dated November 13, 1911, it gave him "no end of trouble."[40] The controversy not only illustrates the eternally fascinating interaction of the reviewer and the reviewed but casts a revealing light on the era's standards and rituals of scholarly conduct, on the drawing of disciplinary boundaries as economics became a more distinct academic discipline, and on the differing treatment of men and women in academic life. It also reveals the powerful influence of the academic association as gatekeeper and the encroachment of the academic journal in the life of women writers in the form of the review as the journal article increased in status as evidence of academic accomplishment.

8

GENDER, THE OLD BOY NETWORK, AND THE SCHOLARLY JOURNAL

At the age of twenty-six and without a profession, Eleanor Lansing Dulles decided to pursue a doctorate in economics. Her previous studies and experience were in industrial management at Bryn Mawr College with no background in economics. To address this deficiency, she traveled to the London School of Economics where, in her words, "the level of thinking was high but where the competitive struggle in the classroom was at a minimum."[1]

After fourteen months in London, Dulles decided she would seek a "Radcliffe-Harvard doctorate." As she later described it, her classes included thirty men and six women and were taught by Harvard faculty. When choosing a dissertation topic, she had two criteria: she wanted the most stimulating faculty advisor possible and she wanted to do the work in France.

Dulles chose to work with Allyn Young, whom she later described as "a perfect teacher" and one whose "views were never frozen." What brought admiration from Dulles brought condemnation from others. Frank Fetter had dropped Young's course in money and banking because Young had said that "he didn't believe everything he had written." Fetter explained that he "didn't want to spend a term getting the ideas of a man who didn't know what he believed."[2] Dulles's work culminated in a successful defense of her thesis in June 1926. She returned to France to turn her thesis into a book.

What Dulles did not expect was a visit from two professors—Robert Murray Haig of Columbia University and (James) Harvey Rogers of the University of Missouri. According to Dulles, Haig made his reason for the visit quite clear: "You are here on a small grant and working alone, studying the nature of French inflation. Professor Rogers is working with our group and can do a more searching and complete job. We want you to turn over your notes to us and we'll carry on your work as part of our comprehensive project." Perhaps as a note of reassurance, Haig added, "I'm sure Professor Young will approve."[3]

Young, it appears, did *not* approve and admonished Dulles to "stick to your guns" and not let "Columbia men change plans in any way."[4] Dulles did not share her research notes and went on to publish *The French Franc* in 1929. Yet the sense of entitlement of some faculty over student research—especially women students' research—certainly did not end with Dulles. Nonetheless, her experience demonstrated many of the obstacles facing women in their efforts to publish research.

THE RISE OF THE SCHOLARLY JOURNAL

As economics was developing as a separate discipline and institutions of higher learning were emerging across the country, the drive to gain status in producing and disseminating knowledge accelerated. One way for universities to gain status was by hiring more faculty experts in a variety of fields. The moniker of "expert" was easily and quickly displayed through the appendage of "PhD" after one's name. This placed growing pressure on faculty to demonstrate their serviceability by displaying their doctorates. Following the path of least resistance, existing faculty sought this approbation by securing an honorary doctorate. The rise of the honorary doctorate in the 1870s and 1880s was doomed when the U.S. Bureau of Education, learned societies, and professional organizations "joined forces in deploring the sham Ph.D."[5] After peaking in 1890, the practice quickly diminished.

At the same time, institutions worked to develop a framework to facilitate faculty's emerging role as producers of knowledge by establishing an occupational hierarchy with three grades of permanent faculty appointments, an apparatus of the department to organize this occupational hierarchy, and a measurement of status or output in the form of the publications. The university press of the late nineteenth century, such as those at Johns Hopkins University (press established in 1878), the University of Pennsylvania (1890), the University of Chicago (1891), the University of California (1893), Northwestern University (1893), and Columbia University (1893), provided a mechanism for publishing a growing number of dissertations and other scholarly output along with the new scholarly journal.

University presidents were increasingly clear about where their priorities lay, and it was not in teaching students but in what was considered a productive use of faculty time. As Frederick Rudolph so aptly put it, "For although one might be a most excellent teacher, and although effective teaching might lead untold students to self-discovery and self-mastery, the organization demanded something else: it fed on research, it regurgitated research, it promoted research."[6]

This status-seeking required a vast bureaucracy. Whereas previous university presidents had exerted direct control in curating a faculty as part of their duties, the growing number of faculty members required departments to play an increasing role in these efforts. At the same time, some skirmishes between economics faculty and university presidents and trustees emerged in the late 1880s and early 1890s, putting presidents at odds with faculty and bringing unwanted public attention to these altercations.[7] In the end, there were benefits to the professionalization of the academy for presidents and at least some faculty.

The professionalization of higher education ultimately resulted in an expanded role for faculty as they asserted autonomy over their standards, and this autonomy was a source of professional power. Presidents continued to exert pressure on faculty members to publish, but the increasing role that faculty played in their own disciplinary associations and on editorial boards served both the president in need of a visible expert and the faculty member in need of a receptive audience and expanded network of friendships. In the growing arena of journal publications, faculty found visibility and developed networks to facilitate their professional careers.

In the discipline of economics, the scholarly journals published in the United States began with the *Quarterly Journal of Economics* (QJE) published by Harvard University in 1886. Following the *QJE* was the *Journal of Political Economy* (JPE) in 1892, published by the University of Chicago. The *American Economic Review* (AER) began in 1911 and was published by the American Economic Association (AEA). The *Review of Economics and Statistics* (REStat), launched in 1919, became the second Harvard journal for economists.

The role of the editor in the growing list of scholarly journals was critical in the evolution of disciplinary communities, signaling recent developments and establishing boundaries of disciplinary conversation. Moreover, the editor (and to a lesser extent the editorial board) played a crucial role in determining whose views were salient, seemingly relevant, and forceful. Drummond Rennie points out that peer review did not become widespread until after World War II and even then, the practice varied by journal. Instead, the editor exerted a great deal of control over the articles solicited and chosen for publication.[8]

It is an important question in the history of higher education to determine how the institutional framework surrounding a discipline shaped not only the intellectual contours of the discipline but the selection of those who came to be known as experts. To better understand the constellation of factors affecting the publication of articles in scholarly journals in the early years of the economics profession, two important journals—*AER* and *QJE*—are particularly instructive.

The *AER* is an archetypal association journal published by the AEA, maintaining an editorial board of faculty from many different universities. In contrast, the *QJE* is an archetypal university journal managed through Harvard University and, at the time, maintaining an editorial board consisting solely of Harvard faculty. A careful examination of relationships that were important determinants in the success of publishing in these journals will expand our understanding of the gendered nature of professionalization in economics and shed light on what has come to be known as the "old boy network."[9]

INSIDER TRADING

Thanks to the financial support of Yale's Henry Farnam, the New Haven Railroad heir who was then serving as AEA president, the association began publishing the *AER* in March 1911. Davis Rich Dewey of MIT (an authority on U.S. financial history, former AEA president, and brother of philosopher John Dewey) was editor for the *AER*'s first three decades. Although Dewey noted that he was "given no instruction or even a particle of advice" on assuming the editorship of the *AER*, he was far from being a novice editor, having previously edited the quarterly of the American Statistical Association in its first fifteen years.

AEA records reveal a total of 265 person-years of service for those people in the position of editor or on the editorial board of the *AER* from its inception in 1911 through 1948. Looking further, we see that a total of seventy-two individuals served in such an editorial role—two of whom were women. Alzada Comstock of Mount Holyoke College served for three years (1937, 1938, and 1939) and Mabel Newcomer of Vassar College served four years (1942, 1943, 1944, and 1945) as editorial board members.

Although there were only two editors of the *AER* during this period—Davis R. Dewey and Paul T. Homan—there were a total of sixty-eight men serving as editorial board members. An examination of the institutional affiliations of these men shows a fairly diverse set of scholarly affiliations (and only a few government affiliations). In all, thirty-six different schools provided academic homes for male members of the editorial board, with Harvard University being the most frequently identified institution with five editorial board members. Harvard was followed by the University of Minnesota and the University of Wisconsin, each with four members.[10]

Although both women on the editorial board of the *AER* during this period held doctorates (both in economics and from Columbia University), the situation for male editorial members was slightly different. Around 90 percent held doctoral degrees, but not all of them were in economics. Of those male members with doctoral degrees, 75 percent were in economics and 25 percent earned their degree in a different field. It is perhaps not surprising that a majority of male and female *AER* editorial board members also maintained a membership in the AEA. Only two men did not.[11]

In the period from 1911 to 1948, the *AER* published 980 articles. Of these articles, 94 percent were written by men and nearly 6 percent were written by women. This compares only slightly less favorably for women than the publication of books, which, as we saw by examining the lists of "New Books" published in the *Economic Bulletin* and *AER*, included 92 percent by men and 8 percent by women. Although the lead article in the inaugural issue of the *AER* was written by a woman, it was eight years before another (non-proceedings) article by a woman author was published. Katharine Coman of Wellesley College published the lead article at the age of fifty-four. She was a well-published author whose work appeared in some of the most prestigious journals.[12]

About half of the women authors publishing in the *AER* from its inception to 1948 held doctorates, and most of their degrees (about 87 percent) were in economics. The women authors with doctorates earned them about equally from Columbia University, University of Wisconsin, and Radcliffe College. In contrast, 61 percent of male authors held doctorates, with a slightly lower proportion (81 percent) of them in economics. The largest number of male authors earned their doctorate from Columbia University, followed by Harvard University and then the University of Wisconsin.

The oldest professional journal in economics in the English language, the *QJE*, began publishing in 1886—during the first year of the AEA. Edited at Harvard University, *QJE* was founded with the aid of a gift by Harvard alumnus, John Eliot Thayer. Its first editor was Charles F. Dunbar, who served for ten years before turning over the editorship to Frank W. Taussig in 1897. So successful was Taussig in guiding the journal in those early years that the *AER* editorship was first offered to him with the hope that the *QJE* might be converted into the official AEA periodical.[13] Perhaps out of loyalty to Harvard, Taussig declined.

Records for those serving on the editorial board of the *QJE* show a total of 354 person-years of editorial service for those serving as editor, managing editor, and associate editor from 1886 through 1948. When we look at individuals, we see that a total of thirty-one people served in the role of associate editor for the *QJE*—none of whom were women. In other words, those serving on the *AER* editorial board did so, on average, for fewer years than those serving in an editorial position (other than editor) for *QJE*—by quite a bit. The average number of years served as associate editor with the *QJE* was eight, while the average number of years served in an editorial position with the *AER* (excluding editors) was only three.

There were only three editors of the *QJE* during this period—Charles Dunbar, who served for ten years; Frank Taussig, who served for twenty-nine years; and Edward Chamberlin, who served only one year. A total of thirty-two men served as associate editor. Examining the institutional affiliations of these men shows that all editorial positions were held by men with an academic home at Harvard. There were no exceptions and no women.[14]

As for the educational status of those people with an editorial role at the *QJE*, 84 percent held doctoral degrees. However, most of these doctoral degrees were in economics. Of those members with doctoral degrees, 86 percent were in economics and 14 percent received their doctorate in a field other than economics. Members of the editorial team of the *QJE* were also highly predisposed to belonging to the AEA. Again, only two members of the editorial team of the *QJE* did not maintain a membership in the AEA.[15]

From 1886 to 1948, the *QJE* published 1,534 articles—1,483 or 97 percent were published by men and only 51 or 3 percent of articles were published by women. The first woman to publish an article in the *QJE* was Alice Rollins Brewster in 1894.[16] It was eighteen years before the next article by a woman was published when Minnie Throop England of the University of Nebraska and Anna Pritchett Youngman of Wellesley College published in the *QJE* in 1912. More than a few women published multiple articles in the *AER* (eight) and in the *QJE* (twelve).

Of the thirty-two women authors publishing in the *QJE* in this period, about 38 percent held doctorates, the majority of which were in economics. Of those women holding a doctorate, most were from Radcliffe College which, it should be noted, had no women faculty in economics; students who received their degrees were taught by Harvard faculty.[17] As for their membership in the AEA, it appears that this was not altogether very important to these women authors. Less than half of the women publishing in the *QJE* were AEA members.

A FIRST LOOK AT "HIGH ACHIEVERS"

A total of thirty-six women published at least one article in the *AER* in the first thirty-seven years of its existence—a small proportion of the total 980 articles published. In the *QJE*, which began publishing in 1886, a total of thirty-two women published at least one article from its inception to 1948—an even smaller proportion of the 1,534 total articles published during these years.

It is perhaps surprising to note that nine women published in both the *AER* and the *QJE* in these years—Dorothy Wolff Douglas (Smith College), Elizabeth Waterman Gilboy (advisor for economics at the graduate school at Radcliffe College), Grace Thompson Gunn (U.S. Bureau of the Budget), Amy Hewes (Mount Holyoke College), Gladys Louise Palmer (Hollins College and later the Industrial Research Unit of the University of Pennsylvania), Rita Ricardo-Campbell (a teaching fellow at Harvard University and later Tufts University), Margaret Loomis Stecker (Social Security Administration), Maxine Yaple Sweezy (Woolston) (Radcliffe College), and Anna Pritchett Youngman (Wellesley College). Most of these women authors published without a coauthor, and all but Gunn held a doctorate.[18]

When we examine the backgrounds of these "high achievers," we see that not only did almost all of them have a doctorate, most of them had one in economics. Only Douglas (political science) and Hewes (sociology) had doctorates in other fields. Another commonality among these women was their affiliation with one of the Seven Sisters. As previously discussed, women with doctorates in economics had difficulty finding positions in areas other than women's colleges and government. Five of the nine women successful in publishing in the *AER* and the *QJE* were at one of these women's colleges at some point, and four were elsewhere: Palmer at Hollins College and then the University of Pennsylvania; Ricardo-Campbell at Harvard and then Tufts University; Stecker at the Social Security Administration; and Gunn at the U.S. Bureau of the Budget.

The success in publishing that these high achievers accomplished is all the more remarkable given the lack of support for research at these institutions compared with what was provided to male faculty at research institutions. High teaching loads were not uncommon. By 1900, professors at Wellesley College typically taught three full courses per term, but it was not uncommon for professors to be responsible for four or five courses.[19] Also limiting women faculty were the low salaries for their teaching activities, often necessitating multiple appointments to make ends meet. Mary Ann Dzuback notes that universities had far more resources to support faculty research, including reduced teaching loads to free up time for research activities and access to funding sources in support of travel and research materials.[20]

It was more than just the expectations of regular (often high) teaching loads or the "missionary pay" that made it difficult for women teaching at women's colleges to engage in research. There was the expectation that women faculty were to have substantial monitoring duties, unlike their male colleagues. Women faculty were to be role models for undergraduate women students and, as Helen Horowitz points out, a "two-tier system" emerged where women faculty were to live on campus while male faculty were provided off-campus housing for their families. Moreover, despite their rank, women at Smith College were referred to as "teachers" in official publications of the college while male faculty held the title of "professor." According to Horowitz, "Women professors lacked professional respect and their private lives remained controlled by the assumption that they provided proper models for students."[21]

A few of these women authors had careers at a single institution spanning decades—Amy Hewes at Mount Holyoke College from 1905 to 1943 and Dorothy Douglas at Smith College for thirty years—but another commonality was the lack of a stable long-term affiliation. Of course, male faculty also had occupational mobility, and it was not altogether unusual for them to change institutional affiliation. Nonetheless, the unique and itinerate nature of women's faculty work added additional time stress and diminished their ability to engage in research.

Finally, women who chose careers as professional faculty were limited in their options as to institutions, and they were destined, as they would characterize it, to a "life a solitude." In the 1890s, Margaret Rossiter writes, marriage for a woman faculty member automatically ended her employment.[22] Yet the two-tier system did not preclude marriage for male faculty. In fact, men who were married were viewed as reliable faculty. A "family man" was a good thing, while a "family woman" was an oxymoron in higher education. In other words, marriage was seen as incompatible with career.

When we examine the marital status of these high achievers, we find some interesting clues as to how women negotiated these troubled waters. While the marriage rate for women in general in the early twentieth century was slightly above 90 percent, four out of nine women or 44 percent of high achievers did not marry.[23] The five remaining women did marry—a fact that might seem to suggest that marriage was not incompatible with aspiring women faculty. Three of those marriages ended in divorce, and a fourth ended a rather robust research and publishing agenda.[24]

One may wonder if these high-achieving women published articles that were more or less likely to include women as subjects in their discussion than were other women publishing in AER and QJE. An examination of all of the articles published by women in the AER and QJE from 1885 to 1948 shows that only one article included the word "women" or "woman" in the title. This was an article by Dorothy Wolff Douglas published in 1920 in the *QJE*. Douglas's article was only the second one published by a woman in either journal that formally included women in the discussion. The first article was published only a year earlier; it was also by Douglas but was published in the *AER*.

In all, there were fourteen articles published by women that included women in the discussion in more than a passing way. Most of these appeared in the 1930s and 1940s. When we examine these women-authored articles, we find that five of the fourteen (about 36 percent) were published by one of the high achievers. When we compare this to the likelihood of women authors in general, we see that high achievers were more likely to publish work that explicitly included a reference to women than were other women publishing in the *AER* and *QJE*. Whereas only 13 percent of the 109 articles published by women in the *AER* and *QJE* during this time included women in the analysis, a much higher percentage of articles by high achievers did so. Although we don't know if these women were more likely to run toward what surely must have been somewhat controversial or if editors were less likely to reject an article by one of these high achievers, we know that these women were not reluctant to include gender in their analysis.[25]

AN EMPIRICAL ANALYSIS OF THE OLD BOY NETWORK

What do we know about the authors publishing in the *AER* and the *QJE*? Were those with doctorates more likely to publish in these journals? Would it matter if their doctorates were in economics or in another field? Were authors with doctorates more likely to coauthor articles or were they sole authors? When they did coauthor, did they do so with members of their own sex or members of the opposite sex? Finally, what role did their academic relationships play in their ability to get their work published? Were authors with a doctorate or current affiliation from the same institution as a member of the editorial team more likely to be published? The answers to these questions allow us to see how relationships determined by institutional access shaped academic success for scholars in economics during this period.

We examine in more detail the role that several factors may have played in determining the likelihood of publishing more than one article in the *AER* and the *QJE* during the early years of the economics profession. Specifically, we examine the role of having a doctorate in a field other than economics or a doctorate in economics in publishing multiple articles in these journals. We examine a series of relationships between authors and editors, such as whether the author has a doctorate from the same institution as an editor, is employed in the same institution as an editor, or has earned a doctorate from the same institution where an editor is located and the possible effect of these relationships on the likelihood of publishing multiple articles.[26] Because there were so few women publishing in the *AER* and *QJE* during this time, most of what is revealed concerns the effect of these relationships for male scholars. We examine male authors, male authors who are AEA members and those who were not, and where possible what can be learned about female authors. These relationships tell us a great deal about the contours of what more recently has come to be known as a "old boy network" and its effect on publishing in the economics profession in the early years.

THE *AER*

Looking first at *AER* male authors, we begin by analyzing the influence that holding a doctorate in a field other than economics or having a doctorate in economics may have played in publishing more than one article during the periods 1911–1919, 1920–1929, 1930–1939, and 1940–1948. One would expect that having more credentials, such as a doctorate in economics, would increase the likelihood of multiple publications. Likewise, one might expect that having a doctorate in a field other than economics may signal one's credentials—particularly when doctorates in economics were not prevalent.

It is surprising, then, to learn that in none of the decades examined does having a doctorate in economics increase the likelihood of multiple publications for male authors. We do find that holding a doctorate in a different field increases the likelihood of multiple publications in the 1920s, 1930s, and 1940s by 25, 28, and 39 percentage points respectively, over authors without a doctorate. Credentials seem to matter, but not just credentials narrowly defined as a doctorate in economics.

It is noteworthy that connections between male authors and editors do not seem to influence the likelihood of having multiple publications in the *AER* in its first three decades. Yet in the 1940s, these relationships began to be important. Those male authors with a doctorate from the same institution as an editor or board member had an increased likelihood of multiple publications by 13 percentage points over authors without such a relationship. Likewise, male authors at the same institution as an editor were 14 percentage points more likely to have multiple publications. In contrast, being a male author with a doctorate from the same institution where a member of the editorial team was located did not bode well for multiple publications. This relationship actually reduced the likelihood of multiple publications by about 23 percentage points over authors without such a relationship.

Because the *AER* is an association journal, we can examine the role that AEA membership may play in influencing multiple publications for authors. To better understand the role of AEA membership in publishing outcomes, we can compare the effect of having a doctorate for those authors who were AEA members versus those who were not, as well as the influence of relationships. The data show that AEA member male authors with a doctorate in a field other than economics had an increased likelihood of multiple publications in the 1920s of 26 percentage points and in the 1940s of 28 percentage points over similar male authors without a doctorate. Again, holding a doctorate in economics was not influential on the likelihood of multiple publications for such authors.

Examining relationships for male AEA members also shows that these relationships were not important until the 1940s. However, in the 1940s, male AEA member authors with a job at the same institution as a member of the editorial team increased the likelihood of publication by 16 percentage points, while having a doctorate from the same institution where an editorial team member was located reduced the likelihood of multiple publications by about 27 percentage points.

Although relatively few authors were not members of the AEA in this time period, those who were not members did not appear to share the benefit of having a doctorate. In no decade did having a doctorate (in any field) result in an increased likelihood of multiple publications in the *AER*. When we consider the influence of relationships for male non-AEA members, the data show that in the 1920s, authors with an appointment at the same institution as an editor or member of the editorial board did have a rather large increased likelihood of multiple publications: about 53 percentage points. In the 1940s, non-AEA member male authors with a doctorate from the same institution as a member of the editorial team were 65 percentage points more likely to have multiple publications. No other relationships were important in influencing the likelihood of multiple publications. That is, nonmembers did not suffer the same negative effect of having a doctorate from the same institution where an editor was located.

Because there are so few women authors, results on women and publishing are extremely limited. We can examine the effect of having a doctorate and the effect of relationships on the likelihood of having multiple publications for women in the 1930s. The evidence shows that none of these factors were significant.

As previously mentioned, the practice of coauthorship in journal publications increased during this period. In the *AER* only 4 percent of articles were coauthored in the period 1911–1929. The incidence more than doubled in the 1930s and 1940s, when 10 and 11 percent of articles were coauthored. The following analysis allows us to see if the same factors influencing sole authors is present for those who chose to coauthor their articles.

When we consider only male coauthors publishing in the *AER*, we see that in the 1920s, male coauthors with a doctorate from the same institution where an editor was located again pay the price with reduced likelihood of multiple publications of 8 percentage points over male coauthors without this relationship. In the 1930s, male coauthors with a doctorate in economics had an increased likelihood of multiple publications of about 9 percentage points compared with male coauthors without a doctorate.[27]

When we consider relationships between editors and female coauthors, the only measurable effect occurs in the 1930s. Women coauthors with an appointment at the same institution as a member of the editorial team were 73 percentage points more likely to have multiple publications over women coauthors without this relationship. During the 1930s, the *AER* had its first female editorial board members—Alzada Comstock of Mount Holyoke College—which may have benefited women coauthors at the time.

Examination of the situation for same-sex coauthors shows that being a women who writes an article with another woman reduces the likelihood of publishing multiple articles by about 70 percentage points in the 1930s and about 96 percentage points in the 1940s. Women coauthoring with other women was apparently not the recipe for publishing multiple articles in the *AER*.

The *AER* was an association publication, not supported by a particular university. As a result, editorial team members were spread throughout the United States, and their academic homes were located in a variety of universities. We can compare the influence of relationships between authors and editors in the *AER* to the *QJE*, which provides a look at another highly influential publication—one that was located at Harvard University and had only Harvard faculty on the editorial team. As such, we might expect to see a stronger influence of relationships on the likelihood of multiple publications.

THE *QJE*

The *QJE* began publishing twenty-five years earlier than the *AER* in 1886. We examine seven decades of publications including the 1880s (1886–1889), 1890s (1890–1899), the first decade of the twentieth century (1900–1909), and the periods 1910–1919, 1920–1929, 1930–1939, and 1940–1948 to determine the influence of doctorates and relationships between authors and editors on the likelihood of multiple publications for authors.

We would expect credentials in the form of a doctorate in economics and perhaps to a lesser extent, a doctorate in a different field to increase the likelihood of multiple publications. Yet the evidence on publications for male authors in *QJE* shows little evidence that these credentials were important. Looking at the influence of doctorates for male authors we see that in the 1880s, having a doctorate in a field other than economics increases the likelihood of publishing multiple articles by 36 percentage points over authors without a doctorate. In no other period does having a doctorate in a field other than economics change the likelihood of having multiple article publications in *QJE*. The results also show that holding a doctorate in economics does not influence publications in any decade examined.

If credentials are not significant in determining multiple publications for authors in the *QJE*, perhaps relationships were significant. The relationship we might expect to be significant here concerns authors who are employed in the same institution as an editor. Here data show that male authors with an appointment at the same institution as an editor (in the case of *QJE*, this is Harvard) increases the likelihood of multiple publications by 36 percentage points over authors not on the Harvard faculty in the 1880s and 18 percentage points in the 1890s. Thus, we see that male authors on the Harvard faculty are more likely to have multiple articles published in two of the seven periods examined—a relationship established because all editorial board members are Harvard faculty members.[28]

An examination of membership (and nonmembership) in the AEA shows that for male authors who were AEA members, credentials influenced publications only in the 1940s, when male AEA member authors with a doctorate in a field other than economics were 27 percentage points more likely to have multiple publications than were male AEA member authors without a doctorate.

In terms of relationships, male AEA member authors on the Harvard faculty were more likely to have multiple publications in three out of the seven periods examined. Here we see that male AEA member authors with an appointment at the same institution as an editor were more likely to have multiple articles published in *QJE* in the 1890s, 1930s, and the 1940s by 14, 9, and 17 percentage points, respectively. Thus, AEA member authors with an appointment at Harvard (the same location as the editorial team) increased the likelihood of multiple publications in several decades.

Things get interesting for male authors who are not members of the AEA. There are results for non–AEA members starting in 1900 and continuing on through the 1940s. It appears that these faculty were viewed as outcasts in some ways—either by their own choosing or through the decisions of others. In 1900–1909 and continuing through 1910–1919 and 1920–1929, non–AEA member male authors with an appointment at Harvard were 60, 72, and 57 percentage points less likely to have multiple publications in *QJE*. This unusual outcome stands in contrast to AEA member authors who were employed at Harvard who experienced a positive effect from this relationship on publications.

Also in contrast to male AEA member outcomes, male non–AEA member authors in the period from 1910–1919 with a doctorate in economics were 72 percentage points less likely to publish multiple articles in *QJE*. This unusual outcome might suggest that being a non-AEA member was likely to result in punishment for those with credentials often lacking in others. However, in the 1920s and 1940s, non–AEA member authors who had earned their doctorate from the same institution as an editor were more likely to have multiple publications by 53 and 62 percentage points, respectively. In general, being a member of the AEA was perhaps a sign of a "company man," and not being a member was a signal that the relationships between author and editor would be more difficult to maintain. Only in the 1920s do we see the often found negative relationship between authors with a doctorate from (in this case) Harvard repeat itself. Those authors were 56 percentage points less likely to have multiple publications.

When we consider coauthorship relationships, it is important to note that the likelihood of coauthorship was slightly lower in *QJE* than in *AER*. Of the total 748 articles published in the *AER* by authors with more than one publication during this period, only 58 (8 percent) were coauthored. Of the total 1,222 articles published in the *QJE* by authors with more than one publication during this period, only 70 (6 percent) were coauthored. Likewise, most of the coauthored papers in the *QJE* were concentrated in the 1930s and the 1940s.[29]

Due to the paucity of male coauthors—especially in the early years of the *QJE*—we have limited results that include the 1930s and 1940s. Examining male coauthors only in the 1930s shows no significant relationships. In the period 1940–1948, male coauthors on the faculty of Harvard University were more likely to have multiple articles published. Specifically, male coauthors employed at Harvard were 17 percentage points more likely to publish multiple articles in *QJE* than were coauthors without this connection.

Finally, because of the lack of women authors in *QJE*, results are very limited. When examining the effect of being a woman, we find that in the 1890s women were 75 percentage points less likely to have multiple articles than were men. In no other period did being a woman produce measurable results to compare the likelihood of multiple publications to men. When we examine women authors alone, we can examine the influence of doctorates on their publications during the 1930s and 1940s. We find that in the 1930s, women with a doctorate in a field other than economics were 87 percentage points less likely to publish multiple articles in *QJE*. No other factors were significant determinants of multiple publications for women in the 1940s.

What can we conclude from our examination of authors and their relationships with *AER* editors from 1911 to 1948 and *QJE* editors from 1886 to 1948? A few patterns emerge. First, when examining the likelihood of authors having multiple publications, one would expect credentials to play a role. In economics, we could expect that having a doctorate in economics or (to a lesser extent perhaps) in another field would provide a signal of proficiency that might result in a higher number of publications. Doctorates in economics were not prevalent in the early decades of this period, but it is surprising that in no decade for male authors does having a doctorate in economics increase the likelihood of publishing more than one article in *AER* or *QJE*.

The data do, however, show that having a doctorate in a field other than economics was a factor in success for authors publishing in the *AER* in several decades, which include the 1920s, 1930s, and 1940s. These credentials were not helpful to authors publishing in the *QJE*. For no decade from 1886 to 1948 did men publishing in the *QJE* with any kind of doctorate increase their likelihood of publishing more than one article.

If credentials had only a limited role in success for male authors, perhaps relationships might better explain how these authors were able to publish more than one article in these journals. We see that for the *AER*, relationships of any sort were not significant determinants of success in publishing until the 1940s. In the 1940s, those authors with an appointment in the same institution as an editorial team member did benefit, as did those authors with a doctorate from the same institution as an editor. For the *QJE*, when tied to AEA membership, male authors with an appointment in the same institution as an editorial team member also benefited in the 1890s, 1930s, and 1940s. It seems that being a "team player" and being a "Harvard man" often led to success for authors in the *QJE*.

There is one relationship that stands out as particularly interesting, and that is the author who earned a doctorate from the same institution where an editorial team member had a current appointment. These unfortunate chaps found that this relationship resulted in a reduced likelihood of more than one publication in the 1940s for *AER*, the 1920s for non–AEA members in *QJE*, and for coauthors in the 1920s publishing in *AER*. The analysis of coauthors also shows that male coauthors with a doctorate in economics were perhaps valued, at least in the 1930s.

As for women authors and coauthors, the relatively small number of women authors publishing articles in *AER* and *QJE* limits what we can learn about factors influencing the likelihood of their success in publishing. We do find that women authors with appointments at the same institution as an editor was beneficial in the 1930s in *AER* and in the 1930s and 1940s in *QJE*. More important perhaps, we find that in these decades, women with same-sex coauthors appear to have paid a penalty, at least in *AER*. Those women reduced their likelihood of publishing more than one article. The message to women was that if you are going to collaborate, best to do so with a man . . . even if he has a doctorate in a field other than economics.

GENDER AND THE JOURNAL ARTICLE IN PERSPECTIVE

Discussion of success in the academy often begins and ends with the notion that those with talent rise to the top. The cultural pull of a meritocratic mindset is well established in the United States, and nowhere more so than in the field of economics, where the virtues of a free market receive their fullest and most dispositive formal treatment.

It is a widely held belief that knowledge is advanced by sharing of research published in journal articles, reviewed by peers, and with the oversight of experts in the field as editors. In her discussion of publishing in science, Diane Crane talks about the presumptions and often unspoken norms underlying the review process and their importance for the advancement of knowledge.[30]

One linchpin of the review process is the notion that scientific achievements should be judged without reference to the scientists' personal or social characteristics—including their position in the social structure of science. Crane points out that advances can be stifled if the academic stratification system inhibits some from performing scientific roles as a result of a personal or social characteristic. This kind of stratification is unfair to the individual scientist and can affect the diffusion of scientific ideas.[31]

Barbara F. Reskin and Denise D. Bielby explained that "social differentiation" refers to the social processes that mark certain personal characteristics as important. Sex is indeed a "master status," a social position that is a primary identifying characteristic of an individual— one that is central in organizing social and economic life.[32]

This reality is central in explaining women economists' role in the production of knowledge in the late nineteenth and early twentieth centuries. The reality facing these women economists was that their sex channeled them into entry-level positions that were different from those of men. They faced barriers in their selection of graduate training and had doors closed to them in terms of their choice of a professional home. This marginalization had profound implications for women's careers and their ability to participate in knowledge production. As Francine Blau, Marianne Ferber, and Anne Winkler put it, "Once men and women are channeled into different types of entry jobs, the normal, everyday operation of the firm—'business as usual'—will virtually ensure sex differences in productivity, promotion opportunities, and pay."[33]

Women scholars in the late nineteenth and early twentieth centuries were often drawn to the settlement house movement as one of the few outlets for educated women. Here they became strong proponents of social reform and exercised their voices in various studies and in government reports not subject to peer review or an editor's interests. In contrast, male scholars took a divergent path, eschewing overt advocacy for seeming objectivity, preferring to concentrate on the new professional journal as a means of gaining professional authority and testimony as experts as a means of influencing policy.[34]

In this chapter we became aware of the subtle ways this overt marginalization works to shape what generally has come to be known as an old boy's network. The reality of how this gendered network actually functioned was partly revealed, and we became aware of how the relationships between mostly male economists shaped outcomes in the publication of journal articles. We find that that being located in the same institution as an editor or gatekeeper played a role in improving one's success in publishing. Holding a doctoral degree from the same institution as an editor occasionally improved the odds of publishing, and having a doctoral degree from the same institution where an editor is currently employed worked against these odds.

9

NOT A FREE MARKET

Women's Employment After the Doctorate

When Leahmae Brown graduated with a doctorate in economics from the University of Illinois in 1937, the U.S. economy was struggling. She had spent most of her student years in higher education while the economy was in a depression, which may explain why her father talked her out of her first calling of chemistry. He believed she would not be able to find a job in that field.[1]

When Brown took a job as a secretary in a law office, her parents were perhaps satisfied, but she was not. At the urging of the lawyers that she worked for, who saw her as a bright and talented young woman, she entered college. She went on to earn a bachelor's degree in economics from the University Kansas in 1933, a master's degree from Tufts University in 1935, and a doctorate in economics from the University of Illinois in 1937.

After graduation, Brown became involved in research at Princeton University, where she met and married Charles F. McCoy in 1939. She went on to have four children and decided to apply for a teaching position at the University of Arizona in the 1950s. Despite her academic credentials and early experience, the department of economics "wouldn't have her," according to a former colleague. In his words, the head of the department "absolutely refused to have anything to do with her." McCoy instead took a part-time teaching job in the marketing department.[2]

Things eventually changed when the economics department launched a doctoral program in 1957 and it was learned that "no one in the department was qualified to teach in it." McCoy was then hired. One might imagine that her career was much improved—and in some ways it was. She earned teaching awards and by all accounts was a popular professor with her students. It took sixteen years for her to be promoted to full professor. She remained the only woman in the economics department during her years at the University of Arizona and, according to her daughter, her office was "always in the darkest, deepest corner, and she knew it was because she was a woman." Summing up her experience as a female faculty member, her daughter remarked, "They treated her like dirt."[3]

TO WORK OR TO WED

When Leahmae McCoy approached the chair of the department she hoped to join, it was, of course, a man. In 1948, the American Economic Association (AEA) published a list of 175 department chairs titled "Chairmen or Heads of Departments of Economics, Deans of Schools of Business, and Directors of Business Research Bureaus and Institutions in Selected Colleges and Universities."[4] This extensive list shows that of the 175 institutions listing chairs of economics departments, only 6 reported having women chairs in economics. In other words, only 3 percent of those listed were women, and 97 percent were men.

The six institutions with women department chairs in economics were all women's colleges.[5] Although Viva B. Boothe was listed as director of the Bureau of Business Research at Ohio State University, no women chairs were found at Ivy League schools, state universities, or smaller coeducational colleges. This reality reflected the lack of women faculty outside women's colleges and the gendered nature of the labor market for scholars at institutions of higher learning.

Several subsequent studies have shown the benefits of having women managers in academic settings on women's earnings and the number of women entering graduate school, but in the early years of the profession, the doors to faculty employment were closed for most women, and one means of closing the door was through the "marriage bar."[6]

Most often, those few women who did secure positions in research universities were disproportionately single and not married. Many universities and colleges had what historians refer to as marriage bars, which prevented married women from being hired or, if already employed, called for their firing once they married or their marriage was discovered. Such was the case for Caroline F. Ware, who kept her maiden name upon marrying economist Gardner Means and was not allowed to fulfill her contract for summer teaching at the University of Wyoming in 1935 when it was discovered that she was married. When national attention was brought to the incident, the university reported that the rule was to "spread employment." Unsurprisingly, Ware pointed out that the university was an educational institution and "not a work-relief organization."[7]

Like other universities, the University of Wyoming had provisions prohibiting the appointment of married women as instructors and calling for the dismissal of female teachers who marry. According to Claudia Goldin, marriage bars arose in teaching and clerical work in the late 1800s and remained for the first two decades of the twentieth century. When formal marriage bar policies were not in place, informal practices effectively prevented women from being hired in higher education. In Goldin's view, women who graduated between 1900 and 1920 were required to choose "family or career."[8]

During the 1920s, women began to openly challenge views on marriage and career. Barbara Solomon notes that educated women started to consider another choice—marriage *and* career.[9] These changing views were reflected in alumni surveys, such as the one conducted by the Radcliffe College Alumnae Association on the fiftieth anniversary of the college. In this survey, 73 percent of respondents thought that women could successfully combine marriage and a career.[10] Changing views were also evident in national surveys like one conducted by

Fortune magazine in 1936, which showed that three-fifths of women hoped to marry within one or two years of graduation and two-fifths expressed the desire to work after marriage.[11] Finally, changing views about marriage and career were apparent in the public pronouncements of educational leaders such as Ada Comstock, president of Radcliffe College, who proclaimed in 1929 that "We have come to see, I believe, that marriage is essentially far more compatible with continuation of a woman's career than has been assumed."[12]

The challenging of existing norms about marriage and career for women was, however, dealt a blow when unemployment rose sharply and the notion of work as a gender-based privilege emerged again during the Great Depression. The implementation of marriage bars rose sharply in the 1930s, even finding their way into legislation.

The Economy Act of 1932, signed into law by President Herbert Hoover, contained a famous provision (Section 213) known as the "married persons clause," indicating that whenever personnel reductions took place in the Executive Branch of the government, "married persons were to be the first discharged if their spouse was also a government employee."[13] Controversial from its inception, the married persons clause remained in place until June 1937. Despite the gender-neutral language, the administration of the act was certainly not gender neutral. The act adversely affected women in government jobs throughout much of the Great Depression, and was a model for state legislation in many instances.[14] In the end, differing cultural norms related to marriage, reflected in law or practice, were only one reflection of the economy that made the notion of a "free market" ring hollow for women—even those trained in the catechism of the free market.

ECONOMICS AS THE STUDY OF CHOICE (FOR SOME)

Economics is often defined as the study of choice.[15] Yet for women in economics from 1885 to 1948, few employment options were available, and constraints were many. The more modest notion of constrained choice in occupations for women, even for those few who had earned a doctorate in economics, falls far short of explaining the limits imposed on women. In short, the labor market for highly educated women in economics was anything but a free market.

One of the difficulties in analyzing occupational outcomes for women in economics in the early years is a lack of data. Limited information is available from the U.S. Census Bureau for women teaching in higher education and working for the federal government. However, the establishment of the Women's Bureau in 1920 made this information somewhat more available and visible.

There have been few sources for data on the number of women teaching in higher education in the United States. One of the most highly cited comes from U.S. Census data, which was reported by the Women's Bureau. We see that among "all college presidents, professors and instructors," the proportion of women was 19 percent in 1910, 30 percent in 1920, 32 percent in 1930, and 27 percent in 1940.[16] These data suggest that the proportion of women faculty expanded in the 1920s, began leveling off in the 1930s, then fell in the 1940s.

Data on Black women college presidents and professors are even more limited. U.S. Census data does report that Black women held about 30 percent of jobs recorded for "Black college presidents and professors" in 1910 and about 48 percent in 1930, although they indicate that this last figure probably includes some teachers in schools below the college level.[17] Hence, we see a growing presence of women as faculty overall during the early decades of the twentieth century and for Black women in relation to Black men during this period.[18]

The Women's Bureau offers information on the growth of women working for the federal government, causes for that growth, and information on which agencies employed women from 1923 to 1939.[19] Women's federal government employment increased from 14.9 percent of total employment in 1923 to 19.5 percent in 1938, with much of the growth occurring after 1935.[20] The gains for women were interrupted in the early 1930s by the Economy Act of 1932. According to the Women's

Bureau, the Economy Act resulted in a "sharp drop" in women's employment from 1932 through 1934.

The Women's Bureau played a significant role in improving opportunities for women in the 1920s when they reported that in 1919, women were excluded from more than half of the civil service examinations. Shortly after this information was reported, the Civil Service Commission passed a rule opening all examinations to both men and women. A uniform salary was established for each specified grade and class of work as part of the Classification Act of 1923.[21]

By the end of the 1930s, women employed by the federal government were typically concentrated in the Treasury and State Departments along with the Labor Department. The Women's Bureau reported that women constituted 36.3 percent of total employees in the Treasury Department, 36 percent of total employees in the State Department, and 33.3 percent of all employees in the Labor Department.[22]

OCCUPATIONAL OUTCOMES FOR WOMEN DOCTORATES IN THE DISMAL SCIENCE

Although U.S. Census data are not helpful in illuminating women economist's occupational outcomes in this period, we have identified women who earned a doctorate in economics and follow their occupational outcomes. These women are compared to a random sample of male doctoral recipients to examine various differences, including labor market outcomes.[23]

As previously noted, 302 women have been identified as having received doctorates in economics or a closely related field from 1890 to 1948. Examining the occupational outcomes of those women, we find that the largest number held academic employment, albeit often temporarily, as a primary job classification. On average, about 63 percent of women had an academic job following completion of their degree.[24] The preponderance of women with doctorates in economics who took academic jobs were employed in women's colleges, including Mount Holyoke College, Bryn Mawr College, Barnard College, Smith College, and Hunter College.[25] Women employed in faculty positions in coeducational environments were often located in home economics departments and sometimes sociology, law, and geography.

The next largest category of employment for women with doctorates in economics was government employment, which accounted for 16 percent of the total number of women earning economics doctorates during this period. Women employed in government were often employed by the Bureau of Labor Statistics, Women's Bureau, and other agencies in the Department of Labor. Other women were employed in the Department of Agriculture and the Social Security Administration, U.S. Treasury, and the Federal Reserve.

The final category where occupations identified were at least 5 percent of the total, was the nonprofit sector. Here we see that 8 percent of women were involved in these activities. Women employed in not-for-profit organizations were widely dispersed among groups that are typically thought of as advocacy organizations, such as the American Association of University Professors, Association of American Pen Women, International Ladies Garment Workers' Union, Tax Policy League, American Management Association, American Child Health Association, the United Nations, and the Cowles Foundation.

Important differences emerge when we compare the outcomes for women with doctorates in economics to those of men with doctorates in economics from 1890 to 1948 in our sample. Again, academic employment was the largest category for men, but 83 percent of men with doctorates chose academic employment in contrast to only 63 percent of women who were classified as such. Whereas women were concentrated in women's colleges and a handful of state universities, men were employed in a wide range of institutions. Those employing the largest number of male economics doctorates were the University of Pennsylvania, the University of Wisconsin, Harvard University, Ohio State University, the University of Illinois, Yale University, Columbia University, Pennsylvania State University, and Cornell University. One cannot help but notice that five of these top nine schools were Ivy League schools.

Likewise, 8 percent of men were classified as holding government employment, in contrast to 16 percent of women. Unlike women, men in government occupations were most often employed by the Agriculture Department, followed by a few employed in the Labor Department, Treasury Department, and the Federal Reserve. Hence, women doctorates were more likely to end up with government jobs than were their male counterparts and were far less likely to be employed in academic pursuits. Only 4 percent of men were classified as having for-profit employment as their primary job classification, and 5 percent were employed at nonprofit institutions. Seven women became high school teachers, while no men were found in this category. In addition, far more women had no occupational affiliation after earning a doctorate.[26] The top occupational outcomes for women and men, academic work and government work, constitute roughly 79 percent of all outcomes for women with doctorates in economics and about 91 percent of all outcomes for men.

Table 9.1 displays information on the sample means of various occupational outcomes and factors affecting occupational outcomes of men and women with doctorates in economics by decade. This allows us to identify gender differences in the likelihood of male and female doctorates in economics working for government or academia, differences in marriage rates, AEA membership, and the likelihood of working in the academic institution where one matriculated. Finally, we examine gender differences in the likelihood of earning a doctorate in economics and then moving out of the field for employment.

Looking first at government employment, the data show that there are no statistical differences between male and female doctorates in economics who work for government in the first four decades under review. Only in the 1930s and 1940s do we begin to see gender differences emerge. In the 1930s, women doctorates were almost twice as likely to work for government than were men; in the 1940s, about 13 percent of women doctorates worked for government compared with only 5 percent of men.

Examining occupational outcomes for male and female doctorates in economics, we also see that significant gender differences in the

TABLE 9.1 Doctorates in Economics, Occupational Outcomes, and Demographic Information Sample Means by Decade and by Sex

Variable	1890–1899 Male	1890–1899 Female	1900–1909 Male	1900–1909 Female	1910–1919 Male	1910–1919 Female	1920–1929 Male	1920–1929 Female	1930–1939 Male	1930–1939 Female	1940–1948 Male	1940–1948 Female
Government employment	0.13	0.13	0.00	0.20	0.05	0.15	0.08	0.14	0.10	0.19*	0.05	0.13*
Academic employment	0.75	0.75	0.80	0.60	0.75	0.45*	0.86	0.66*	0.84	0.61*	0.85	0.64*
Married	1.0	0.50*	0.80	0.50	1.0	0.45*	0.99	0.63*	0.93	0.57*	0.96	0.55*
AEA member	0.63	0.63	0.70	0.80	0.85	0.50*	0.73	0.62	0.70	0.57*	0.63	0.48*
Matriculated/employment	0.38	0.25	0.30	0.20	0.35	0.15	0.30	0.18*	0.30	0.20	0.34	0.13*
Move out of economics	0.57	0.57	0.33	0.44	0.26	0.50	0.22	0.41*	0.20	0.41*	0.24	0.37*

Source: The source used to identify doctoral degrees for women members is ProQuest. Biographical information is determined by examination of historical documents such as newspapers, obituaries, educational institution records, and census records.

Note: All values are in percentage terms.
*Indicates female/male means differ: *p*-value < .10.

likelihood of having academic employment are present since 1910.[27] Although the proportion of women doctorates employed in academic work was lower than that of men since 1890, this difference was not large enough to be statistically significant until 1910. From 1910 to 1948, for each decade examined, the likelihood of women's academic employment is significantly lower than that of men. In 1910–1919, 75 percent of male doctorates were employed in academic pursuits, compared with 45 percent of women doctorates. In the 1920s, 86 percent of men doctorates were employed in academic pursuits, compared with 66 percent of women doctorates. Finally, in the 1930s and 1940s, respectively, 84 and 85 percent of male doctorates were employed in academic pursuits, compared with 61 and 64 percent of women doctorates.

When we examine other important factors such as marriage rates, AEA membership, and occupational ties to previously attended educational institutions, additional aspects of the gendered nature of the professional culture for economists are revealed. Concerning the likelihood of marriage, we find a statistically significant difference in marriage rates between men and women for individuals earning doctorates in five of six decades examined. The only decade without a significance difference in the marriage rate occurred from 1900 to 1909. The data show that 50 percent of women with doctorates in economics earned in the period 1890–1899 were married at some point in their lives, compared with 100 percent of men with economics doctorates. Likewise, in 1910–1919, the proportion of married women with doctorates fell to 45 percent, while 100 percent of men were married.

The proportion of women with doctorates who married began to increase to 63 percent for those earning doctorates in the 1920s—the highest rate during the entire period 1890–1948. The marriage rate for women doctorates in the 1930s fell to 57 percent and continued to decline to 55 percent in the 1940s. At the same time, the proportion of male doctorates in economics who were married remained in the area of 99 percent for those completing their doctorates in the 1920s, falling only slightly to 93 percent in the 1930s, and going to 96 percent in the 1940s.[28] These differences are compatible with the historical trends that brought increased interest on women combining marriage and work in the 1920s and the constraints introduced by the reintroduction of marriage bars in the 1930s.

AEA membership indicates professional ties at the same time providing networks with others in the profession who might offer access to job opportunities, information, and professional development in a variety of forms, including coauthorship. The results show that there was no difference in the likelihood of being an AEA member for men and women with doctorates in economics in the first two decades examined (1890 to 1899 and 1900 to 1909). From 1910 to 1919, there is a statistically significant difference in the likelihood of membership between men and women. The mean proportion of women earning a doctorate in 1910–1919 who joined the AEA fell to 50 percent, while 85 percent of men joined. In the 1930s and 1940s, there was a significant difference in AEA membership between men and women doctorates in economics even though the likelihood of membership fell for both men and women. In the 1930s, roughly 70 percent of male doctoral recipients were likely to join the AEA, compared with 57 percent of women; in the 1940s, 63 percent of men joined and only 48 percent of women joined the AEA.

When we examine the likelihood that a doctoral recipient will be employed at some point in their life at an institution where they matriculated, we see additional gender differences emerge. There were no significant differences between men and women doctorates employed at an institution where they had matriculated in the last decade of the nineteenth century and first two decades of the twentieth century. We begin to see gender differences in this connection emerge in the 1920s. The results show that in the 1920s and the 1940s, male doctorates in economics were more likely to find jobs in an institution where they matriculated than were women doctorates. Specifically, 30 percent of these men in the 1920s found academic employment in an institution where they had matriculated, compared with only 18 percent of women. Likewise, 34 percent of men earning their doctorates in the 1940s displayed this connection, but only 13 percent of women did. Although men have been more likely to find employment in academic institutions where they had matriculated, the significant gender differences in the

1920s may reflect the growing number of women pursuing academic roles. The differences in the 1940s may reflect the postwar bias toward male employment, resulting in the growth of male academic employment especially after the war's end.

FINDING A HOME FOR (SOME) WOMEN ECONOMISTS

The results from our investigations show that women with doctorates in economics were more likely to move outside their discipline than were men. These differences began to appear in the 1920s and continued through the 1940s. The movement of women doctorates employed in academic pursuits into other fields was a troublesome aspect of the economics profession in these formative years. This raises the question of where these people were moving and if there were gender differences in the fields providing academic homes for doctorates in economics.

These results show that although women with doctorates in economics have been more likely to move outside the discipline for their employment since the beginning of the twentieth century, when we examine academic employment more narrowly, we begin to see where these women and men were going. First, with the growth of home economics as a discipline in the 1920s, women with doctorates in economics were increasingly employed in departments related to home economics, whereas men showed no such movement. Home economics provided an academic home for 23 of the 187 women academics with doctorates in economics, followed by history, social sciences in general, administration, and then sociology.[29]

For men with academic employment in fields other than economics, most prevalent were fields that came to form the core of a business curriculum, including accounting, finance, business administration, business education and business statistics, marketing, and management. Nearly half of the 60 male doctorates in economics over 1890–1948 who moved to a different academic field went to these business core areas. Only 32 percent of male doctorates who moved were employed in the traditional social sciences, such as history, political science, sociology, sociology, and geography.

For women in administration, the role of "dean of women" was one of the few administrative opportunities in the state university system. In this role, women were able to hold faculty appointments and provide substantive input, shaping the educational environment for women graduate and undergraduate students.[30] Ada Comstock at the University of Minnesota (later president of Radcliffe College), Lucy Sprague Mitchell and Lucy Ward Stebbins at the University of California at Berkeley, and Alice Freeman Palmer and Marion Talbot (both at the University of Chicago), played important roles in shaping higher education for women through their administrative roles.

Marion Talbot had significant influence, not only on the curriculum for women at the University of Chicago but on the expansion of a new field of thought.[31] She pushed for and was able to establish a new academic department—the Department of Household Administration—in 1904. She secured employment for women faculty like Sophonisba Breckinridge who, upon moving to the University of Chicago, brought many doctorates into this growing field.[32]

Edith Abbott, who had completed her doctorate in economics in 1905, and Breckinridge pushed for the joint appointment for Hazel Kyrk in the departments of home economics and economics. Kyrk brought the issue of women's nonmarket labor to the forefront with her book *Economic Problems of the Family*.[33] Her later student, Margaret Gilpin Reid, provided a definition of work that argued for the recognition of unpaid work in national income accounting. Reid's work was an important contribution to the discipline of economics and, in the words of Nancy Folbre, was "a basis for classification and measurement of household members' activities that is widely utilized today."[34]

Data suggest that the growth of women doctorates in home economics increased significantly in the 1920s, fell somewhat in the 1930s, and rapidly expanded in the 1940s. Importantly, the University of Chicago awarded more than three times the number of doctorates in this field as did the next institution, Pennsylvania State University.[35] Clearly, Evelyn

Forget's argument that women began to disappear from economics as part of the general decrease in their academic employment, which was partly influenced by rising interest in home economics, rings true.[36] The rise of doctorates in home economics and the movement of women with economics doctorates into this new field contributed to the diminished role of women in economics in the 1930s and 1940s.

The influence of women in the role of dean of women waned in the 1940s following World War II. Along with the decline in the proportion of women's undergraduate enrollment, which fell from 47 percent in 1920 to only 21 percent by the mid-1950s, came what historians have described as the "social reconstruction of the 19th century concept of 'separate spheres,' with women's place being located exclusively in the home."[37] The change in attitudes toward women resulted in the demise of the position of dean of women and its gradual replacement with dean of students—a role that was filled by men and not women.

There has long been the impression that the war years brought women back into the labor market—even if temporarily—and that women were drawn into previously male-dominated jobs. These impressions were captured in the infamous "We Can Do It" Rosie the Riveter poster of World War II. What do the data on women and men in the United States with doctorates in economics reveal about the conditions for women during the war years and the immediate postwar period, and what effect did the war years have on women with doctorates in economics?

By examining the sample of women and men earning doctorates in economics in the 1940s, we can see that the proportion of women with academic jobs in 1940–1948 declined from the 1920s. About 64 percent of women with doctorates in economics in the 1940s held academic jobs, compared with 66 percent of doctorates in the 1920s. At the same time, the proportion of men earning doctorates in economics in the 1940s and employed in academic work increased slightly, from 84 to 85 percent.[38]

In terms of government employment for women with doctorates in the 1940s, the proportion of women employed in government jobs fell from 17 percent to 13 percent. Large increases in demand for war-related goods prompted a shift in the labor supply for women in general during the war years, but there is little evidence that the war expanded opportunities for women with doctorates in economics in the 1940s.[39] Among all women earning doctorates from 1890 to 1948, many found employment in the federal government in the 1940s. Although some (such as Margaret Garritsen de Vries with the International Monetary Fund, Florence Helm with the Federal Deposit Insurance Corporation, and Elisabeth Paschal with the Social Security Administration) had long careers in government, many found only intermittent employment, moving frequently throughout the working lives.[40]

WOMEN AND WORK IN PERSPECTIVE

What we gain from our examination of the careers of women earning their doctorates in economics from 1890 to 1948 is a deeper appreciation for how work, even academic work, as a gender-based privilege affected women's lives. The working lives of these highly educated women reveals most clearly how a basic human right, such as the right to marry, was used as a cudgel—segregating women in the workplace and forcing them to make a choice between family and career.

Antinepotism rules established at many universities were used to fire women whose marriage was discovered and those who married while employed. The same rules also limited the hiring of women in so-called ladder jobs where the full benefits of faculty status were available. Even when formal antinepotism rules were not present, informal practices prevented women from being hired in many institutions of higher learning.

When women were allowed into the hallowed halls, as in women's colleges, they had high teaching loads, earned low pay, and were expected to provide monitoring duties not expected of male faculty. Once again, in very real ways, the underlying message continued: work was a gender-based privilege that benefited men and worked against women.

The use of marriage bars to limit women's ability to participate in the academic labor market diminished somewhat in the 1920s as women began to call for opportunities to work and marry, but reemerged in the 1930s because of rising unemployment. What made the Great Depression particularly harmful to women was the introduction of a marriage bar to federal law through the Economy Act of 1932. This act, which remained in law until 1937, contained a "married persons clause" mandating that whenever personnel reductions were to take place in the Executive Branch, married persons were to be the first discharged if their spouse was also a government employee. Despite gender-neutral language, the law was used to fire women. In the end, the Economy Act had a limiting effect on women's employment in federal government and state government employment, as many states followed with similar legislation.

Decisions that excluded women as potential faculty in many educational institutions limited their access to graduate students and no doubt further depressed the interest of women considering graduate education. Moreover, the absence of women faculty contributed greatly to a male-dominated editorial network in journals that certainly altered knowledge production in the discipline. The notion that work was a gender-based privilege significantly marginalized women in the discipline. In the closing chapter, we shall see how the 1940s in many ways represented the culmination of efforts directed toward the professionalization of economics and the role women would play in fulfilling this destiny.

10

A DESTINY FULFILLED

Defining the Professional Economist

When we examine the 1940s, we begin to see that many ongoing efforts directed toward professionalizing economics as a distinct discipline culminated in this period. Jurisdictional disputes aimed at defining the borders of the discipline eventually resulted in concrete expressions defining who is (and who is not) an economist. Academic professions such as economics emerged through efforts to define what counts as knowledge and eventually resulted in the development of fields of study in the discipline identified by what we now know as JEL codes.

Academic professions were independent precisely because they were self-regulating and articulated their own professional standards. The American Economic Association (AEA) leadership, urged to develop professional standards in the 1940s, moved to establish a committee for improving professional standards and recruitment in 1941.[1] Throughout the 1950s and into the 1960s, with the encouragement of governmental entities and foundations such as the Ford Foundation, the AEA worked to bring concrete meaning to the notion of "professional standards." These efforts emphasized the importance of graduate training in research institutions and oversaw the standardization of student training in economics.[2] Moreover, these efforts brought grants and government funds to research institutions. These efforts at professionalization culminated in a particular type of professional organization the 1940s.

From its early years as an organization, when the AEA was a fledging institution struggling to pay its bills, there was debate about who might be allowed to join the association and how that might influence what counts as economics while shaping the status of the profession. The ideological debates of those influenced by the German Historical School and those more inclined to use the language of science to label others as propagandists, as well as ending the branch associations, narrowed the contours of a new profession by defining who is (and who is not) an economist.[3] Although efforts to include businessmen as members were present from the beginning of the AEA, when the organization became self-supporting, efforts to reach out to the business class for membership declined. A. W. Coats has argued that the concern with classifying economists was "an obvious byproduct of the AEA's heterogenous membership and the desire to preserve the Association's scholarly and scientific character."[4] Perhaps the word "preserve" was a little optimistic. Efforts to define who is (and is not) an economist were certainly at the core of efforts to gain professional status.

Efforts by Davis R. Dewey to develop an organizational format of topics for reviews, notes, and annotated titles represented additional efforts framing this debate about professional identity. Although Dewey's original list was developed in his role as editor to organize literature in the *American Economic Review* (*AER*), Beatrice Cherrier notes that "it was the growing—and now largely forgotten—need to classify AEA *members* that prompted open discussion of the methodology of classification."[5]

ROUNDING UP (SOME OF) THE BRAINS OF THE COUNTRY

It is important to note the significant role of wartime (World War I and especially World War II) in further shaping the identity of economics and economists. The debates on how to categorize legitimate research in the field along with the influence of AEA leadership in shaping the identity of those who might rightfully be called "economist" has had a long history and was solidified in the 1940s.

While Dewey introduced a format for categories of study in economics to organize material included in the *AER*, as Coats points out, during the interwar years the preoccupation with defining economics and who is an economist, along with growing concern over professional standards, began to emerge in earnest.[6] Would the professional leadership in the AEA play a significant role in settling these "jurisdictional disputes," and what role did these discussions have in creating borders in the discipline? Most important, would these borders include women as valued members in the discipline or work to marginalize their work as outside the discipline?

During World War I, the association was presented with an opportunity to more formally identify real economists from imposters. In spring 1914, Secretary Allyn Young sought to raise the visibility of AEA leadership with the federal government.[7] Writing to Secretary of Agriculture David F. Houston, Young complained about the poor quality of the statistical work of the Department of Agriculture, offering to improve their work by sponsoring sessions at the annual meetings. When met with a positive response by Houston, Young moved quickly to contact those with expertise in statistics to follow through on the suggestion, and the American Statistical Association joined the AEA in sponsoring sessions. As the program for the Twenty-Seventh Annual Meeting of the AEA showed, none of the participants offering their insights in the jointly sponsored session were women.[8]

In March 1917, the AEA leadership of the also began to discuss how the organization might contribute to the war effort by mobilizing "all of our resources, intellectual as well as physical."[9] To that end, Young sent a letter to members indicating that the Executive Committee would soon meet to discuss plans "for the cooperation of economists in the work of national defense."[10] One of the likely acts that the committee might take up, Young indicated, would be to appoint committees on subjects related to national defense. As it turns out, the Executive

Committee did consider appointing committees on subjects of national defense, but this proposal was voted down.[11] Young also alluded to another important act—taking a census of economic experts in connection with the U.S. Civil Service Commission.

Only a month later, in April 1917, Young sent a survey to the AEA membership inquiring after their expertise. The next step, requested by the Civil Service Commission, was to request that the roster be purged of "the names of persons who did not properly come within the classification of economic expert." According to Michael A. Bernstein, three "eminent members"—George Barnett of Johns Hopkins University, John Bates Clark of Columbia University, and Frank Taussig—along with Young were given the task of purging the list of those not considered economic experts. Unfortunately for some, the work, which was completed in June 1918, was never put to use because the war ended.[12]

The list of people properly classified as economic experts may not have been put to use, but the idea of classifying economists was far from dead. The Classification Act of 1923 may have reflected an effort to regularize pay in Civil Service employment, but the attempt to clarify pay categories once again brought the issue of who might count as an expert to the AEA. The issue became even more heated when the introduction of mail ballots for AEA leadership was introduced in the mid-1930s, making it possible for those not able to attend the annual meetings to express their preference in the choice of candidates and vote in the election of officers.[13] As Coats saw it, the introduction of a "more democratic" process for electing officers reignited proposals to restrict voting to "properly qualified" members.[14]

The issue of identifying "properly qualified" experts continued (unresolved) until World War II brought it to the attention of the association's leadership again.[15] The work of creating a list of bona fide economists began in earnest when Vannevar Bush approached President Franklin Delano Roosevelt in 1940 to recommend establishing a National Defense Research Committee to coordinate wartime labor needs using a National Roster of Scientific and Specialized Personnel (NRSSP). The AEA Executive Committee was approached and took up the matter of professional subfield classifications along with developing a list of experts. By fall 1940, plans were in place regarding the association's possible contribution to the NRSSP under the direction of the National Resource Planning Board.

James Washington Bell, then secretary of the AEA, began by providing the 1938 list of members to Princeton's Carl Brigham who was collecting data for the roster. Brigham suggested omitting the reference to the "economic history of this and that," and when he suggested that the list of experts "should be drastically reduced and simplified," the challenge of who and what to include began.[16]

The list of categories of interest became an ongoing project. Dewey's list served as a starting point, Bell produced a list of categories by January 1940 that many thought "too elaborate," and Paul Homan, the new editor of the *AER*, offered a compromise. The Executive Committee eventually adopted Bell's scheme. Bell's victory was short-lived when Brigham immediately rejected Bell's scheme.

The lesson would eventually be learned about the difficulty of developing one list that could serve as a taxonomy to categorize literature for use by academics and for personnel decisions in the war effort. In the end, the decision was made to produce two classifications—one focused on problems studied by economists and the other on commodities and manufactured goods. Neither was especially useful for editors of economics journals, but for the war effort, they were deemed appropriate. Working with the association, the NRSSP was maintained throughout the war years.

Several surveys were conducted in the 1940s to solicit names of experts along with their areas of expertise. An initial roster was established by 1941. In June 1942, the NRSSP prepared a report on the distribution of professionals by field, sex, and extent of education—the results of which reveal the lack of gender balance in some professions.[17] The report shows that women made up only 6 percent of the personnel in economics compared with other social sciences such as history and political science, where women were 15 percent; sociology, where women were 16 percent; and geography, where women were 17 percent of personnel. What is surprising is that women were far more represented in statistics and mathematics, where they were 13 and 18 percent of personnel, respectively, than they were in economics.[18]

With Bell's assistance, a final list of membership personnel with areas of expertise was published in the *AER* in 1949 using information from a member survey distributed in 1948. Ninety-five percent of those listed were male members and only 5 percent were women. The AEA membership in 1948 was such that the survey appears to have successfully elicited responses from 38 percent of female members and 63 percent of male members. Although the final list of names included in the roster was taken from this list, the desire to maintain confidentiality leaves open the question of whose names were included and whose were not.

We don't know the reason for the difference in the response rate for male and female members in the 1948 survey.[19] We do know that women were not compelled to respond at the same rate as men with one possible reason being differences in areas of interest that were solicited. Specifically, the survey form did not include home economics but did include business administration and subfields in the business core, such as accounting, marketing, and advertising.

THE PROFESSION OF ECONOMIST

The final exhibit in the first issue of volume 39 of the *AER* published in January 1949 contained a statement of the AEA's definition of who is (and is not) an economist. The two-and-a-half-page description was the third draft of an effort begun by the secretary, redrafted by the NRSSP staff, and edited by an AEA committee consisting of Frank Whitson Fetter, Fritz Machlup, Howard Sylvester Ellis, and James Washington Bell.[20]

The "brief statement" contained ten male pronouns (he and his), no female pronouns (she or hers), along with the use of the word "man" twice. No reference was made to women. The first sentence set the tone when it declared that "Economists study the whole process through which man makes a living and satisfies his wants for food, shelter, service or amusement, and the conditions favoring or hampering his economic development."[21] Included in the description are major branches of economics, which include economic theory; money, banking, and finance; industry; industrial trade; agricultural economics; labor economics; and socioeconomics.

As for the functional activities of the professional economist, they were said to involve: (1) Teaching: "teaching at the college or university level" where "he usually but not always engages in part-time research." (2) Research: "he conducts research on a full-time basis in government, in business and industrial establishments, in banks, in labor unions, and at private research foundations." (3) "Management or Administration of industry or government." (4) "Technical editing and writing of books, magazines, pamphlets, and newspaper articles." Finally, the professional economist may engage in (5) "Consulting and advisory work for government, business and financial institutions, and investors."[22]

It is revealing that the AEA took effort to point out that "membership in a national or local professional organization is no criterion of professional status since such membership is open to anyone interested in the objectives or activities of the society." Noting that the professional economist usually has a master's or doctorate in economics, the description goes on to identify who is not an economist. We learn that high school teachers who have a bachelor's degree in economics are classified as "teachers, high school" rather than professional economists. Journalists and radio news commentators may be interested in economics but are not professional economists. Bankers, bank cashiers, and related banking, insurance, and finance occupations are classified as managers and not economists. Finally, to be clear, "home economists are classified as such." In other words, don't be confused into thinking that a home economist is an economist.[23]

These statements offer a fairly clear indication of the borders drawn around the discipline at the end of World War II. No mention is made of nonprofit occupations that might employ a professional economist except those considered to be "private research institutions." This reflects the general disregard for advocacy work most typically done by women. It explicitly rejects those teaching high school but also argues that bankers—courted by the AEA in their membership drives—are not professional economists. Finally, women who had been drawn to economics, some even earning a doctorate, who found employment in departments of home economics, might have been somewhat surprised to learn that they are not economists.

It is telling and perhaps not surprising to learn that the efforts made throughout almost all of the AEA's early history that culminated in the 1940s to define who is an economist, what counts as knowledge, and efforts to set professional standards were directed entirely by male leadership. None of the committees established to review and draft statements in the 1940s, none of the members of the Executive Committee who approved final documents, and none of the officers who communicated with government officials were women.[24] In many ways, women's voices were effectively silenced in the organization that assumed the role of speaking on behalf of the profession.

KNOWLEDGE, POWER, AND GENDER IN THE PROFESSIONALIZATION OF ECONOMICS

An examination of AEA history and the professionalization of the discipline offers a unique lens into gender bias in economics. The emergence of the professional association offered scholars a mechanism to establish ties with colleagues, an opportunity to meet annually to discuss new techniques and refine theories, and a venue for establishing themselves as experts. As Cynthia Epstein points out, "Professional friendships develop into personal relationships at the cocktail hours, and at committee and dinner meetings."[25] Membership and participation in the association became a central aspect of professional development—but not for women.

Despite the presence of one woman at the original organizing meeting of the AEA and growing interest by women in branch meetings, it was thirty-two years before women served in any capacity in AEA leadership and twenty-six years before a woman would serve on the editorial board of the *AER*. The first woman to serve as president of the AEA was Alice M. Rivlin in 1986—one hundred years after the association's founding. The first woman to serve as editor of the *AER* was Pinelopi K. Goldberg in 2011—at the one hundredth anniversary of the founding of the journal.

When the AEA annual meetings were established to bring economists together and cull consensus from a wide variety of opinions, women were seldom on the program. In fact, Robert W. Dimand, Geoffrey Black, and Evelyn L. Forget note that "at twenty six of the thirty six annual AEA annual meetings from 1899 to 1934 inclusive, the number of women among the speakers and discussants was zero, as was also the case for five of the six AEA meetings held from 1887 to 1894."[26]

The few women who did attend the annual meetings were often made to feel like unwelcomed intruders at "the professors' party." With attention to mentoring young economists, local organizers were encouraged to schedule receptions, or "smokers," bringing together young members with older, established members. It was seen inappropriate for women and men to mix in such a setting, so when a reception was held at the home of the Stuart Wood in 1886, interested women were offered a lady's reception at another location. None showed up.[27] In future annual meetings, it was suggested that local organizers set aside certain tables for women members, many of whom felt "out of it" when they were not allowed to be present at such functions.[28]

It is important to state that the marginalization of Black women economists was deep and pervasive, and not all women faced the same degree of marginalization. Sadie Mossell Alexander, who had earned her doctorate in economics from the University of Pennsylvania in 1921, had to change professions to gain a degree of professional recognition. Becoming a lawyer allowed her an opportunity to exercise agency and professional autonomy not afforded to her in economics. Irene Malvan Hypps, who earned her doctorate in economics from New York University in 1943, taught high school, becoming a school superintendent over her long career. Finally, Phyllis Ann Wallace, who earned her doctorate from Yale University in 1948, was successful by first working for the

National Bureau of Economic Research and then working on the faculty of Atlanta University—a historically black college. She became chief of technical studies at the Equal Employment Opportunity Commission's Office of Research. After serving as a visiting professor of MIT's Sloan School of Management, she was finally granted the rank of full professor in 1975.[29]

For all women economists, external pressures of varying kinds stifled their careers, creating barriers to entry for those trained in the finer points of a free market. When Sadie Mossell Alexander, Irene Malvan Hypps, and Phyllis Wallace were taking graduate courses, they could not eat in a restaurant or ride freely in public transportation. When Caroline Ware applied for work teaching courses at the University of Wyoming as a married woman, she experienced the full force of the "marriage bar" and was not allowed to teach courses when it was discovered that she was a married woman. What most women learned was that it was more acceptable to be a consumer of someone else's knowledge than to be a producer of knowledge. One activity added to the status of the insider, while the other held the threat of competing with it.

As women economists faced external pressures, they were channeled into different types of entry jobs. Some white women were allowed to teach in women's colleges while being turned away from state universities—universities their tax dollars helped support. Black women scholars were accepted in historically black colleges while being turned away from women's colleges and a burgeoning state university system. This channeling had long-term effects. As Francine Blau and Marianne A. Ferber have argued, "Once men and women are channeled into different types of entry jobs, the normal everyday practices of the firm will virtually ensure sex differences in productivity, promotion opportunities, and pay."[30]

By the 1950s, the stage was set to marginalize women in the economics profession. The cruel irony was that women were excluded from the so-called free labor market at the same time the profession waxed poetic about the virtues of a free market. This marginalization has had lasting effects on the production of knowledge, and although there have been considerable improvements in the status of women in economics, considerable problems remain.

EPILOGUE

When the American Economic Association (AEA) passed a resolution establishing the Committee on the Status of Women in the Economics Profession (CSWEP) in 1971, the paucity of women in economics was given formal recognition. At the December 1971 AEA business meeting and at the behest of the newly formed Women's Caucus, Carolyn Shaw Bell presented a set of resolutions addressing the "woman problem" in economics. The final resolutions declared that "economics is not exclusively a man's field" and established the ad hoc CSWEP, whose first task would be to gather data and produce a report on the status of women in the profession.[1] The resolutions also stated that no discrimination in recruitment, salary, or promotion be allowed by university departments; that a roster of women economists be established; and that women be nominated for editorial boards at economics journals. Also included were provisions making it easier for participants with children to attend the annual conference by making child care available.[2]

When CSWEP began collecting data on the number of women graduate students and faculty, they received responses from only 22 percent of surveyed departments. The schools that did not respond were smaller. To provide meaningful data, they identified institutions known as the "Chairman's Group"—forty-three schools or, as they referred to them, the "cartel," that produced over two-thirds of the graduate students in the field. All but one school in this group, the University of Rochester, responded to the survey.[3] This was the data CSWEP used to gain an overall picture of the status of women in the economics profession.

At the time of the first survey, the cartel reported a total of 1,194 economics faculty, 80 (6.7 percent) of whom were women. Almost half of the women in the census had joined their intitutions since 1970. Only twenty-two, or less than a third of women, held the rank of associate or full professor. Two-thirds of male faculty held senior ranks. Clearly, women were not just a minority but a lower-ranked minority of faculty. Moreover, Bell reported that CSWEP's results showed that women constituted only 12 percent of graduate students in economics.[4]

The data on women faculty and graduate students presented in the first CSWEP report reveal the lack of progress for women academic economists in the decades following World War II. The GI Bill brought expanded education to millions of returning veterans, but resulted in what Margaret Rossiter has referred to as the "remasculinization" of science. This generous program provided five years of full tuition and a living allowance to veterans, most of whom were white men. As Hilary Herbold points out, "the segregationist principles of almost every institution of higher learning effectively disbarred a huge proportion of Black veterans from earning a college degree." Likewise, as Rossiter points out, of the nearly 8 million returning veterans returning to universities after the war, only 400,000 were women.[5]

The 1950s and 1960s brought expansion, growth, and government grants to the discipline of economics. However, few women participated in this expansion. Those few who held faculty positions were often removed by antinepotism policies. Most were never hired in a faculty position if they were married to a scholar employed in the same institution. Women such as Margaret S. Gordon, wife of Robert Aaron Gordon, earned her doctorate from Radcliffe University in 1935. Despite her credentials, she was disqualified from becoming "ladder faculty" at the University of California at Berkeley because of antinepotism policies.[6]

There were some notable exceptions. Margaret Reid, who had earned her doctorate from the University of Chicago in 1931, taught in the department of economics and in home economics at Iowa State until 1943, when she left academia and began working for the federal government. Five years later, she became professor of economics at the University of Illinois at Urbana-Champaign. Dorothy Brady, who received a doctorate in mathematics in 1933, was employed for several decades as a home economist in the Department of Agriculture. In 1951, she returned to academia and joined the department of economics at the University of Illinois, later moving to the University of Chicago.[7]

These notable women were indeed exceptions. As the case of Anne P. Carter demonstrates, most departments experiencing growth in the postwar era were not welcoming to women, however qualified they might be. Despite earning her doctorate from Harvard University in 1949 and serving as a research fellow at Harvard for fifteen years, Carter was finally hired as an assistant professor in 1966—the first woman assistant professor in the Department of Economics at Harvard. As she later recalled it, she "never felt welcome" at Harvard. Carter left for Brandeis University in 1971 and became a full professor in 1972.[8]

The lack of an academic home for women in the 1950s and 1960s also resulted in a lack of representation in the work of the burgeoning professional association, the AEA. Between 1949 and 1970, only five women served on the Executive Committee of the AEA—Eveline M. Burns (New York School of Social Work), Ruth Prince Mack (National Bureau of Economic Research), Faith Moors Williams (U.S. Department of Labor), Mabel Frances Timlin (University of Saskatchewan), and Mary Jean Bowman (University of Chicago). The institutional affiliation of these women members of the AEA Executive Committee is telling. Only one woman was in a U.S. university, where she received a faculty appointment in 1958 after a change in nepotism rules. As for representation on editorial boards in economics journals such as the *American Economic Review* (*AER*), no women served on the editorial board from 1945, when Mabel Newcomer served, until 1970, when Barbara Bergmann became a member of the editorial board.[9]

Women's lack of access to so-called ladder appointments during this period stiffled their professional development. This no doubt discouraged women from choosing economics as a field of study in their graduate work. As the work of Sarah Thébaud and Maria Charles suggests, the lack of women in a field contributes to cultural stereotypes about work. If women don't see anyone who looks like them doing a particular job, this contributes to cultural stereotypes that reproduce occupational segregation.[10] The lack of women in faculty positions in the 1950s and 1960s surely had long-term consequences stiffling gender balance in the dismal science for decades to follow.

Likewise, the lack of women with faculty positions in universities offering graduate training also has an effect on what counts as knowledge. A faculty graduate adviser has enormous influence in overseeing graduate student reserach and dissertation work—from topics to approachs and often policy conclusions. The lack of women available to serve as graduate adviser limits the universe of topics suggested. There is evidence, as we saw in chapter 1, that this also constrains the approaches used.

Another consequence of women's lack of access to faculty positions in economics in the 1950s and 1960s concerns the impact on what counts as knowledge through the review process. The lack of women faculty resulted in an extreme lack of women serving on editorial boards, not to mention as editor in the *AER* and other journals in the field. When publications in journals were exanding and becoming more important in terms of faculty development and promotion, there was no formal mechanism for including women's intellectual perspectives. If, as we have since verified, the views of women economists differ from those of men, we must conclude that women's absence as editors and on editorial boards altered research on a variety of topics—many affecting large numbers of people in important ways.[11]

It has been fifty years since the founding of CSWEP in 1971, and the profession still finds gender balance to be elusive among faculty, graduate students, and editors of economics journals. Although the representation of women as faculty and graduate students has increased somewhat in economics, as it has in every other field in higher education, these missing women continue to haunt the discipline. Only 32 percent of doctorates in economics are awarded to women, and only 14 percent of full professors are women as of 2018. Likewise, only eleven minority (African American, Hispanic, and Native American) women earned doctorates in economics in 2014 and, while about 30 percent of the U.S. population is Black or Hispanic, only 6.3 percent of tenured and tenure-track economics faculty are identified as such.[12]

The AEA has once again begun to take steps to address this imbalance—collecting and publishing the results of surveys on the views of economists on gender issues such as pay inequity and sexual harassment. The results of the 2019 climate survey provide evidence of the difference in men's and women's views on gender equity in economics and the prevalence of sexual harassment in the field. Perhaps as a result of the shocking responses of the survey, the AEA has developed a Policy on Harassment and Discrimination, putting in place an ombdsperson to address concerns of unequal or discriminatory treatment.[13]

While recent years have marked a renewed effort by the AEA to address its "gender and diversity problem," research on inequities in the discipline is expanding. This research provides evidence on the underrepresentation of women as faculty by rank and institution and the underrepresentation of women as graduate students. It also allows us to drill down into the policies and practices generating a variety of inequities.

Evidence is accumulating on gender differences in tenure rates between men and women faculty by type of institution and over time.[14] Research on publishing in economics is revealing gender differences. Tommaso Colussi's research demonstrates the importance of ties between editors and authors based on their academic histories. Other research, such as that by Erin Hengel on the length of time in reviews (which are longer for women), may also explain part of the gender gap in tenure rates.[15]

Other research examines the effect of coauthorship in a male-dominated field such as economics. Heather Sarsons's study of the effect of coauthorship for women on tenure decisions suggests that credit attribution depends on the sex of the coauthor. Women's research coauthored with men seems to "count less" when tenure decisions are made than research coauthored with other women, which appears not to suffer in credit attribution.[16]

As studies in the sociology of the discipline continue, the contours of a better roadmap to identify gender gaps and for whom they exist will emerge along with remedies to promote better gender balance and racial equity. Certainly the lack of progress in the past two decades in terms of these dimensions in economics deserves attention, and we need to further examine the effectiveness of remedies to redress these shortcomings.

The examination of remedies suggests that we need to begin to look more closely at why women undergraduates are less likely to choose economics as a major than are male students. There is promising work suggesting that women show greater grade sensitivity and this influences their choice of majors more than it does for male students.[17] If this sensitivity is in part due to a tendency for women to attribute negative feedback to a lack of ability (rather than something arbitrary such as luck), then sharing information with students on these differences in decision-influencing factors may help mitigate them.[18]

Other research is focused on the influence of role models for women. Tatyana Avilova and Claudia Goldin's work on the Undergraduate Women in Economics project suggests that exposure to women faculty and female role models other than women faculty can have a positive effect on women students and their decision to major in economics.[19]

Other studies examine sources of faculty bias on teaching evaluations. For example, Lillian MacNell, Adam Driscoll, and Andrea Hunt find that students evaluate female instructors more harshly than male instructors. Disguising the gender of the instructor in online teaching revealed this bias and showed students often referring to men as "brilliant" and women as "annoying."[20] Better instruments for evaluating teaching and information on possible bias provided to chairs may help mitigate this additional challenge for women faculty.

As Amanda Bayer and Cecilia Rouse have shown, implicit bias is present at all stages of the academic pipeline—often embedded in formal decisions and decision-making structures, as well as routine interactions. The routines and practices shaping the academic work-place in economics need to be thoughtfully and critically examined. Remedies need to be offered and tested for effectiveness. Finally, accountability and transparency should be expected.

The professional association has a large role in promoting equity in the dismal science, and we can no longer rely on women and faculty of color to identify shortcomings and biases. As Sadie Tanner Mossell Alexander pointed out long ago, "when you do these things, you're a troublemaker." Unfortunately, there are often severe professional costs to such troublemaking, and what may be good for the institution in the long run may not be so good for faculty with the courage to uncover biases where they exist.

Increasing research is making it possible for the discipline to better understand its biases and we will at least have some tools to promote better gender balance and racial equity. In the years ahead, the expansion of gender research on the discipline will either mark progress or document the impediments to change in the recalcitrant discipline of economics.

NOTES

1. CURRENT CHALLENGES, HISTORICAL ORIGINS

1. Ben Casselman and Jim Tankersley, "Female Economists Push Their Field Toward a #MeToo Reckoning," *New York Times*, January 10, 2019.
2. Finance & Economics, Free Exchange, "Barriers to Entry," *The Economist*, May 10, 2018. See also Ben Casselman, Jim Tankersley, and Jeanna Smialek, "A Year After a #MeToo Reckoning, Economists Still Grapple With It," *New York Times*, January 7, 2020; Heather Long, "'Please, Listen to Us': What It's Like Being Female at America's Biggest Economic Conference," *Washington Post*, January 18, 2019; David Harrison, "Female Economists, in Survey, Cite Gender Discrimination," *Wall Street Journal*, March 18, 2019; Heather Long, "Female Economists Report Widespread Discrimination and Sexual Assault, Prompting Calls for Major Change," *Washington Post*, March 18, 2019; Leaders, Women and Economics, "Economics Is Uncovering Its Gender Problem," *The Economist*, March 21, 2019; Finance & Economics, Academic Sexism, "A Dispiriting Survey of Women's Lot in University Economics," *The Economist*, March 23, 2019; Noah Smith, "Economics Starts Reckoning with Its Gender Bias Problem," *Bloomberg Opinion*, January 10, 2018. For specific criticisms concerning the economics profession and race, see Randall Akee, "The Race Problem in Economics," *Brookings*, January 22, 2020, https://www.brookings.edu/blog/up-front/2020/01/22/the-race-problem-in-economics/, and Ben Casselman and Jim Tankersley, "Economics, Dominated by White Men, Is Roiled by Black Lives Matter," *New York Times*, June 10, 2020.
3. National Science Foundation, National Center for Science and Engineering Statistics, "Doctorate Recipients from U.S. Universities: 2018," Special Report NSF 20-301, NSF (2009), https://ncses.nsf.gov/pubs/nsf20301/.
4. Each year CSWEP provides the results of a survey of departments with doctoral programs in economics on the number of women faculty. See Shelly Lundberg,

"Report: Committee on the Status of Women in the Economics Profession (CSWEP),"
AEA Papers and Proceedings 108 (2018): 704–21.

5. Kim A. Weeden, Sarah Thébaud, and Dafna Gelbgiser, "Degrees of Difference: Gender Segregation of U.S. Doctorates by Field and Program Prestige," *Sociological Science* 4 (2017): 123–50.

6. See Weeden, Thébaud, and Gelbgiser, "Degrees of Difference," 143.

7. Amanda Bayer and Cecilia Elena Rouse, "Diversity in the Economics Profession: A New Attack on an Old Problem," *Journal of Economic Perspectives* 30, no. 4 (2016): 221 and 223.

8. Donna Ginther and Shulamit Kahn, "Academic Women's Careers in the Social Sciences," in *The Economics of Economists: Institutional Setting, Individual Incentives, and Future Prospects*, ed. A. Lanteri and J. Vromen (Cambridge: Cambridge University Press, 2014), 307.

9. Erin Hengel, "Publishing While Female: Are Women Held to Higher Standards? Evidence from Peer Review," Cambridge Working Papers in Economics 1753, University of Cambridge (2017), 3.

10. See Marianne A. Ferber and Michelle Teiman, "Are Women Economists at a Disadvantage in Publishing Journal Articles?," *Eastern Economic Journal* 6, no. 3–4 (1980): 189–94; and John M. McDowell and Janet Kiholm Smith, "The Effect of Gender-Sorting on Propensity to Coauthor: Implications for Academic Promotion," *Economic Inquiry* 30, no. 1 (1992): 68–82; and Donna K. Ginther and Shulamit Kahn, "Women in Economics: Moving Up or Falling Off the Academic Career Ladder?," *Journal of Economic Perspectives* 18, no. 3 (2004): 193–214. These studies all report a pattern in gender sorting in coauthorship in economics such that women write more single-authored articles than men. McDowell and Smith find that women were more than five times more likely than men to have female coauthors. See also Shulamit B. Kahn, "Women in the Economics Profession," *Journal of Economic Perspectives* 9, no. 4 (1995): 193–206.

11. Heather Sarsons, "Recognition for Group Work: Gender Differences in Academia," *American Economic Review* 107, no. 5 (2017): 141–45.

12. The woman Dewey spoke of was Lucile Eaves, and a full discussion of the saga of her review in the inaugural issue of the *AER* is the subject of chapter 7 in this volume. See correspondence from Davis R. Dewey to Ira Cross dated October 2, 1911, American Economic Association Records, Box 64–69, "Correspondence of Davis R. Dewey with editors and authors of articles and communications, 1910–1917," David M. Rubenstein Rare Book & Manuscript Library, Duke University.

13. Eleanor Lansing Dulles, *Eleanor Lansing Dulles, Chances of a Lifetime: A Memoir* (Englewood Cliffs, NJ: Prentice Hall, 1980), 101–2.

14. Rachel McCullough, "Interview with Anne Carter," *Newsletter of the Committee on the Status of Women in the Economics Profession (CSWEP)* (Spring/Summer 2009).

15. Carolyn Shaw Bell, "Report of the Committee on the Status of Women in the Economics Profession," *American Economic Review* 63, no. 2 (1973): 508–11.

16. Evelyn L. Forget, "American Women and the Economics Profession in the Twentieth Century," *Economia: History/Methodology/Philosophy* 1, no. 1 (2011): 9–30.

17. CSWEP engaged in a number of initiatives, including writing to challenge sexism in textbooks and a boycott of the Atlanta AEA meetings on the basis that Georgia had not ratified the ERA, an initiative that failed. See Cleo Chassonnery-Zaïgouche, Beatrice Cherrier, and John D. Singleton, "Economics Is Not a Man's Field: CSWEP and the First Reckoning in Economics (1971–1991)," AEA/ASSA Conference 2020, https://www.aeaweb.org/conference/2020/preliminary/1872 .

18. Shelly Lundberg and Jenna Stearns, "Women in Economics: Stalled Progress," *Journal of Economic Perspectives* 33, no. 1 (2019): 3–22.

19. See Jacob Mincer, "Labor Force Participation of Married Women: A Study of Labor Supply," in *Aspects of Labor Economics*, ed. Universities-National Bureau Committee for Economic Research (Princeton, NJ: Princeton University Press, 1962), 63–106; Gary S. Becker, *The Economics of Discrimination* (Chicago: University of Chicago Press, 1957); and Gary S. Becker, *A Treatise on the Family* (Cambridge, MA: Harvard University Press, 1981).

20. Claudia Goldin, Lawrence F. Katz, and Ilyana Kuziemko, "The Homecoming of American College Women: The Reversal of the College Gender Gap," *Journal of Economic Perspectives* 20, no. 4 (2006): 133–56.

21. See Donald Tomaskovic-Devey, *Gender and Racial Inequality at Work: The Sources and Consequences of Job Segregation* (Ithaca, NY: Cornell University Press, 1993); Joe R. Feagin and Clairece Booher Feagin, *Discrimination American Style: Institutional Racism and Sexism* (Upper Saddle River, NJ: Prentice Hall, 1978); Stephen Kulis, "Gender Segregation among College and University Employees," *Sociology of Education* 70, no. 2 (1997): 151–73; and David Colander and Joanna Wayland Woos, "Institutional Demand-Side Discrimination Against Women and the Human Capital Model," *Feminist Economics* 3, no. 1 (1997): 53–64.

22. Rosabeth Moss Kanter, *Men and Women of the Corporation* (New York: Basic Books, 1977).

23. For an examination of standards and rituals of scholarly conduct and hiring, see Pamela S. Tolbert and Alice A. Oberfield, "Sources of Organizational Demography: Faculty Sex Ratios in College and Universities," *Sociology of Education* 64, no. 4 (1991): 305–14 and Alison M. Konrad and Jeffrey Pfeffer, "Understanding the Hiring of Women and Minorities in Educational Institutions," *Sociology of Education* 64, no. 3 (1991): 141–57. John C. Smart, "Gender Equity in Academic Rank and Salary," *Review of Higher Education* 14, no. 4 (1991): 511–25 provides a discussion of gender and promotion. For a discussion of performance reviews, see Jeanne S. Hurlbert and Rachel A. Rosenfield, "Getting a Good Job: Rank and Institutional Prestige in Academic Psychologists' Careers," *Sociology of Education* 65, no. 3 (1992): 188–207 and J. Scott Long, Paul D. Allison, and Robert McGinnis, "Rank Advancement in Academic Careers: Sex Differences and the Effects of Productivity," *American Sociological Review* 58, no. 5 (1993): 703–22.

24. Sarah Thébaud and Maria Charles, "Segregation, Stereotypes, and STEM," *Social Sciences* 7, no. 111 (2018): 1–18. See also Londa Schiebinger, *Has Feminism Changed Science?* (Cambridge, MA: Harvard University Press, 1999), 68–91.

25. Thébaud and Charles, "Segregation, Stereotypes, and STEM," 2.

26.   Laurie A. Rudman, Corinne A. Moss-Racusin, Julie E. Phelan, and Sanne Nauts, "Status Incongruity and Backlash Effects: Defending the Gender Hierarchy Motivates Prejudice Against Female Leaders," *Journal of Experimental Social Psychology* 48, no. 1 (2012): 165–79.

27.   Linda Hutcheon, "Rhetoric and Competition: Academic Agonistics," *Common Knowledge* 9, no. 1 (2003): 42–49.

28.   Hutcheon makes the connection between the idealized behavior of the modern academic and the model of competitive capitalism explicit. See also Donald Goellnicht, "From Novitiate Culture to Market Economy: The Professionalization of Graduate Students," *English Studies in Canada* 19, no. 4 (1993): 475. For a broader look, see Sandra Harding, *The Science Question in Feminism* (Ithaca, NY: Cornell University Press, 1986).

29.   American Economic Association, "AEA Professional Climate Survey: Final Report," September 15, 2019. https://www.aeaweb.org/resources/member-docs/final-climate-survey-results-sept-2019.

30.   The AEA provides important results by additional groups such as LGBT, Black, Asian, and Latinx economists and by age and religion. American Economic Association, "AEA Professional Climate Survey."

31.   See Alice H. Wu, "Gendered Language on the Economics Job Market Rumors Forum," *AEA Papers and Proceedings* 108 (2018): 175–79; and Alice H. Wu, "Gender Bias Among Professionals: An Identity-Based Interpretation," *Review of Economics and Statistics* 102, no. 5 (2020): 867–80; and Alice H. Wu, "Gender Stereotyping in Academe: Evidence from Economics Job Market Rumors Forum," undergraduate thesis, University of California, Berkeley, September 2017, https://scholar.harvard.edu/alicewu/publications/gender-stereotyping-academia-evidence-economics-job-market-rumors-forum.

32.   Although it is also true that "homosexual" and "homo" were frequently used when describing men, the list of words associated with men were more often relevant to economics, while words associated with women were personal and, in Justin Wolfers's words, "make for uncomfortable reading." See Justin Wolfers, "Evidence of a Toxic Environment for Women in Economics," *New York Times*, August 18, 2017. Reaction to the results of Alice Wu's research on the Economics Job Market Rumors (EJMR) website was swift. Following Wolfers's story about this research, where Berkeley economist David Romer summarized the paper as depicting "a cesspool of misogyny," more than 1,000 economics professors, lecturers, and graduate student instructors in the United States signed a petition urging the AEA to develop a "fact-based" and moderated wiki to provide an alternative source for current job market information. See Kathleen Maclay, "Berkeley Economist Leads Petition Drive to Fight Pervasive Misogyny," *Berkeley News*, October 31, 2017.

33.   Katherine W. Phillips, Sun Young Kim-Jun, and So-Hyeon Shim, "The Value of Diversity in Organizations: A Social Psychological Perspective," in *Social Psychology and Organizations*, ed. David De Cremer, Rolf van Dick, and J. Keith Murnighan (New York: Routledge, 2011), 253–72. See also Scott E. Page, *The Difference: How the Power of Diversity Creates Better Groups, Firms, Schools, and Societies* (Princeton, NJ: Princeton University Press, 2007).

34. Ann Mari May, Mary G. McGarvey, and Robert Whaples, "Are Disagreements Among Male and Female Economists Marginal at Best? A Survey of AEA Members and Their Views on Economics and Economic Policy," *Contemporary Economic Policy* 32, no. 1 (2014): 111–32 and Ann Mari May, Mary G. McGarvey, and David Kucera, "Gender and European Economic Policy: A Survey of the Views of European Economists on Contemporary Economic Policy," *Kyklos* 71, no. 1 (2018): 162–83.

35. May, McGarvey, and Whaples, "Are Disagreements," 126–227.

36. May, McGarvey, and Kucera, "Gender and European Economic Policy," 178.

37. See, for example, Andrew Abbott, *The System of Professions: An Essay on the Division of Expert Labor* (Chicago: University of Chicago Press, 1988).

38. Magali Sarfatti Larson, *The Rise of Professionalism: Monopolies of Competence and Sheltered Markets* (Piscataway, NJ: Transaction, 2013).

39. Larson, *The Rise of Professionalism*, xvi.

40. Eliot Freidson, *Profession of Medicine: A Study of the Sociology of Applied Knowledge* (Chicago: University of Chicago Press, 1988), 71–72.

41. Larson, *The Rise of Professionalism*, 48.

42. Larson, *The Rise of Professionalism*, xiii.

43. Larson specifically excludes the discussion of gender and her analysis, although it is clearly a framework that is most useful when analyzing gender. See Larson, *The Rise of Professionalism*.

44. Larson, *The Rise of Professionalism*, 46.

45. Larson, *The Rise of Professionalism*, 48.

46. Larson, *The Rise of Professionalism*, 155.

47. Margaret Rossiter notes that the Geological Society of America required a PhD, but only for its women members. See Margaret W. Rossiter, *Women Scientists in America: Struggles and Strategies to 1940* (Baltimore, MD: Johns Hopkins University Press, 1982), 83.

48. Abbott, *The System of Professions*, 33–111.

49. As the press clippings for the AEA annual meetings show, the growing disdain for sociology by economists did not go unnoticed. See American Economic Association Records, Box 3, "Annual Meetings, 1908–1924," David M. Rubenstein Rare Book & Manuscript Library, Duke University.

50. See A. W. Coats, "The American Economic Association and the Economics Profession," *Journal of Economic Literature* 23, no. 4 (1985): 1697–727.

51. See, for example, Frederick Rudolph, *The American College and University: A History* (New York: Knopf, 1962), 406–7.

52. Perhaps most telling is the conversation reported by Abraham Flexner in *The Atlantic Monthly*, where he asked a college dean about who was the best teacher in his institution. The dean named a certain instructor, and the conversation evolved:

> Q: "What is his rank?"
> A: "Assistant Professor."
> Q: "When will his appointment expire?"
> A: "Shortly"

Q: "Will he be promoted?"
A: "No."
Q: "Why not?"
A: "He hasn't done anything!"

See Abraham Flexner, "The Problem of College Pedagogy," *Atlantic Monthly*, 104 (1909): 844.

53. Thomas Wakefield Goodspeed, *A History of The University of Chicago: The First Quarter Century* (Chicago: University of Chicago Press, 1916), 319.

54. Dorothy Ross, *The Origins of American Social Science* (Cambridge: Cambridge University Press, 1991), 102.

2. THE POLITICAL ECONOMY OF GENDER IN THE HALLS OF IVY

1. Photographic images of Ivy Day at Smith College were captured by an unknown photographer and preserved in the Smith College Archives. See Smith College Archives, "Smith College Ivy Day 1895," Smith College, https://www.smith.edu/lib raries/libs/archives/gallery/images/womenseducation/sc_ivy.JPG (accessed October 16, 2020).

2. The image of Otelia Cromwell in the Ivy Day procession at Smith College, 1900, was captured by an unknown photographer. See Smith College Archives, "Mabel Milham Roys and Otelia Cromwell in the Ivy Day Procession at Smith College, 1900," Class of 1900 Records, Smith College, https://libex.smith.edu/omeka/exhibits/show /black-students-alliance/item/414 (accessed October 16, 2020).

3. Black women students graduating from the Seven Sisters colleges in the nineteenth century include Hortense Parker (1883) and Martha Ralston (1898) from Mount Holyoke College; Harriet Alleyne Rice (1887) and Ella Lavina Smith (1888) from Wellesley College; Alberta Scott (1898) and Gertrude Mabel Baker (1900) from Smith College; and Anita Hemmings (1897) from Vassar College. By 1913, Mount Holyoke's official policy, voted in 1845, was not to accept Black students. However, two Black students were unknowingly admitted (Hortense Parker and Martha Ralston) in the 1880s and 1890s. See Linda M. Perkins, "The Racial Integration of the Seven Sister Colleges," *Journal of Blacks in Higher Education* 19 (Spring 1998): 104–8; and Joan Marie Johnson, *Southern Women at the Seven Sister Colleges: Feminist Values and Social Activism, 1875–1915* (Athens: University of Georgia Press, 2008), 99–100.

4. Anita Florence Hemmings of Vassar College was accepted without the knowledge that she was an African American student. Bryn Mawr College did not allow Black women to live on campus until 1942, and only nine Black women graduated from Bryn Mawr before 1960. See Johnson, *Southern Women at the Seven Sisters*, 99.

5. Although there were limited opportunities for free Blacks and slaves to become literate in the Southern states before 1830, by 1863 every Southern state had laws

prohibiting the education of slaves or prohibiting slaves from congregating for the purposes of education. For an in-depth discussion, see Carter G. Woodson, *The Education of the Negro Prior to 1861* (Washington, DC: Associated Publishers, 1919). For a discussion of efforts to limit the literacy of Blacks in the South see Heather Andrea Williams, *American Slavery: A Very Short Introduction* (Oxford: Oxford University Press, 2014). The University of South Carolina was a lone exception where, until racial segregation was strictly imposed in the 1880s, Black students did attend in the years following the Civil War. See Robert Bruce Slater, "The First Black Graduates of the Nation's 50 Flagship State Universities," *Journal of Blacks in Higher Education* 13 (1996): 72–85.

6. Separate Black colleges and universities were established in Pennsylvania, Ohio, Kentucky, Delaware, Missouri, and West Virginia. See Slater, "The First Black Graduates," 73 and 74.

7. Slater, "The First Black Graduates," 72.

8. Tiffany K. Wayne reports that Oberlin College alone accounted for a full quarter of the undergraduate degrees held by Black women in the nineteenth century. See Tiffany K. Wayne, "Education and the Professions," in *Women's Roles in Nineteenth-Century America*, ed. Tiffany K. Wayne (Westport, CT: Greenwood, 2007), 87.

9. For example, see the discussion of the push for coeducation at the University of Michigan in Lynn D. Gordon, *Gender and Higher Education in the Progressive Era* (New Haven, CT: Yale University Press, 1990), 22–23.

10. See National Center for Educational Statistics, *120 Years of American Education: A Statistical Portrait*, ed. Thomas D. Snyder (Washington, DC: U.S. Department of Education, 1993), 55.

11. Lynn Gordon has argued that older women played a significant role in pushing for coeducation. See Gordon, *Gender and Higher Education*, 24. It has also been argued that the role of alumni influenced the transformation of many institutions from single-sex to coeducational status. See Claudia Goldin and Lawrence F. Katz, "Putting the 'Co' in Education: Timing, Reasons, and Consequences of College Coeducation from 1835 to the Present," *Journal of Human Capital* 5, no. 4 (2011): 377–417.

12. Early on, land-grant colleges met the shortfall in student enrollment in part by expanding preparatory work to make up for inadequate high school training. Because the Morrill Act of 1862 provided support in the form of land grants, and land sales to fund endowments for new colleges and universities were often not as favorable as expected, financial pressures emerged. Legislatures were often in search of some elusive formula for this dilemma from tuition, fees, the sale of produce from the college farm, and more. Passage of the Morrill Act not only provided support for historically black colleges and university, it also provided much needed appropriations to existing land-grant universities. See Elton L. Johnson, "Misconceptions About the Early Land-Grant Colleges," *Journal of Higher Education* 52, no. 4 (1981): 333–51.

13. Frederick Rudolph, *The American College and University: A History* (New York: Knopf, 1962), 323.

14. Objection to coeducation was not confined to the United States, as the widely attended protest of students at the University of Cambridge in 1897 showed when male students were found mutilating an effigy of a woman on a bike. These students were protesting the presence of women students who were allowed merely to take classes but not to graduate with degrees. See BBC News, "Cambridge University Anti-women Students 'Confetti and Rockets' Digitized," August 11, 2018, https://www.bbc.com/news/uk-england-cambridgeshire-45096690.

15. See Kim Clarke, "Madelon's World," Heritage Project, University of Michigan https://heritage.umich.edu/stories/madelons-world/, accessed October 16, 2020.

16. In 1924, the University of Michigan Alumni Association sent a questionnaire to every woman who had attended the university to date. For a summary of the project and some of the responses see James Tobin, "The First Women," Heritage Project, University of Michigan https://heritage.umich.edu/stories/the-first-women/ (accessed October 16, 2020). See also Doris E. Attaway and Marjorie Rabe Barritt, eds., *Women's Voices: Early Years at the University of Michigan*, Ann Arbor, MI: Bentley Historical Library 2000; Ruth Bordin, *Women at Michigan: The "Dangerous Experiment," 1870s to the Present* (Ann Arbor: University of Michigan Press, 1999).

17. Rosalind Rosenberg, "The Limits of Access: The History of Coeducation in America," in *Women and Higher Education in American History*, ed. John Mack Faragher and Florence Howe (New York: Norton, 1988), 112. See also Rosalind Rosenberg, *Changing the Subject: How the Women of Columbia Shaped the Way We Think About Sex and Politics* (New York: Columbia University Press, 2004), 8–47.

18. Barbara Miller Solomon, *In the Company of Educated Women: A History of Women and Higher Education in America* (New Haven, CT: Yale University Press, 1985), 53.

19. Edwin Mims, *History of Vanderbilt University* (Nashville, TN: Vanderbilt University Press, 1946), 130–31.

20. Linda M. Perkins, "The History of Black Women Graduate Students, 1921–1948," in *The SAGE Handbook of African American Education*, ed. Linda C. Tillman (Thousand Oaks, CA: Sage, 2009), 54.

21. Anne Firor Scott, "The Ever Widening Circle: The Diffusion of Feminist Values from the Troy Female Seminary, 1822–1872," *History of Education Quarterly* 19, no. 1 (1979): 3–25.

22. Linda M. Perkins, "The Impact of the 'Cult of True Womanhood' on the Education of Black Women," *Journal of Social Issues* 39, no. 3 (1983): 24.

23. Perkins notes that when the first Black American Learned Society was founded in 1897, the constitution limited membership to men. When Fanny Coppin was forced to retire in 1901 from the Institute for Colored Youth in Philadelphia, the school was headed by Black men. See Perkins, "The Impact of the 'Cult of True Womanhood,'" 24.

24. See Helene Lange, *Lebenserinnerungen* (Berlin: Herbig, 1928), 111–12, quoted in Patricia M. Mazón, *Gender and the Modern Research University: The Admission of*

Women to German Higher Education, 1865–1914 (Palo Alto, CA: Stanford University Press, 2003), 54–56.

25. Londa Schiebinger, "Skeletons in the Closet: The First Illustrations of the Female Skeleton in Eighteenth-Century Anatomy," *Representations* 14 (Spring 1986): 71.

26. See Mazón, *Gender and the Modern Research University*, 71 and 89.

27. See Lelia McNeill, "The Statistician Who Debunked Sexist Myths about Skull Size and Intelligence" *Smithsonian Magazine*, January 14, 2019; and James C. Albisetti, *Schooling German Girls and Women* (Princeton, NJ: Princeton University Press, 1988), 185.

28. Edward H. Clarke, *Sex in Education or, A Fair Change for the Girls* (Boston: James R. Osgood, 1873).

29. Clarke, *Sex in Education*, 103–6.

30. Clarke, *Sex in Education*, 83.

31. Clarke, *Sex in Education*, 97.

32. See Sue Zschoche, "Dr. Clarke Revisited: Science, True Womanhood, and Female Collegiate Education," *History of Education Quarterly* 29, no. 4 (1989): 545–69.

33. As early as the 1850s, William B. Carpenter began to apply Hermann von Helmholtz's principle of conservation of energy to the physiology of the body. While Carpenter's work relating the principle of conservation of energy was developed in the 1850s, it was the British political philosopher and popularizer of Darwin, Herbert Spencer, who is often credited with applying concentration of energy, or as he preferred to call it, "persistence of force," to the human body. See Vance M. D. Hall, "The Contribution of the Physiologist, William Benjamin Carpenter (1813–1885), to the Development of the Principles of the Correlation of Forces and the Conservation of Energy," *Medical History* 23, no. 2 (1979): 129–55.

34. Herbert Spencer, *Social Statics; or, the Conditions Essential to Human Happiness* (London: John Chapman, 1851), 155.

35. Herbert Spencer, "Psychology of the Sexes," *Popular Science Monthly* 14 (November 1873): 30–38; and Herbert Spencer, *The Study of Sociology* (London: Henry S. King, 1873), 341–42.

36. See Patricia Vertinsky, "Exercise, Physical Capability, and the Eternally Wounded Woman in Late Nineteenth-Century North America," *Journal of Sport History* 14, no. 1 (1987): 15.

37. Board of Regents, University of Wisconsin, *Annual Report for the Year Ending September 30, 1877* (Madison: University of Wisconsin Press, 1877), 45.

38. Rudolph, *The American College and University*, 326–27.

39. In a letter to the Chancellor Benjamin Andrews dated September 15, 1905, Ross and his colleague W. G. Langworthy Taylor admonished Andrews to establish a program of courses in commercial education to retain male students. The argument was apparently successful. The Regents Report of 1905–6 stated that it was indeed imperative that a commercial college be established. See Richard F. Crees, *CBA: The First 75 Years* (self-published booklet, 1994), 11–12.

40. Rudolph, *The American College and University*, 323–24.

41. Thorstein Veblen, *The Theory of the Leisure Class* (New York: Prometheus Books, [1899] 1998), 376.

42. Mary Roth Walsh, *Doctors Wanted, No Women Need Apply: Sexual Barriers in the Medical Profession, 1835–1975* (New Haven, CT: Yale University Press, 1977), and Rita McWilliams Tullberg, *Women at Cambridge* (Cambridge: Cambridge University Press, 1998).

43. When women traveled to Europe to pursue an advanced degree, they were often treated much worse than their male colleagues. See Mazón, *Gender and the Modern Research University*, 7.

44. Veblen, *The Theory of the Leisure Class*, 376.

45. Andrea G. Radke-Moss, *Bright Epoch: Women and Coeducation in the American West* (Lincoln: University of Nebraska Press, 2008), 145.

46. See Henry Kiddle and Alexander J. Schem (eds.), *The Yearbook of Education for 1878* (New York: E. Steiger, 1878).

47. The University of Kentucky also charged special fees for music and "several branches of handicraft." See "Kentucky," in Kiddle and Schem, eds., *The Yearbook of Education for 1878*, 98. For information on fees at the University of Nebraska, see Nebraska History Museum, "University of Nebraska, 1878," https://history.nebraska.gov/pub lications/university-nebraska-1878 (accessed July 15, 2020).

48. Clarence D. Long, *Wage and Earnings in the United States, 1860–1890* (Princeton, NJ: Princeton University Press, 1960), 42.

49. Charles Eliot, "Remarks of President Eliot of Harvard College before the Trustees of The Johns Hopkins University," binder labeled "Johns Hopkins University 1874," Special Collections Holdings, Ferdinand Hamburger Jr. Archives, Johns Hopkins University, 1874, 50–53.

50. Eliot, "Remarks of President Eliot," 50–53.

51. See Michèle A. Pujol, *Feminism and Anti-Feminism in Early Economic Thought* (Aldershot, UK: Edward Elgar, 1992), 17–34.

52. U.S. Bureau of the Census, *Historical Statistics of the United States, Colonial Times to 1970*, Bicentennial Edition, part 1 (Washington, DC: U.S. Government Printing Office, 1975), 129.

53. See Joseph A. Hill, *Women in Gainful Occupations, 1870 to 1920: A Study of the Trend of Recent Changes in the Numbers, Occupational Distribution, and Family Relationship of Women Reported in the Census as Following a Gainful Occupation*, Census Monograph IX (Washington, DC: U.S. Government Printing Office, 1929), 45 and 76.

54. Hill, "Women in Gainful Occupations," 109 and 78.

55. Mary Elizabeth Pidgeon, *Changes in Women's Occupations 1940–1950*, Women's Bureau Bulletin No. 253 (Washington, DC: U.S. Department of Labor, 1954), 57.

56. U.S. Census data is not available for Black women professors and instructors for 1940. For all other years, see U.S. Bureau of the Census, *Occupation Statistics, 1910* (Washington, DC: U.S. Government Printing Office, 1914), 430–31, https://www

.census.gov/library/publications/1914/dec/vol-4-occupations.html; U.S. Bureau of the Census, *Fifteenth Census of the United States, 1930*, Population, vol. 5, General Report on Occupations, chap. 3 (Washington, DC: U.S. Government Printing Office, 1930), 84; Hill, *Women in Gainful Occupations*, 182–83.

57. See Julian B. Roebuck and Komanduri S. Murty, *Historically Black Colleges and Universities: Their Places in American Higher Education* (Westport, CT: Praeger, 1993).

58. U.S. Bureau of the Census, *Historical Statistics of the United States, Colonial Times to 1970*, part 2, 386.

59. Margaret W. Rossiter, "Doctorates for American Women, 1868–1907," *History of Education Quarterly* 22, no. 2 (1982): 157. For a full discussion of the struggles of women scientists in many disciplines, see Margaret W. Rossiter, *Women Scientists in America: Struggles and Strategies to 1940* (Baltimore, MD: Johns Hopkins University Press, 1982).

60. See Lori Thurgood, Mary J. Golladay, and Susan T. Hill, *U.S. Doctorates in the 20th Century*, NSF 06-319, (Arlington, VA: National Science Foundation, Division of Science Resources Statistics, 2006), 17.

61. The way Veblen defines how "feminine" and "unfeminine" fields are determined is both curious and compelling and may go far in understanding where women's work has been accepted and where it is likely to be marginalized. Specifically, Veblen identifies "unfeminine" knowledge as that which expresses the unfolding of the learner's own life, "the acquisition of which proceeds on the learner's own cognitive interest . . . without reference back to a master whose comfort and good repute is to be enhanced by the employment or the exhibition of it." See Veblen, *The Theory of the Leisure Class*, 376.

62. Jo Freeman, "Women on the Social Science Faculties Since 1892," paper delivered at the Political Science Association Conference, Winter 1969, https://eric.ed.gov/?q=%2 2male+chauvinism%22&id=ED041567 (accessed October 16, 2020).

63. Catherine L. Coghlan, "Please Don't Think of Me as a Sociologist: Sophonisba Preston Breckinridge and the Early Chicago School," *American Sociologist* 36, no. 1 (2005): 3–22.

64. Gender schemas are implicit, nonconscious hypotheses about sex differences that play a central role in occupational outcomes. For a full discussion of gender schemas and their influence on occupational outcomes, see Virginia Valian, *Why So Slow? The Advancement of Women* (Cambridge, MA: MIT Press, 1998).

65. See, for example, Thomas S. Kuhn, *The Structure of Scientific Revolutions* (Chicago: University of Chicago Press, 1962); and Paul Feyerabend, *Against Method: Outline of an Anarchistic Theory of Knowledge* (Atlantic Highlands, NJ: Humanities Press, 1975).

66. Helen E. Longino, *Science as Social Knowledge: Values and Objectivity in Scientific Inquiry* (Princeton, NJ: Princeton University Press, 1990); Sandra Harding, *The Science Question in Feminism* (Ithaca, NY: Cornell University Press, 1986); and Sandra Harding, *Whose Science? Whose Knowledge? Thinking from Women's Lives* (Ithaca, NY: Cornell University Press, 1991).

67.   Sandra Harding, "Rethinking Standpoint Epistemology: What Is 'Strong Objectivity?," in *Feminist Epistemologies*, ed. L. Alcoff and E. Potter (London: Routledge, 1993), 54.

68.   Tullberg, *Women at Cambridge*, 149.

3. A LIMINAL SPACE: GRADUATE TRAINING IN THE DISMAL SCIENCE

1.   Elizabeth Webb Wilson (Radcliffe College, 1934) was one of the first "human computers"; Julia J. Henderson (University of Minnesota, 1946) served as secretary-general of the International Planned Parenthood Federation; Juanita Morris Kreps (Duke University, 1948) was the first female secretary of Commerce and first female director of the New York Stock Exchange. In addition to her work as a research analyst for the Foreign Economic Administration of the U.S. government, Helen Elizabeth Boyden Lamb (Lemont) was included on President Richard Nixon's enemies list of 1973. Lucile Eaves (Columbia University, 1910) was the only woman among eight Stanford scholars who was forced out or resigned in protest following the 1901 ouster of Edward A. Ross. Sadie Tanner Mossell (Alexander) (University of Pennsylvania, 1921) was the first African American woman to earn a doctorate in economics, and Mabel Frances Timlin (University of Washington, 1941) went on to become the first female full professor in Canada. Phyllis Ann Wallace completed her doctorate in economics from Yale University, joined the staff of the Equal Employment Opportunity Commission, joined the faculty of the Massachusetts Institute of Technology (MIT) as a visiting professor, and became the first woman to earn tenure at the Sloan School of Management at MIT. Wallace was an African American economist whose work focused on racial and gender discrimination. Penelope Hartland Thunberg began her career teaching at Mount Holyoke College and Brown University before moving to Washington and working on the staff of the Council of Economic Advisers (1951–53), becoming a member of the U.S. Tariff Commission (1965–69), and then taking several high-level positions with the CIA (1954–1966 and 1970–1978).

2.   Others earning a doctorate in economics from the University of Pennsylvania in 1921 were Ueda Tatsunosuke and William Duncan Gordon. Tatsunosuke went on to have a long career in Japan as an academic economist at Hitotsubashi University, and Gordon went on to become a professor at the University of Pennsylvania, serving as deputy secretary of Banking for the state from 1923 to 1926 and as secretary of Banking from 1931 to 1935. See *Prabook*, s.v. "Ueda Tatsuosuke," https://prabook.com/web/tatsunosuke.ueda/3752713, and the *Pennsylvania State Archives*, s.v. "William Duncan Gordon," http://www.phmc.state.pa.us/bah/dam/mg/mg510.htm (accessed July 19, 2021).

3.   Sadie Tanner Mossell Alexander (interviewee), "Sadie Tanner Mossell Alexander Oral History," interview by Walter M. Phillips, October 20, 1976, Special Collections

Oral Histories Repository, Temple University Libraries, 3–4, https://libdigital.temple
.edu/oralhistories/catalog/transcript:AOHWMPJZ2014110010xp16002coll22x0.

4.   Alexander (interviewee), "Sadie Tanner Mossell Alexander Oral History," October 20, 1976, 4–5.

5.   Alexander (interviewee), "Sadie Tanner Mossell Alexander Oral History," October 20, 1976, 4.

6.   Alexander (interviewee), "Sadie Tanner Mossell Alexander Oral History," October 20, 1976, 5.

7.   See Sadie Tanner Mossell Alexander (interviewee), "Sadie Tanner Mossell Alexander Oral History, interview by Walter M. Phillips, October 12, 1977," Special Collections Oral Histories Repository, Temple University Libraries, https://libdigital.temple.edu/oralhistories/catalog/transcript:AOHWMPJZ2014120029xp16002coll22x1.

8.   Alexander (interviewee), "Sadie Tanner Mossell Alexander Oral History," October 12, 1977, 14–15.

9.   Alexander (interviewee), "Sadie Tanner Mossell Alexander Oral History," October 12, 1977, 15.

10. Irwin Collier, "Economics in the Rear-View Mirror: Archival Artifacts from the History of Economics," *Irwin Collier*, 2017, http://www.irwincollier.com/harvard-nine-radcliffe-graduate-students-petition-to-attend-economics-seminary-1926/. Original source: Harvard University Archives, *Department of Economics, Correspondence and Papers (1902–1950)*, Box 25, Folder: "Economics Seminary 1925–33."

11. The only institutions among the Seven Sisters providing graduate training or access to graduate training were Bryn Mawr College and Radcliffe College (through Harvard University).

12. Although Harriet Alleyne Rice was allowed to live on campus, she was given a single room. See Linda M. Perkins, "The Racial Integration of the Seven Sisters Colleges," *Journal of Blacks in Higher Education*, no. 19 (Spring 1998): 104.

13. According to Perkins, sixty-nine Black women had attended or graduated from Smith College by 1964. See Perkins, "The Racial Integration," 105.

14. Twenty-two of the identified women earning doctorates in economics from 1890 to 1948 completed their undergraduate training at Bryn Mawr College.

15. Helen Lefkowitz Horowitz, *The Power and Passion of M. Carey Thomas* (Urbana: University of Illinois Press, 1999), 23032 and 342–43.

16. Enid Cook went on to earn a doctorate in bacteriology in 1937 from the University of Chicago. During her time at Bryn Mawr College, she was not allowed to live on campus. See Grace Pusey, "Enid Cook, 1927–1931: Bryn Mawr's First Black Graduate," *Black at Bryn Mawr*, February 9, 2015, https://blackatbrynmawr.blogs.brynmawr.edu/2015/02/09/enid-cook-first-black-graduate/.

17. Olivia Mancini, "Passing as White: Anita Hemmings 1897," *Vassar: The Alumni Quarterly* 98, no. 1 (2001), https://vq.vassar.edu/issues/2002/01/features/passing-as-white.html.

18. See Perkins, "The Racial Integration," 105.

19. For example, Irving Fisher (president of the AEA in 1918) earned his doctorate from Yale University in economics in 1891, yet the department of economics did not come into being until 1937. See M. Ann Judd, "The Yale Economics Department: Memories and Musings of Past Leaders," 1999, https://web.archive.org/web/20000816052151/www.econ.yale.edu/depthistory.html.

20. See Walter Crosby Eells, "Earned Doctorates for Women in the Nineteenth Century," *AAUP Bulletin* 42, no. 4 (1956): 644–51.

21. Ethel Muir went on to teach at Wilson College and Lake Erie College. No records were located to indicate in what department she taught.

22. The digital source used to identify doctoral degrees in economics is ProQuest. ProQuest is a global information contact and technology company founded in 1938. ProQuest provides the largest repository of graduate dissertations.

23. See Yale University, *Obituary Record of Yale Graduates, 1922–1923* (New Haven, CT: Yale University, 1923), 904–5.

24. The assignment of disciplinary affiliation is complicated and requires an examination of the department name, academic background, and later teaching and research. Kate Holladay Claghorn studied political economy at Bryn Mawr College under Franklin H. Giddings and "industrial history, advanced economics, political science and anthropology" with William Graham Sumner and Arthur Hadley at Yale University. See William H. Hills, *The Writer: A Monthly Magazine for Literary Workers*, vol. 10 (Boston: Writer Publishing, 1897), 102–3. Mary Roberts Smith is listed in ProQuest as having earned her doctorate in sociology, yet the Department of Economics at Stanford lists her as having been the first woman to get a doctorate in economics from Stanford. It is noteworthy that she received it from the Department of Economics and Social Science, which included political science, economics, and sociology. See Department of Economics, "Our Mission," Stanford University, https://economics.stanford.edu/about/our-mission (accessed November 13, 2021). Nellie Neilson is also listed in ProQuest has having completed her doctorate in economics from Bryn Mawr College in 1898. Neilson's dissertation was titled "Economic Conditions on Ramsey Manors." Neilson attended Bryn Mawr College as an undergraduate but went on to teach history at Mount Holyoke College. She later became the first woman to serve as president of the American Historical Association.

25. See John B. Parrish, "Rise of Economics as an Academic Discipline: The Formative Years to 1900," *Southern Economic Journal* 34, no. 1 (1967): 11.

26. Eells, "Earned Doctorates for Women," 647.

27. Women earning doctorates in economics, economic history, political economy, labor relations, welfare, business commerce, finance, and agricultural economics are included in the sample.

28. The 1940s includes only the years 1940 through 1948.

29. The sample of men is taken from ProQuest, searching for doctorates in economics. Doctorates of men were identified by first name; when unsure, biographical information was sought via U.S. Census Records, newspaper articles, and obituaries.

30. The coefficient of variation for men earning doctorates is 168 percent, while for women it is 186 percent. The higher the coefficient of variation, the greater the level of dispersion around the mean. Hence, women doctorates are more dispersed among schools in this sample than are male doctorates.

31. The coefficient of variation for men completing undergraduate degrees in our sample is 148 percent, and for women it is 200 percent. The higher the coefficient of variation, the greater the level of dispersion around the mean. Hence, women undergraduate students are more dispersed among schools in this sample than are male undergraduate students.

32. The coefficient of variation for men and women doctorates was found to be 168 percent and 186 percent, whereas the coefficient of variation for men and women undergraduates (going on to obtain a doctorate) was found to be 148 percent and 200 percent. Hence, we see more dispersion for women (higher coefficient of variation) than for men at the undergraduate and graduate levels.

33. Cynthia F. Epstein, "Encountering the Male Establishment: Sex-Status Limits on Women's Careers in the Professions," *American Journal of Sociology* 75, no. 6 (1970): 974–75.

34. This outcome is consistent with results showing that women in general are less likely to join professional associations. See Jessie Bernard, *Academic Women* (University Park: Pennsylvania University Press, 1964).

35. The *p*-values for testing the null hypothesis that the female mean in membership is equal to that of men shows a value of .02 for 1910–1919, .04 for 1930–39, and .08 for 1940–49.

36. Of the 302 women earning doctoral degrees in economics during this period, 188 are classified as having worked primarily in an academic job. The results show that 49 out of these 188 (26 percent) had an occupational connection with the institution where they were educated.

37. Of the 302 men earning doctoral degrees in economics during this period, 250 are classified as having worked primarily in an academic job. The results show that 90 out of these 252 men (36 percent) had an occupational connection with the institution where they were educated.

38. The *p*-values for testing the null hypothesis that the female mean of holding a job at the same institution where one received their doctorate by decade is equal to that of men shows a value of .07 for 1920–1929 and .0 for 1940–49. Thus, for the 1920s and 1940s, we can reject the null hypothesis that the mean values are the same for men and women.

39. Julianne Malveaux, "Tilting Against the Wind: Reflections on the life and work of Dr. Phyllis Ann Wallace," *American Economic Review* 84, no. 2 (1994): 93–97.

40. See Malveaux, "Tilting Against the Wind," 94, and American Economic Association, "Past Annual Meetings," https://www.aeaweb.org/conference/past-annual-meetings.

41. Jo Anne Preston, "Negotiating Work and Family: Aspirations of Early Radcliffe Graduates," in *Yards and Gates: Gender in Harvard and Radcliffe History*, ed. Laurel Thatcher Ulrich (New York: Palgrave Macmillan, 2004), 174.

42. From the sample of 302 women graduate students earning doctorates in economics, 171 were married at some point in their lives and 3 had no information available to confirm their marital status. Evidence of marital status was found in records maintained by Ancestry.com, obituary records, and newspaper articles.

43. From the sample of 302 men graduate students earning doctorates in economics, 288 were married at some point in their lives, and 1 man had no information available to confirm their marital status. Evidence of marital status was found through records maintained by Ancestry.com, obituary records, and newspaper articles.

44. Regional Oral History Office, "Elizabeth Paschel, Pioneering Career Woman: New Deal Labor Economist, Social Security Administration Program Chief, Ford Foundation Executive," Bancroft Library, University of California, Berkeley, 37, https://californiarevealed.org/islandora/object/cavpp%3A21820 (accessed November 13, 2021).

45. Regional Oral History Office, "Elizabeth Paschel, Pioneering Career Woman," 61.

46. Regional Oral History Office, "Elizabeth Paschel, Pioneering Career Woman," 37.

4. A MEMBERSHIP BEYOND THE PROFESSORIATE

1. Charlotte Perkins Gilman, *Women and Economics: A Study of the Economic Relation Between Men and Women as a Factor in Social Evolution* (Boston: Small, Maynard, 1898), 164.4

2. Larry Ceplair, *Charlotte Perkins Gilman: A Nonfiction Reader* (New York: Columbia University Press, 1991), 25–83.

3. Ceplair, *Charlotte Perkins Gilman*, 44.

4. As a public intellectual, Gilman was thought by some to be "the greatest writer that the feminists ever produced on sociology and economics." See Andrew Sinclair, *The Emancipation of the American Woman* (New York: Harper & Row, 1966), 272. Being at the margin of the discipline was not the same as being completely outside it. Gilman later published a discussant's comment on child labor in the proceedings of the AEA annual meeting. See Charlotte Perkins Gilman and Francis H. McLean, "Child Labor in the United States: Discussion," *Publications of the American Economic Association*, 3rd series, 8 no. 1 (1907): 260–67. Gilman was also possibly the only woman on the program of any AEA annual meeting or conference proceedings in the period between Katharine Coman (1891) and Crystal Eastman (1909). See Robert W. Dimand, Geoffrey Black, and Evelyn L. Forget, "Women's Participation in the ASSA Meetings," *Oeconomia: History/Methodology/Philosophy* 1, no. 1 (2011): 33–49 for further discussion. See https://journals.openedition.org/oeconomia/1821.

5. For example, see Barbara Libby, "Women in Economics Before 1940," *Essays in Economic and Business History* 3 (1984): 273–90; Barbara Libby, "Statistical Analysis of Women in the Economics Profession," *Essays in Economic and Business History* 5 (1987): 179–89; Barbara S. Libby, "Women in the Economics Profession 1900–1940: Factors in Their Declining Visibility," *Essays in Economic and Business History* 8

(1990): 121–30; Claire H. Hammond "American Women and the Professionalization of Economics," *Review of Social Economy* 51, no. 3 (1993): 347–70; Evelyn L. Forget, "American Women and the Economics Profession in the Twentieth Century," *Oeconomia: History/Methodology/Philosophy* 1, no. 1 (2011): 19–31; Robert W. Dimand, "Women Economists in the 1890s: Journals, Books and the Old Palgrave," *Journal of the History of Economic Thought* 21, no. 3 (1999): 269–88.

6. Marion Fourcade, *Economists and Societies: Discipline and Profession in the United States, Britain, and France, 1890s to 1990s* (Princeton, NJ: Princeton University Press, 2009), 65, and Richard Hofstadter, *Anti-Intellectualism in American Life* (New York: Vintage Books, 1963).

7. For a full discussion of professionalization see Fourcade, *Economists and Societies*, 79–81.

8. See A. W. Coats, "The First Two Decades of the American Economic Association," *American Economic Review* 50, no. 4 (1960): 556.

9. Coats, "The First Two Decades," 557.

10. For a full discussion of academic freedom cases at the turn of the century, see Fourcade, *Economists and Societies*, 79–80; and Richard Hofstadter and Walter Metzger, *The Development of Academic Freedom in the United States* (New York: Columbia University Press, 1955).

11. Mary O. Furner, *Advocacy and Objectivity: A Crisis in the Professionalization of American Social Sciences, 1865–1905* (Lexington: University of Kentucky Press, 1975), 157–59.

12. Dorothy Ross, *The Origins of American Social Science* (Cambridge: Cambridge University Press, 1991), 158.

13. American Economic Association Records, Box 1, "AEA Histories. A. W. Coats, 1952–1963: *Journal of Economic Literature*, Mark Perlman, editor. Correspondence, [1968] 1970–1980." David M. Rubenstein Rare Book & Manuscript Library, Duke University.

14. In 1890, AEA Secretary Richard T. Ely posted a notice for "Prize Essays on Women Wage-Earners." The notice read, "Through the generosity of various persons interested in this subject, the American Economic Association has received the sum of Five Hundred dollars to be awarded as prizes for the best essays on the subject of Women Wage-Earners." In describing the essay, the notice indicated that "It is desired to know the early and present condition of Working-Women, their growth in numbers, both absolutely and in proportion to the population, the present extent of their sphere of labor, the economic and social evils connected with their various occupations as wage-earners, and remedies for these evils." Although the notice did not reveal who sponsored the prize, the Treasurer's Report of 1889–90 did. It showed that Mrs. Rives-Chanler supported the prize for the child labor essay (which was awarded to Miss Clare de Graffenried and William F. Willoughby) and that Messrs. Morgan, Lowell, Shearman, White and Seligman supported the prize for essays on women wage earners. This is particularly curious because the only AEA member with the last name of "Lowell" was Mrs. C. R. Lowell (Josephine Shaw

Lowell). Mrs. Lowell was a widow whose husband died during the Civil War. She was active reformer and author of numerous articles on charity, poverty, and child labor. *The Saint Paul Daily Globe* reported on March 9, 1889, that Mrs. Lowell presided over the Woman's Conference, where the condition of working women in the United States was discussed. Claire De Graffenried read the paper of the day and "gave some interesting facts regarding the condition of the workingwomen in the various parts of the country." See American Economic Association, "Report of the Treasurer," *Publications of the American Economic Association* 6, no. 1/2 (1891): 183, and "The Woman's Conference," *Saint Paul Daily Globe*, March 9, 1889.

15.   Alan Trachtenberg, *The Incorporation of America: Culture and Society in the Gilded Age* (New York: Hill and Wang, 1982), 80.

16.   See Richard Barker, "The Big Idea: No, Management Is Not a Profession," *Harvard Business Review* 88, no. 7/8 (2010), 54; and A. Lawrence Lowell, "The Profession of Business," *Harvard Business Review* 1, no. 2 (1923): 129.

17.   A. W. Coats, *The Sociology and Professionalization of Economics: British and American Economic Essays*, vol. 2 (London: Routledge, 1993), 241 and 256.

18.   One might also conclude that the desire for status in the relationship between businessmen and AEA leaders went both ways. As the AEA records show, Stuart Wood, a businessman and AEA member, expressed surprise when he learned that the AEA allowed women to participate in the annual meetings as, in his experience, the presence of women lessened the "seriousness" of proceedings. See Stuart Wood, "Letter to Richard T. Ely," dated December 12, 1888, American Economic Association Records, Box 4, "Correspondence. Incoming, 1888 March–1896 February," David M. Rubenstein Rare Book & Manuscript Library, Duke University.

19.   See Ann Mari May and Robert W. Dimand, "Women in the Early Years of the American Economic Association: A Membership Beyond the Professoriate Per Se," *History of Political Economy* 51, no. 4 (2019): 671–702.

20.   Data on AEA membership are taken from the membership lists found in the American Economic Association Records, *Publications of the American Economic Association*, *Handbook of the American Economic Association*, in supplements to *Economic Studies*, *Bulletin of the American Economic Association*, and *AER*. The sex of the member is determined by first name and, when in question, by searches of historical documents such as newspapers, obituaries, and census records.

21.   Edward Bemis reported a total member of sixty-two with eleven women among them, making women about 18 percent of the membership of the Connecticut Valley Branch. See Richard T. Ely, "Constitution By-Laws and Resolutions of the American Economic Association," *Publications of the American Economic Association* 1, no. 1 (1886): 42; and Richard T. Ely, "Proceedings of the Second Annual Meeting of the American Economic Association, Boston and Cambridge. May 21–25, 1887," *Publications of the American Economic Association* 3, no. 3 (1888): 62–63.

22.   American Economic Association, "Constitution, By-Laws, and Resolutions of the American Economic Association with List of Officers and Members," *Publications of the American Economic Association* 4, July supplement (1889): 12–13.

23. See American Economic Association, "The Sixth Annual Meeting," *Publications of the American Economic Association* 9, no. 1 (1894): 44.

24. See American Economic Association, "The Seventh Annual Meeting," *Publications of the American Economic Association* 10, no. 3 (1895): 43.

25. Membership figures are reported here as of January 1894. See American Economic Association, "The Seventh Annual Meeting," 44.

26. See membership list in American Economic Association, "American Economic Association," *Publications of the American Economic Association* 3, no. 1 (1902): 15–39, and American Economic Association, "American Economic Association," *Publications of the American Economic Association* 5, no. 1 (1904): 12–36.

27. See Bradley W. Bateman and Ethan B. Kapstein, "Between God and the Market: The Religious Roots of the American Economic Association," *Journal of Economic Perspectives* 13, no. 4 (1999): 249–58.

28. Coats, *The Sociology and Professionalization of Economics*, 130.

29. Coats, *The Sociology and Professionalization of Economics*, 241.

30. American Economic Association, "The Thirteenth Annual Meeting," *Publications of the American Economic Association* 2, no. 1 (1901): 47.

31. American Economic Association, "The Fourteenth Annual Meeting," *Publications of the American Economic Association* 3, no. 1 (1902): 48.

32. Coats, *The Sociology and Professionalization of Economics*, 241.

33. American Economic Association, "The Fourteenth Annual Meeting," 49.

34. For a complete gender analysis of the history of American social science, see Helene Silverberg, *Gender and American Social Science: The Formative Years* (Princeton, NJ: Princeton University Press, 1998).

35. American Economic Association, "The Twenty-Second Annual Meeting," *American Economic Association Quarterly* 11, no. 2 (1910): 49–79.

36. American Economic Association, "Business Meetings at Washington D.C: December 27–30, 1911," *American Economic Review* 2, no. 1 (1912): 133. Coats reports that earlier in 1899 there was serious consideration of the desirability of electing a businessman as AEA president. Although the proposal was rejected, it was seriously considered, which is an indication of the desire to bring businessmen into the fold. See Coats, "The First Two Decades," 571.

37. American Economic Association Records, Box 64–69, "Correspondence of Davis R. Dewey with editors and authors of articles and communications, 1910–1917," David M. Rubenstein Rare Book & Manuscript Library, Duke University.

38. American Economic Association, "Report of the Secretary for the Year Ending December 15, 1913," *American Economic Review, Supplement* 4, no. 1 (1914): 202.

39. Michael A. Bernstein, *A Perilous Progress: Economists and Public Purpose in Twentieth Century America* (Princeton, NJ: Princeton University Press, 2001), 18.

40. Letter from Davis R. Dewey to Miss Benedict, May 13, 1918, is found in the American Economic Association Records, Box 16, "Correspondence, 1918–1919. Allyn A. Young, Secretary-Treasurer," David M. Rubenstein Rare Book & Manuscript Library, Duke University.

41.   American Economic Association Records, Box 70–71, "Correspondence of Davis R. Dewey with editors and authors of articles and communications, 1918–1919," David M. Rubenstein Rare Book & Manuscript Library, Duke University

42.   American Economic Association Records, Box 16, "Correspondence 1918–1919."

43.   Seligman's committee was the special committee on War Finance—a committee established to undertake a thorough study of the war revenue system of the United States and other countries. See American Economic Association, "Report of the Secretary for the year ending December 18, 1918," *American Economic Review* 9, no. 1 (1919): 355. See American Economic Association Records, Box 16, "Correspondence 1918–1919."

44.   While Eph. A. Straus joined the AEA in 1916, Thomas Lamont did indeed join in 1918.

45.   See letter from Irving Fisher to H. S. J. Sickel, dated October 30, 1918, in American Economic Association Records, Box 16, "Correspondence 1918–1919."

46.   Letter from E. E. Pratt to Young, dated November 8, 1915, in American Economic Association Records, Box 14, "Correspondence, including reports, 1914–1915. Allyn A. Young, Secretary-Treasurer," David M. Rubenstein Rare Book & Manuscript Library, Duke University.

47.   The letter from Erastus W. Bulkley to Secretary Young is dated July 15, 1918. In this letter, Bulkley had many suggestions for the AEA leadership in working more closely with businessmen. For example, he asked if it would not be an excellent idea for the committee on War Finance to include a working financier. See American Economic Association Records, Box 16, "Correspondence 1918–1919."

48.   The letter from Erastus W. Bulkley to Secretary Young dated July 15, 1918, in American Economic Association Records, Box 16, "Correspondence 1918–1919."

49.   Letter from President Fisher to Erastus W. Bulkley dated July 16, 1918, in American Economic Association Records, Box 16, "Correspondence 1918–1919."

50.   Letter from Erastus W. Bulkley to Secretary Young dated July 17, 1918, in American Economic Association Records, Box 16, "Correspondence 1918–1919."

51.   Letter from Secretary Young to Erastus W. Bulkley dated July 22, 1918, in American Economic Association Records, Box 16, "Correspondence 1918–1919."

52.   Letter from Erastus W. Bulkley to Secretary Young dated July 24, 1918, in American Economic Association Records, Box 16, "Correspondence 1918–1919."

53.   Letter from Bulkley to Young dated October 1, 1918, in American Economic Association Records, Box 16, "Correspondence 1918–1919." Bulkley died in 1923.

54.   Coats, *The Sociology and Professionalization of Economics*, 249.

55.   American Economic Association, "Report of the Secretary for the Year Ending December 29, 1919," *American Economic Review* 10, no. 1 (1920): 234.

56.   American Economic Association, "Report of the Membership Committee," *American Economic Review* 13, no. 1 (1923): 256.

57.   American Economic Association, "Report of the Auditing Committee," *American Economic Review* 10, no. 1 (1920): 237; and American Economic Association, "Report of the Auditing Committee," *American Economic Review* 11, no. 1 (1921): 189.

58.   American Economic Association, "Report of the Special Committee on Finance of the American Economic Association," *American Economic Review* 13, no. 1 (1923): 255.

59.   See American Economic Association, "Report of the Auditing Committee" (1921): 189; and American Economic Association, "Report of the Auditing Committee," *American Economic Review* 20, no. 1 (1930): 190.

60.   American Economic Association, "Report of the Membership Committee," 256.

61.   American Economic Association, "Report of the Finance Committee," *American Economic Review* 20, no. 1 (1930): 192–93.

62.   American Economic Association, "Report of the Secretary for the Year Ending December 15, 1930," *American Economic Review* 21, no. 1 (1931): 275.

63.   See American Economic Association, "Report of the Secretary for the Year Ending December 12, 1931," *American Economic Review* 22, no. 1 (1932): 282.

5. A NATURAL CONSTITUENCY

1.   It may be noted that William Graham Sumner and J. Laurence Laughlin long refused to join the AEA (Laughlin until 1905) because they disapproved of Richard Ely's Chautauqua and *Verein für Socialpolitik* style of social reform emphasis. Membership lists for the AEA are published in the *Publications of the American Economic Association*, *Handbook of the American Economic Association*, in supplements to *Economic Studies*, *Bulletin of the American Economic Association*, and *American Economic Review* after 2011. There are several years between the founding of the AEA and 1948 where full lists were not provided. Those missing years are 1887, 1891, 1892, 1893, 1912, 1915, 1917, 1918, 1921, 1923, 1925, 1927, 1929, 1930, 1932, 1934, 1935, 1937, 1939, 1941, 1943, 1944, 1945, and 1947. Membership is reported in the year published. Membership lists in the 1890s were maintained by hand and are found in the American Economic Associations Records, Box 2, "Organization, [1885]; Minutes, 1886–1908; Membership 1890–1896; Accounts, 1889–1894; Annual Meetings, 1886–1905," David M. Rubenstein Rare Book & Manuscript Library, Duke University.

2.   See Richard T. Ely, "The American Economic Association 1885–1909," *American Economic Association Quarterly* 11, no. 1 (1910): 58.

3.   Also members in the first year of the association were Mary W. (White) Bond; Imogene (C.) Fales, who co-organized the Sociologic Association of America; and Jeannie R. Lippman, educator of the Mary Institute, a school for girls founded by William Greenleaf Eliot. See Richard T. Ely, "Constitution By-Laws and Resolutions of the American Economic Association," *Publications of the American Economic Association* 1, no. 1 (1886): 43–46.

4.   Jane D. Kelly Sabine, also a member, earned her MD in 1894 from the Northwestern University Women's Medical School.

5.   Also listed as members were Emma M. Batcheller, the daughter of Francis Amasa Walker, president of MIT and first president of the AEA; Emma Helen Blair, who did

graduate work at Wisconsin State University and went on to edit numerous works, including work on the Lewis and Clark expedition; Grace H. (Hoadley) Dodge, a philanthropist who donated roughly $1.5 million to various organizations and played a large role in supporting the Teachers College of Columbia University; Ida M. Mason, who was active in the Women's Educational and Industrial Union, a philanthropist, and a major contributor to the Tuskegee Five Year Fund; Emily Tracy (Swett) Parkhurst, who worked on behalf of women writers and helped to found the Pacific Coast Women's Press Association; and Clare de Graffenreid, who received two AEA prizes for her studies on child labor and conditions of women's labor, taught at the Georgetown Female Seminary, and followed a nonacademic (and controversial) career as an investigator with the Bureau of Labor. See Robert W. Dimand and Geoffrey Black, "Clare de Graffenreid and the Art of Controversy: A Prizewinning Woman Economist in the First Decade of the American Economic Association," *Journal of the History of Economic Thought* 34, no. 3 (2012): 339–53.

6.   Along with Balch's papers, one can find the engraved box that contained the auspicious prize along with the misspelling of the recipient's name in the Swarthmore College Archives. See Swarthmore College Archives, "Emily Greene Balch Papers," Swarthmore College Peace Collection, Swarthmore College. https://www.swarthmore .edu/friends-historical-library/swarthmore-college-archives.

7.   For changes to the AEA constitution, see various issues of *Publications of the American Economic Association*, the *American Economic Association Quarterly*, and the *AER* from 1886 to 1948.

8.   Excluded from the officer count is what was known as the "Council." Members of the Council were recognized in the constitution from 1886 through 1905 as officers. It consisted of an "infinite number of members" of the society, serving three-year terms and whose responsibility it was to elect the president, vice presidents, secretary, and treasurer. Three of its members served on the Executive Committee. The Council organized itself into a number of committees. In 1905, the Council consisted of 173 members—2 of whom were women (Mary Roberts Smith and Katharine Coman). Obviously, at some point this became unwieldy. That point was apparently 1906, when the Council was discontinued. See various issues of *Publications of the American Economic Association*.

9.   Letter from Thomas Nixon Carver to Dixon, dated April 14, 1911, in American Economic Association Records, Box 12, "Correspondence of 1910–1911; Thomas N. Carver, Secretary-Treasurer," David M. Rubenstein Rare Book & Manuscript Library, Duke University.

10. Among other issues raised (and quickly dispensed with) were how to organize birth control education and research and a suggestion that the association "probe a little into the alcohol problem." See A. W. Coats, *The Sociology and Professionalization of Economics: British and American Economic Essays*, vol. 2 (New York: Routledge, 1993), 251.

11. Letter from Theodora B. Cunningham and Virginia King Frye, dated July 29, 1916, in American Economic Association Records, Box 64–69, "Correspondence of David R.

Dewey with editors and authors of articles and communications, 1910–1917," David M. Rubenstein Rare Book & Manuscript Library, Duke University.

12. What was originally the League of American Pen Women is now the National League of American Pen Women. The organization is still in existence. Information on the group's history is found at the National League of American Pen Women's website: https://www.nlapw.org.

13. See American Economic Association Records, Box 1, "AEA Histories, A. W. Coats, 1952–1963; *Journal of Economic Literature*, Mark Perlman, editor. Correspondence [1968] 1970–1980," David M. Rubenstein Rare Book & Manuscript Library, Duke University.

14. Letter from Dewey to Frye, dated August 9, 1916, in American Economic Association Records, Box 64–69, "Correspondence of David R. Dewey."

15. Also revealed in Dewey's list of editors is his geographic naiveté or his New England–centric perspective, as he lists Johns Hopkins, Vassar, and Princeton among "Middle States" (perhaps meaning Middle Atlantic) and the University of Kansas and the University of Nebraska among "Western States."

16. Coats argues that although the dangers of a "regional split" in the AEA had largely subsided by 1900, disagreements on the choice of the location for the annual meetings reflected "dissatisfaction with the disproportionate influence of the leading eastern academic institution." See A. W. Coats, "The American Economic Association and the Economics Profession," *Journal of Economic Literature* 23, no. 4 (1985): 1707. Likewise, discussions of a membership hierarchy brought with it a concern over changes that "smacked of oligarchy" that might lead the organization to be dominated by, for example, nonacademic economists or the "Eastern academic elite." See Coats, *The Sociology and Professionalization of Economics*, 249 and 444.

17. Michael A. Bernstein, *A Perilous Progress: Economists and Public Purpose in Twentieth-Century America* (Princeton, NJ: Princeton University Press, 2001), 29.

18. Dorothy Ross, *The Origins of American Social Science* (Cambridge: Cambridge University Press, 1991), 102.

19. Mary O. Furner, *Advocacy and Objectivity: A Crisis in the Professionalization of American Social Science, 1865–1905* (Lexington: University of Kentucky Press, 1973); Andrew Abbott, *The System of Professions: An Essay on the Division of Expert Labor* (Chicago: University of Chicago Press, 1988); Marion Fourcade, *Economists and Societies: Discipline and Profession in the United States, Britain, and France, 1890s to 1990s* (Princeton, NJ: Princeton University Press, 2009); Jonathan S. Franklin, *A History of Professional Economists and Policymaking in the United States: Irrelevant Genius* (New York: Routledge, 2016).

20. In describing the period from 1885 to 1904, Coats describes the tensions between economists, pointing out that it was perhaps inevitable that some would interpret the strong religious and ethical tone adopted by others as "soft-headedness." He went to point out that "Ely was indubitably the chief offender." See Coats, *The Sociology and Professionalization of Economics*, 210.

21. Quoted in Bernstein, *A Perilous Progress*, 24.

22. American Economic Association Records, Box 3, "Annual Meetings, 1908–1924," David M. Rubenstein Rare Book & Manuscript Library, Duke University.

23. See Jessica Blanche Peixotto, *The French Revolution and Modern French Socialism* (New York: Crowell, 1901); Susan Myra Kingsbury, *An Introduction to the Records of the Virginia Company of London* (Washington, DC: U.S. Government Printing Office, 1905); Minnie Throop England, "Church Government and Church Control" (PhD thesis, University of Nebraska, 1906); Dorothy Stahl Brady, "On the Solution of Homogeneous Linear Integral Equations" (PhD thesis, University of California, 1933).

24. By 2018, the critique of "mathiness" had become so accepted that Paul M. Romer could coin the word, make an argument, and go on to win the Nobel Prize in Economics. Of course, critiques of the discipline are as old as the discipline itself, but when they come from eminent economists, it is typically after they have served as president of the AEA and not before. See Paul M. Romer, "Mathiness in the Theory of Economic Growth," *American Economic Review* 105, no. 5 (2015): 89–93.

25. For a full discussion of gender schemas, see Virginia Valian, *Why So Slow? The Advancement of Women* (Cambridge, MA: MIT Press, 1998).

6. THE TRADE IN WORDS:
GENDER AND THE MONOGRAPH

1. Andrew Sinclair, *The Better Half: The Emancipation of the American Woman* (New York: Harper and Row, 1965), 272.

2. Virginia Woolf, *Mrs. Dalloway* (London: Hogarth Press, 1925), 109–10.

3. Charlotte Perkins Gilman, *The Living of Charlotte Perkins Gilman: An Autobiography* (New York: D. Appleton-Century, 1935), 96 and 335.

4. Carl F. Kaestle and Janice A. Radway, "Introduction," in *A History of the Book in America*, vol. 4, ed. Carl F. Kaestle and Janice A. Radway (Chapel Hill: University of North Carolina Press, 2009), 49.

5. James L. W. West III, "The Expansion of the National Book Trade," in *A History of the Book*, vol. 4, ed. Carl F. Kaestle and Janice A. Radway (Chapel Hill: University of North Carolina Press, 2009), 79.

6. Data collected here show that of the 158 women writing three or more books listed in the *Economic Bulletin* and the *AER* in "New Books," 50 had doctoral degrees—most of which were from Columbia University and then the University of Chicago.

7. Frederick Rudolph, *The American College and University: A History* (New York: Knopf, 1962), 403.

8. The lists of women authors of "New Books" in the *Economic Bulletin* and *AER* show that 1,537 individual women authors were included, compared with 16,404 individual male authors.

9. Excluded are books written in languages other than English. A complete list of male authors listed in the *Economic Bulletin* and *AER* from 1908 through 1948 was

developed. A random number of male authors for each year were chosen to match the number of female authors for each year.

10. Further examination of the data shows that most authors listed in the *Economic Bulletin* and *AER* who held a doctorate, had their doctorate at the time of publication, and few authors earned their doctorates after their books were listed.

11. This discussion examines the results of a binary response model (or linear probability model) to better understand the relationship between authors with doctoral degrees, doctoral degrees in economics, and the probability of being a coauthor. For information on linear probability models, see Jeffrey M. Wooldridge, *Introductory Econometrics: A Modern Approach* (Mason, OH: South-Western Cengage Learning, 2009), 246–51.

12. For this analysis, the following regression model is used: $Yi = \beta o + \beta 1EconNowi + \beta 2PhDNowi + \varepsilon i$ where i indexes the person publishing a new book listed in the "New Books" section of the *Economic Bulletin* or the *AER* from 1908 through 1948. $Yi = 1$ if individual i is a coauthor, and 0 if i is not a coauthor. $EconNow\ i = 1$ if individual i has an economics PhD as of the publication date, and 0 if i does not have an economics PhD as of the publication date. $PhDNow\ i = 1$ if individual i has a PhD in any field as of the publication date, and 0 if i does not have a PhD as of publication date. To examine the likelihood of same-sex coauthorship, the dependent variable becomes $Y_i = 1$ if the individual is a same-sex coauthor and 0 if individual i is not a same-sex coauthor.

13. To test for differences between the male and female coefficients, interaction terms are added to the model. Interacting the dummy variable *female* with *PhDNow* and *female* with *EconPhD*. This allows an estimate of the difference in the female effect and the male effect and a test for significance. The model thus becomes: $Yi = \beta o + \beta 1EconNowi + \beta 2PhDNowi + \beta 3female + \beta 4FemPhD + \beta 5FemEcon + \varepsilon i$, where the coefficient for *FemPhD* is the coefficient for *PhDNow* (women) – *PhDNow* (men) and the coefficient for *FemEcon* is the coefficient for *EconPhD* (women) – *EconPhD* (men).

14. Results that are significant at the 0.05 level and 0.01 level are discussed.

15. See, for example, Anne Boschini and Anna Sjögren, "Is Team Formation Gender Neutral? Evidence from Coauthorship Patters," *Journal of Labor Economics* 25, no. 2 (2007): 325–65; Marianne A. Ferber and Michelle Teiman, "Are Women Economists at a Disadvantage in Publishing Journal Articles," *Eastern Economic Journal* 6, no. 3–4 (1980): 189–93; John M. McDowell and Janet Kiholm Smith, "The Effect of Gender-Sorting on Propensity to Coauthor: Implications for Academic Promotion," *Economic Inquiry* 30, no. 1 (1992): 68–82.

16. The model used to examine same-sex coauthorship is the same as the previous model except that the dependent variable is same-sex coauthorship rather than simply coauthorship.

17. The model compares results during World War I to nonwar years and World War II to nonwar years to examine the effect of wartime on coauthorship.

18. The results are based on the following regression: $Yi = \beta o + \beta 1WWII + \beta 2EconPhDi + \beta 3WWII^*EconPhDi + \beta 4PhDNowi + \beta 5\ WWII^*PhDNowi + \varepsilon i$, where i indexes the

individual publishing a new book listed in the "New Books" section of the *Economic Bulletin* or the *AER* from 1908 through 1948.

19.   For a useful examination of women and publishing in the early years, see Robert W. Dimand, "The Neglect of Women's Contributions to Economics," in *Women of Value: Feminist Essays on the History of Women in Economics*, ed. Mary Ann Dimand, Robert W. Dimand, and Evelyn L. Forget (Aldershot, UK: Edward Elgar, 1995), 1–24. See also Barbara Libby, "Women in Economics Before 1940," *Essays in Economic and Business History* 3 (1984): 273–290.

20.   See, for example, Boschini and Sjögren, "Is Team Formation," 325–65.

7. TROUBLE IN THE INAUGURAL ISSUE OF THE *AMERICAN ECONOMIC REVIEW*: THE MONOGRAPH AND THE REVIEW

1.   See Patricia M. Mazón, *Gender and the Modern Research University: The Admission of Women to German Higher Education, 1865–1914* (Palo Alto, CA: Stanford University Press, 2003), 145.

2.   Lucile Eaves, "My Sociological Life History—1928," ed. Michael R. Hill, *Sociological Origins* 2, no. 2 (2000): 65–70.

3.   Richard Hofstadter and Walter P. Metzger, *The Development of Academic Freedom in the United States* (New York: Columbia University Press, 1955).

4.   Like other settlement houses, South Park Settlement offered social services and a meeting place for lectures, concerts, and entertainment. In addition, it offered a forum for advocacy, bringing together middle-class reformers and academics interested in social reform and "enlarged civic action." See Ann Mari May and Robert W. Dimand, "Trouble in the Inaugural Issues of *The American Economic Review*: The Cross/Eaves Controversy," *Journal of Economic Perspectives* 23, no. 3 (2009): 189–204.

5.   Ann Wilson, "Settlement Work in a Union Town: Lucile Eaves, the San Francisco Settlement Association, and Organized Labor, 1894–1906," *Ex Post Facto* 11 (Spring 2002): 87.

6.   Mary Ann Dzuback, "Gender, Professional Knowledge, and Institutional Power: Women Social Scientists and the Research University," in *The Woman Question and Higher Education: Perspectives on Gender and Knowledge Production in America*, ed. Ann Mari May (Cheltenham, UK: Edward Elgar, 2008), 62.

7.   For biographical details on Eaves's life, see Mary Jo Deegan, *Women in Sociology: A Bio-Bibliographical Sourcebook* (New York: Greenwood Press, 1991).

8.   Ira B. Cross (interviewee), "Portrait of an Economics Professor," Oral History Transcript, Regional Oral History Office, Bancroft Library, University of California, Berkeley (1967).

9.   Harry A. Millis first wrote to Edwin W. Kemmerer on November 14, 1910, and Kemmerer replied to Millis in a letter dated November 21, 2010. See American Economic Association Records, Box 64–69, "Correspondence of Davis R. Dewey with editors

and authors of articles and communications, 1910–1917," David M. Rubenstein Rare Book & Manuscript Library, Duke University.

10. Davis R. Dewey wrote to Allyn A. Young in a letter dated November 25, 2010. Young replied in his letter dated November 28, 2010. For Dewey and Young correspondence here and elsewhere see American Economic Association Records, Box 64–69, "Correspondence of Davis R. Dewey."

11. For correspondence between Davis R. Dewey and Ira B. Cross here and elsewhere, see American Economic Association Records, Box 64–69, "Correspondence of Davis R. Dewey."

12. Cross accused Eaves of crediting the National Labor Union Party for things done by the Workingmen's Party of the United States (later the Socialist Workers Party) and insisted that Denis Kearney, a very controversial figure who used anti-Chinese sentiments to gain labor support, was never connected with the Workingmen's Party. See Ira B. Cross, "Review of *A History of California Labor Legislation* by Lucile Eaves," *American Economic Review* 1, no. 1 (1911): 106–9.

13. Cross, "Review of *A History of California Labor Legislation*," 108.

14. Ira B. Cross, "Co-operation in California," *American Economic Review* 1, no. 3 (1911): 535–44.

15. Correspondence between Lucile Eaves and Davis R. Dewey here and elsewhere found in American Economic Association Records, Box 64–69, "Correspondence of Davis R. Dewey."

16. Eaves consulted other leading economists as well. One was John Bates Clark of Columbia University (where Eaves earned her doctorate). Clark wrote to Dewey on June 15, 1911, stating: "My only knowledge of the points in controversy comes from a copy of her note to the Economic Review. That appears to have 'made good' as to a number of points; but you are in a better position than I am for judging, and you are so fair that any words of mine would be superfluous." The file contains no record of a response from Dewey to Clark. For correspondence between Dewey and Frank A. Fetter (letter dated May 24, 1911) and Dewey and Henry Farnam (letter dated May 23, 1911), see American Economic Association Records, Box 64–69, "Correspondence of David R. Dewey."

17. This "boys will be boys" letter, dated May 26, 1911, is found in American Economic Association Records, Box 64–69, "Correspondence of David R. Dewey."

18. For Dewey's letter to Eaves dated May 23, 1911, and Eaves's responses dated May 31, 1911, and June 28, 1911, see American Economic Association Records, Box 64–69, "Correspondence of Davis R. Dewey."

19. For Fetter's letter to Dewey dated June 7, 1911, see American Economic Association Records, Box 64–69, "Correspondence of Davis R. Dewey."

20. See Lucile Eaves, "A Communication," *American Economic Review* 1, no. 3 (1911): 587–89.

21. The correspondence with Eaves, Cross, and Young in letters dated September 19, 1911, October 13, 1911, October 22, 1911, November 1, 1911, November 2, 1911, and November 17, 1911 concerning objections to the review and responses are found in

American Economic Association Records, Box 64–69, "Correspondence of David R. Dewey."

22. Davis R. Dewey, "History of California Labor Legislation," *American Economic Review* 2, no. 1 (1912): 115.

23. Ira B. Cross, *A History of the Labor Movement in California* (Berkeley: University of California Press, 1935), 215.

24. See American Economic Association Records, Box 62, "Correspondence of AEA re founding 7journal and Special Editorial Correspondence, *AER*, 1910–1940, Davis R. Dewey, Managing Editor," David M. Rubenstein Rare Book & Manuscript Library, Duke University.

25. Alvin S. Johnson, "Book Reviews: Value and Distribution. Herbert Joseph Davenport," *Journal of Political Economy* 16, no. 6 (1908): 380–85.

26. Johnson, "Book Reviews," 380.

27. Letter from Irving Fisher to Herbert J. Davenport dated October 21, 1908. For correspondence on the issue of book reviews sparked by Davenport, see American Economic Association Records, Box 62, "Correspondence of AEA re founding journal."

28. Letter from Dewey to Fetter dated October 10, 1908, in American Economic Association Records, Box 62, "Correspondence of AEA re founding journal."

29. Letter from Kemmerer to Dewey dated January 21, 1911, in American Economic Association Records, Box 64–69, "Correspondence of Davis R. Dewey."

30. For a full discussion of Dewey's remarks on stepping down from the editorship of the *AER* after thirty years, see Benno Torgler and Marco Piatti, *A Century of American Economic Review: Insights on Critical Factors in Journal Publishing* (New York: Palgrave Pivot, 2013).

31. A. W. Coats, "The American Economic Association and the Economics Profession," *Journal of Economic Literature* 23, no. 4 (1985): 1711.

32. See American Economic Association Records, Box 1, "AEA Histories, A. W. Coats, 1952–1963; Journal of Economic Literature, Mark Perlman, editor. Correspondence, [1968] 1970–1980," David M. Rubenstein Rare Book & Manuscript Library, Duke University.

33. See American Economic Association Records, Box 64–69, "Correspondence of Davis R. Dewey." It should be noted that Eaves was not the only outraged author to write to Dewey about an unjust review in the first issue. In a letter dated July 3, 1911, Carl Vrooman wrote to Dewey, "Your unexpected and utterly incomprehensible refusal to publish my reply to Mr. Dewsnup's deliberately disingenuous and misleading criticisms of my book was received some weeks ago." See American Economic Association Records, Box 64–69, "Correspondence of Davis R. Dewey."

34. Frederick Rudolph, *The American College and University: A History* (New York: Knopf, 1962), 403.

35. See, for example, Najia Aarim-Heriot, *Chinese Immigrants, African Americans, and Racial Anxiety in the United States, 1848–82* (Urbana: University of Illinois Press, 2006); Alexander Saxton, *The Indispensable Enemy: Labor and the Anti-Chinese*

Movement in California (Berkeley: University of California Press, 1971); Michael Kazin, "The Great Exception Revisited: Organized Labor and Politics in San Francisco and Los Angeles, 1870–1940," *Pacific Historical Review* 55, no. 3 (1986): 371–402; Daniel A. Cornford, ed., *Working People of California* (Berkeley: University of California Press, 1995).

36. As Ann Wilson points out, "Eaves astutely observed that the long campaign against the 'common enemy' of Chinese labor 'contributed more than any other factor to the strength of the California labor movement'—an assertion that anticipated arguments put forth by Alexander Saxton and Michael Kazin more than six decades later." See Wilson, "Settlement Work in a Union Town," 89.

37. For a complete list, see Kirsten K. Madden, Janet A. Seiz, and Michèle Pujol, *A Bibliography of Female Economic Thought up to 1940* (London: Routledge, 2004), 161–163.

38. The June 1914 issue of *AER* published an article by Eaves on "Social Politics in California," immediately followed by an article by Cross on "Workmen's Compensation in California"—the last articles either of them published in *AER*. The *AER* invited a review by Eaves of three works on irregularity of employment among women workers, which it published in June 1916. See Lucile Eaves, "Social Politics in California," *American Economic Review* 4, no. 2 (1914), 450–54; Ira B. Cross, "Workmen's Compensation in California," *American Economic Review* 4, no. 2 (1914), 454–60; Elizabeth Donnan, "Reviewed Work(s): *A Legacy of Wage-Earning Women: A Survey of Gainfully Employed Women of Brattleboro, Vermont and of Relief Which They have Received from the Thomas Thompson Trust*, by Lucile Eaves," *American Economic Review* 16, no. 2 (1926): 331–32.

39. Dorothy Ross, *The Origins of American Social Science* (Cambridge: Cambridge University Press, 1991), 101–2.

40. See American Economic Association Records, Box 64–69, "Correspondence of Davis R. Dewey."

8. GENDER, THE OLD BOY NETWORK, AND THE SCHOLARLY JOURNAL

1. Eleanor Lansing Dulles, *Eleanor Lansing Dulles: Chances of a Lifetime, a Memoir* (Englewood Cliffs, NJ: Prentice Hall, 1980), 87.

2. Roger Sandilands, "New Evidence on Allyn Young's Style and Influence as a Teacher," *Journal of Economic Studies* 26, no. 6 (1999): 453–79.

3. Dulles, *Chances of a Lifetime*, 102.

4. Dulles, *Chances of a Lifetime*, 102.

5. Frederick Rudolph, *The American College and University: A History* (New York: Knopf, 1962), 396–97.

6. Rudolph, *The American College*, 404.

7. Three influential academic freedom "trials" of note were Henry Carter Adams at Cornell University, Richard T. Ely at the University of Wisconsin, and Edward

Bemis at the University of Chicago. See Richard Hofstadter and Walter Metzger, *The Development of Academic Freedom in the United States* (New York: Columbia University Press, 1955); A. W. Coats, "Henry Carter Adams: A Case Study in the Emergence of the Social Sciences in the United States, 1850–1900," *Journal of American Studies* 2, no. 2 (1968): 177–97.

8. Drummond Rennie, "Editorial Peer Review: Its Development and Rationale," in *Peer Review in Health Sciences*, ed. Fiona Godlee and Tom Jefferson (London: BJM Books, 1999), 1–13.

9. For a general discussion of the old boy network in academia, see Elizabeth Pleck, "The Unfulfilled Promise: Women and Academe," *Sociological Forum* 5, no. 3 (1990): 517–24. See also Barbara F. Reskin, "Sex Differentiation and the Social Organization of Science," *Sociological Inquiry* 48, nos. 3–4 (1978): 6–37; Debra Renee Kaufman, "Association Ties in Academe: Some Male and Female Differences," *Sex Roles* 4, no. 1 (1978): 9–21.

10. Information on the *AER* editorial board is found in various locations over time, including the *Bulletin of the American Economic Association*, the *American Economic Review Papers and Proceedings*, *AER*, and at the top of official stationery of the AEA.

11. The two men on the *AER* editorial board who did not hold an AEA membership were Frederic B. Garver of the University of Minnesota and David A. McCabe of Princeton University.

12. It has been noted that despite Coman's extensive studies of the developing West, William Baumol neglected to mention her work in his study commissioned for the one hundredth anniversary of the AEA. See Robin L. Bartlett, "Katharine Coman," in *A Biographical Dictionary of Women Economists*, ed. Robert W. Dimand, Mary Ann Dimand, and Evelyn L. Forget (Cheltenham, UK: Edward Elgar, 2000), 115–17.

13. A. W. Coats, "The American Economic Association's Publications: An Historical Perspective," *Journal of Economic Literature* 7, no. 1 (1969): 58–59.

14. The absence of women in any editorial capacity in journals specific to a particular university was not unusual. Vicky M. Longawa demonstrates that those serving as editors in the *Journal of Political Economy* at the University of Chicago were all male faculty, and the first woman to infiltrate this austere group was Mary Jean Bowman, who served for one year in 1960—two years after the University of Chicago changed its nepotism rules. For a full list of editors, see Vicky M. Longawa, "Episodes in the History of the Journal of Political Economy," *Journal of Political Economy* 100, no. 6 (1992): 1087–91.

15. The two men on the editorial board of *QJE* who did not have an AEA membership were Alexander Gerschenkron and William J. Ashley, both of Harvard University.

16. Little is known of Alice Rollins Brewster. She published her article in *QJE* in 1894 and has no known publications after that date.

17. See Jane Knowles, "Harvard's Invisible Faculty: Four Portraits," in *Yards and Gates: Gender in Harvard and Radcliffe History*, ed. Laurel Thatcher Ulrich (New York: Palgrave Macmillan, 2004), 187–94.

18. Grace Thompson Gunn coauthored all three of her publications with Paul Howard Douglas, her colleague at the U.S. Bureau of the Budget and the former husband of Dorothy Wolff Douglas. Elizabeth Waterman Gilboy coauthored one of her nine articles in the *AER* and *QJE* with Helen Sorenson.

19. For a full description of the time stress invoked by these high teaching loads for women faculty at Wellesley College, see Patricia Ann Palmieri, *In Adamless Eden: The Community of Women Faculty at Wellesley* (New Haven, CT: Yale University Press, 1995), 101–20. See also Helen Lefkowitz Horowitz, *Alma Mater: Design and Experience in the Women's Colleges from Their Nineteenth-Century Beginnings to the 1930s* (Amherst: University of Massachusetts Press, 1984).

20. Mary Ann Dzuback, "Women Economists in the Academy: Struggles and Strategies, 1900–1940," in *The Routledge Handbook of the History of Women's Economic Thought*, ed. Kirsten Madden and Robert W. Dimand (London: Routledge, 2019), 211–28.

21. As Horowitz points out, there was no two-tier system as Wellesley College because they hired only women faculty. For an excellent discussion of the expectations placed on women faculty teaching in women's colleges, see Horowitz, *Alma Mater*, 180.

22. Margaret W. Rossiter, "Doctorates for American Women, 1868–1907," *History of Education Quarterly* 22, no. 2 (1982): 159–83.

23. For marriage rates in the early twentieth century, see Diana B. Elliott, Kristy Krivickas, Matthew W. Brault, and Rose M. Kreider, "Historical Marriage Trends from 1890–2010: A Focus on Race Differences," Census Working Paper No. SEHSD-WP2012-12, U.S. Census Bureau, 2012, https://www.census.gov/library/working-papers/2012/demo/SEHSD-WP2012-12.html.

24. Margaret Loomis Stecker, who published three articles in *QJE* and *AER* in 1916, 1917, and 1921, married in 1928. She left academia and continued her work as an economist for the Social Security Administration from 1938 to 1950. No published work is found after her marriage.

25. For a full summary of articles published by women in the early years of the profession, see also Robert W. Dimand, "Women Economists in the 1890s: Journals, Books and the Old Palgrave," *Journal of the History of Economic Thought* 21, no. 3 (1999): 269–88.

26. The analysis in this chapter uses the linear probability model, $Y(i,t) = \beta_0 + \beta_1 female(i,t) + \beta_2 PhDNow(i,t) + \beta_3 PhDEcon(i,t) + \beta_4 SamePhD(i,t) + \beta_5 SameJob(i,t) + \beta_6 PhDEdJob(i,t) + e(i,t)$, where i indexes authors of articles published in *AER* from year $t = 1911$ to 1948. All the regression variables are 0–1 indicators (dummy variables) where the value 1 indicates that the author has a specified characteristic and the value 0 indicates she or he does not. The dependent variable $y(i,t)$ equals 1 if *AER* published another article by author i in a year before year t. The conditioning variables include *female* (if the author is a woman), *PhDNow* (if the author had a doctorate in year t), *PhDEcon* (if the author had a doctorate in economics in year t), *SamePhD* (if the author and an *AER* editor earned their doctorates at the same

institution), *SameJob* (if the author and an *AER* editor have the same current institutional affiliation), and *PhDEdJob* (if an *AER* editor is a faculty member at the author's doctoral institution). To examine the likelihood of same-sex coauthorship, the dependent variable becomes $Y(i,t) = 1$ if the individual is a same-sex coauthor and 0 if individual i is not a same-sex coauthor. The same model is used to examine articles published in *QJE* except that the time period is extended.

27.   The factors affecting multiple publications for all coauthors (male and female) show that only in the 1930s did having a doctorate in a field other than economics have an effect on multiple publications compared to coauthors without a doctorate. Coauthors with such a doctorate were 14 percentage points less likely to have multiple publications. The results also show that coauthors with a doctorate in economics were more likely to have multiple publications by about 10 percentage points in the 1930s, compared to coauthors without a doctorate. As for relationships, the same negative effect of earning a doctorate from the same institution where an editor or editorial board member held an appointment continued, but only in the 1920s. In all other decades, relationships between editors and coauthors did not affect the likelihood of multiple publications for coauthors.

28.   Although no other relationships were significant at the .95 and .99 confidence levels for any other decades, several variables were significant at the .90 confidence level. Specifically, the results for these marginally significant variables suggest that from 1910 to 1919, authors with a doctorate in economics may have been likely to have more than one publication in *QJE* as were authors with a doctorate from the same institution as a member of the editorial team. Likewise, in the 1930s, these marginally significant results suggest that authors with an appointment at the same institution as an author might have had a greater likelihood of multiple publications.

29.   There were no coauthored papers in *QJE* from 1886 to 1908, only five from 1909 to 1919, and three in the 1920s. The proportion of coauthored papers (from multiple article authors) went from 8 percent in the 1930s to 16 percent in the 1940s.

30.   Diana Crane, "The Gatekeeper's of Science: Some Factors Affecting the Selection of Articles for Scientific Journals," *American Sociologist* 2, no. 4 (1967): 195–201.

31.   Crane, "The Gatekeeper's of Science," 195.

32.   Barbara F. Reskin and Denise D. Bielby, "A Sociological Perspective on Gender and Career Outcomes," *Journal of Economic Perspectives* 19, no. 1 (2005): 72.

33.   Francine D. Blau, Marianne A. Ferber, and Anne E. Winkler, *The Economics of Women, Men, and Work* (Upper Saddle River, NJ: Pearson Prentice Hall, 2006), 233.

34.   For a variety of views on these divergent paths, see Robert L. Church, "Economists as Experts: The Rise of an Academic Profession in the United States, 1870–1920," in *The University in Society*, vol. 2, ed. Lawrence Stone (Princeton, NJ: Princeton University Press, 1974), 571–610; Claire H. Hammond, "Women and the Professionalization of Economics," *Review of Social Economy* 51, no. 3 (1993): 347–70; Mary O. Furner, *Advocacy and Objectivity: A Crisis in the Professionalization of American Social Science, 1865–1905* (Lexington: University of Kentucky Press, 1975), 144; Marion Fourcade,

Economists and Societies: Discipline and Profession in the United States, Britain, and France, 1890s to 1990s (Princeton, NJ: Princeton University Press, 2009).

9. NOT A FREE MARKET: WOMEN'S EMPLOYMENT AFTER THE DOCTORATE

1. See Pila Martinez, "Retired Professor Leahmae McCoy; Broke Barriers at UA Economics Dept.," *Arizona Daily Star*, January 1, 1999, 20.
2. Martinez, "Retired Professor Leahmae McCoy," 20. With the exception of Leahmae Brown McCoy, the economics department at the University of Arizona included only male faculty at the time that McCoy was there (1954–1978). See Department of Economics, "Economics Faculty," Arizona Board of Regents, University of Arizona, https://archive.catalog.arizona.edu/faculty/984/econ.html (accessed November 9, 2020).
3. Martinez, "Retired Professor Leahmae McCoy," 20.
4. American Economic Association, "Exhibit II: List of Chairmen or Heads of Departments of Economics, Deans of Schools of Business, and Directors of Business Research Bureaus and Institutions in Selected Colleges and Universities," *American Economic Review* 39, no. 1 (1949): 333–36.
5. The institutions listing female chairs as of 1948 were Barnard College, Bryn Mawr College, Goucher College, MacMurray College for Women, Mount Holyoke College, and Vassar College.
6. See Andrew Langan, "Female Managers and Gender Disparities: The Case of Academic Department Chairs," Working Papers, Princeton, University, https://scholar.princeton.edu/alangan/publications/female-managers-and-gender-disparities-case-academic-department-chairs (accessed November 24, 2020). Also Donna S. Rothstein, "Do Female Faculty Influence Female Students' Educational and Labor Market Attainments?," *IL Review* 48, no. 3 (1995): 515–30.
7. Although Ware was effective in bringing national attention to the unfairness of marriage bars and vowed to fight them in court, she did not bring a case against the University of Wyoming and did not teach the course in summer 1935. For more discussion, see Landon R. Y. Storrs, *The Second Red Scare and the Unmaking of the New Deal Left* (Princeton, NJ: Princeton University Press, 2013), 44–45.
8. See Claudia Goldin, "The Meaning of College in the Lives of American Women: The Past One-Hundred Years," Working Paper No. 4099, National Bureau of Economic Research (1992).
9. See Barbara Miller Solomon, *In the Company of Educated Women: A History of Women and Higher Education in America* (New Haven, CT: Yale University Press, 1985), 173.
10. See Jo Anne Preston, "Negotiating Work and Family: Aspirations of Early Radcliffe Graduates," in *Yards and Gates: Gender in Harvard and Radcliffe History*, ed. Laurel Thatcher Ulrich (New York: Palgrave Macmillan, 2004), 173–74. For more

information, see Barbara Miller Solomon and Patricia M. Nolan, "Education, Work, Family, and Public Commitment in the Lives of Radcliffe Alumnae, 1883–1928," in *Changing Education: Women as Radicals and Conservators*, ed. Joyce Antler and Sari Knopp Biklin (Albany: State University of New York Press, 1990), 139–55.

11. See Solomon, *In the Company of Educated Women*, 174.

12. Ada Comstock, "The Fourth R for Women," *Century Magazine* 117 (1929): 413.

13. Section 213 of the original draft of the employment act called for firing wives over husbands. There was a change in wording in the final version. According to Civil Service Commissioner Jessie Dell, this change was due to "fear, on the part of legislators, of the political effect, if discrimination against women were otherwise so clearly and forcibly shown." See Feminist Majority Foundation, "Founding Feminists: September 25, 1932," https://feminist.org/news/founding-feminists-september-25-1932/ (accessed November 16, 2020).

14. See, for example, Claudia Goldin, *Understanding the Gender Gap: An Economic History of American Women* (Oxford: Oxford University Press, 1990); Matthew P. Nagowski, "Inopportunity of Gender: The G. I. Bill and the Higher Education of the American Female, 1939–1954," DigitalCommons@ILR, 2005, https://digitalcommons .ilr.cornell.edu/student/97; Lois Scharf, *To Work and to Wed: Female Employment, Feminism, and the Great Depression* (Westport, CT: Greenwood Press, 1980), 45; John Thomas McGuire, "'The Most Unjust Piece of Legislation': Section 213 of the Economy Act of 1932 and Feminism During the New Deal," *Journal of Policy History* 20, no. 4 (2008): 516–41.

15. Lionel Robbins is attributed with this definition of economics. See Lionel Robbins, *An Essay on the Nature and Significance of Economic Science* (London: Macmillan, 1932). For a thoughtful critique of this notion for women, see Diana Strassmann, "Not a Free Market: The Rhetoric and Disciplinary Authority in Economics," in *Beyond Economic Man: Feminist Theory and Economics*, ed. Marianne A. Ferber and Julie A. Nelson (Chicago: University of Chicago Press, 1993), 54–68.

16. See Janet M. Hooks, "Women's Occupations Through Seven Decades," *Women's Bureau Bulletin* 218 (1947): 160.

17. See U.S. Bureau of the Census, *Thirteenth Census of the United States: 1910*, Population, vol. 4, *Occupations* (Washington, DC: U.S. Government Printing Office, 1911), 430–31; U.S. Bureau of the Census, *Fifteenth Census of the United States: 1930*, Population, vol. 4, *Occupations* (Washington, DC: U.S. Government Printing Office, 1933), 33.

18. The 1930 U.S. Census shows 1,020 Black women and 18,146 white women in this category. See U.S. Census Bureau, *Fifteenth Census of the United States: 1930*, Population, vol. 5, *General Report on Occupations* (Washington, DC: U.S. Government Printing Office, 1933), 84, table 3.

19. See Rachel Fesler Nyswander and Janet M. Hooks, "Employment of Women in the Federal Government 1923–1939," *Bulletin of the Women's Bureau* 182 (1941): 1–60.

20. See Nyswander and Hooks, "Employment of Women," 17.

21. See Nyswander and Hooks, "Employment of Women," 6.

22. See Nyswander and Hooks, "Employment of Women," 22.

23. A random sample of men with doctorates in economics was obtained by searching all doctorates awarded by U.S. universities for each year from 1890 to 1948. A random sample of male doctoral recipients was selected to match the numbers of women in the sample. ProQuest was used to conduct the search.

24. In classifying the women with doctorates in economics from 1890 to 1948, about 8 percent were either not located after earning their degree or had no found active involvement with the labor market. Another 2 percent were high school teachers. Four percent of women were characterized as having for-profit employment.

25. Hunter College was a women's college until 1946, when it became coeducational.

26. All men in the sample were located and identified, and 8 percent of women had no found occupational affiliation after receiving their doctorate.

27. These results reflect a test for a difference in means between men's and women's employment by decade.

28. Results show that the mean value of male and female academics who are married by decade are significantly different (p-value $< .10$) in the 1920s, 1930s, and 1940s.

29. In the 1930s and 1940s, the most prevalent field drawing women with PhDs in economics was home economics. This field drew about 12 percent of women in economics away from employment in academic economics. Other fields—such as history, followed by social science, administration (dean of women), sociology, political science, geography, and library science—also employed women with PhDs in economics.

30. For a useful discussion of the influential role that women played as dean of women, see Robert A. Schwartz, "How Deans of Women Became Men," *Review of Higher Education* 20, no. 4 (1997): 419–36.

31. As dean of women, Talbot proposed a program in "sanitary science" at the University of Chicago. Her preferred name for the program was not kept, and it was later changed to home economics. See Patricia J. Thompson, "Beyond Gender: Equity Issues for Home Economics Education," *Theory into Practice* 25, no. 4 (1986): 276–83; Sarah Stage, "Home Economics: What's in a Name?," in *Rethinking Home Economics: Women and the History of a Profession*, ed. Sarah Stage and Virginia B. Vincenti (Ithaca, NY: Cornell University Press, 1997), 1–14.

32. See, for example, Ellen Fitzpatrick, "For the 'Women of the University,' Marion Talbot, 1858–1948," in *Lone Voyagers: Academic Women in Coeducational Institutions, 1870–1937*, ed. Geraldine Jonçich Clifford (New York: Feminist Press, 1989), 87–97. For a further understanding of Breckinridge's time at the University of Chicago, see Ellen Fitzpatrick, *Endless Crusade: Women Social Scientists and Progressive Reform* (Oxford: Oxford University Press, 1990).

33. Hazel Kyrk is a real-world example of what Myra Strober sees as one of the benefits of interdisciplinary research. Strober points out that interdisciplinarity is a complement to disciplinarity and not a substitute. See Myra H. Strober, *Interdisciplinary Conversations: Challenging Habits of Thought* (Palo Alto, CA: Stanford University Press, 2011), 20–22.

34. For an excellent discussion of Kyrk's and Reid's contributions to national income accounting and measuring work, see Nancy Folbre, *Greed, Lust and Gender: A History of Economic Ideas* (Oxford: Oxford University Press, 2009). See also Hazel Kyrk, *Economic Problems of the Family* (New York: Harper & Brothers, 1933); Margaret G. Reid, *Economics of Household Production* (New York: Wiley, 1934).

35. An estimate of women doctorates in home economics was obtained by searching ProQuest for all "home economics" doctorates awarded by U.S. universities for each year from 1890 to 1948.

36. See Evelyn L. Forget, "American Women and the Economics Profession in the Twentieth Century," *Economia: History/Methodology/Philosophy* 1, no. 1 (2011): 19–30.

37. See Schwartz, "How Deans of Women Became Men," 433. For statistics on enrollment of women undergraduates, see Patricia Albjerg Graham, "Expansion and Exclusion: A History of Women in American Higher Education," *Signs* 3, no. 4 (1978): 766.

38. Testing the null hypothesis that the female mean = male mean shows that we cannot accept this hypothesis.

39. For a discussion of the impact of World War II on women's labor supply, see Evan K. Rose, "The Rise and Fall of Female Labor Force Participation During WWII in the United States," *Journal of Economic History* 78, no. 3 (2018): 1–39.

40. These results are consistent with those of Linda Eisenmann, who notes that when placed on college faculties, women were "eased out as soon as men became available." She also says that while common perceptions suggested that women "benefited tremendously from wartime opportunities, they in fact did not overtake men's advances, and much of their progress was either short-lived or low-level." See Linda Eisenmann, "Women, Higher Education, and Professionalization," *Harvard Educational Review* (Winter 1996): 11.

10. A DESTINY FULFILLED: DEFINING THE PROFESSIONAL ECONOMIST

1. See Letter from Morris A. Copland to Secretary Bell dated November 14, 1941. In this letter Copeland recommends Edmund E. Day, Isaiah L. Sharfman, Stuart A. Rice, Alvin H. Hansen, Lauchlin B. Currie, Lionel D. Edie, James S. Hatchcock, Walton Hamilton, Oscar C. Stine, Isador Lubin, Howard Piquet, Donald Riley, and William Carson for consideration. See American Economic Association Records, Box 59, "Correspondence: Committees, AEA, and Miscellaneous Business, 1940–1945 (1959) James Washington Bell, Secretary-Treasurer," David M. Rubenstein Rare Book & Manuscript Library, Duke University.

2. See A. W. Coats, "The American Economic Association and the Economics Profession," *Journal of Economic Literature* 23, no. 4 (1985): 1708; Beatrice Cherrier,

"Classifying Economics: A History of the *JEL* Codes," *Journal of Economic Literature* 55, no. 2 (2017): 548.

3. For a discussion of the early debates see Michael A. Bernstein, *A Perilous Progress: Economists and Public Purpose in Twentieth-Century America* (Princeton, NJ: Princeton University Press, 2001), 16–20.

4. Coats, "The American Economic Association," 1708.

5. Cherrier, "Classifying Economics," 548.

6. See A. W. Coats, *The Sociology and Professionalization of Economics: British and American Economic Essays*, vol. 2 (London: Routledge, 1993), 444.

7. Bernstein, *A Perilous Progress*, 36.

8. The joint session with the American Statistical Association (ASA) was chaired by John Koren, president of the ASA, and included Walter F. Wilcox, Edward Dana Durand, Royal Meeker, Wesley C. Mitchell, Walter S. Gifford, Harvey S. Chase, Roger W. Babson, and John Cummings. Discussants were Joseph A. Hill and N. I. Stone. See American Economic Association, "Program of the Twenty-Seventh Annual Meeting," *American Economic Review* 5, no. 1 (1915): 1–2.

9. Letter from John R. Commons, president of the AEA, in response to Henry W. Farnam, April 17, 1917. See American Economic Association Records, Box 64–69, "Correspondence of Davis R. Dewey with editors and authors of articles and communications, 1910–1917," David M. Rubenstein Rare Book & Manuscript Library, Duke University.

10. See letter from Allyn A. Young to membership dated May 23, 1917. See American Economic Association Records, Box 64–69, "Correspondence of Davis R. Dewey."

11. See American Economic Association, "Report of the Secretary for the Year Ending December 18, 1917," *American Economic Review* 8, no. 1 (1918): 300.

12. Bernstein, *A Perilous Progress*, 36–37.

13. There was only one actively contested election for the presidency under the old regime. See Coats, *The Sociology and Professionalization of Economics*, 467.

14. See Coats, *The Sociology and Professionalization of Economics*, 444.

15. The process of coordinating the human resources needs of a country at war resulted in the National Roster of Scientific and Specialized Personnel. At the conclusion of the effort, Bell put it this way, "The resources of the United States Government were employed to round up the brains of the country for the National Roster of Scientific and Specialized Personnel." He observed that "they got most of the social scientists on their list, and perhaps many who really should not be classified as professional economists were also included." See letter from James Washington Bell to Claude E. Hawley, Division of Higher Education, Federal Security Agency, dated June 26, 1950, in the American Economic Association Records, Box 60–61, "Correspondence: Committees, AEA, and Miscellaneous Business, 1946–1950, James Washington Bell, Secretary-Treasurer," David M. Rubenstein Rare Book & Manuscript Library, Duke University.

16. One of the early revisions that Brigham made was to remove the reference to the "economic history of this and that." Of course, economic history was a field where

women were more likely to be found. See letter from Brigham to Bell, dated October 10, 1940, in the American Economic Association Records, Box 59, "Correspondence: Committees, AEA, and Miscellaneous Business."

17. National Roster of Scientific and Specialized Personnel, *Report of the National Roster of Scientific and Specialized Personnel to the National Resources Planning Board* (Washington, DC: U.S. Government Printing Office, 1942).

18. National Roster of Scientific and Specialized Personnel, *Report of the National Roster*, Appendix D, 47.

19. Although we don't know the reasons for the different response rates between men and women, in noting the lower response rate from the previous survey from 1942, Bell expressed his belief that "a number of our newer members and nonprofessional economists apparently feel that they have nothing significant to contribute; hence did not answer our inquiry." See American Economic Association, "Foreword," *American Economic Review* 39, no. 1 (1949), iii.

20. See the preamble to the statement. American Economic Association, "Exhibit IV: The Profession of Economist," *American Economic Review* 39, no. 1 (1949): 341.

21. American Economic Association, "The Profession of Economist," 341.

22. American Economic Association, "The Profession of Economist," 342.

23. American Economic Association, "The Profession of Economist," 342–43.

24. The AEA archives contain numerous documents with correspondence about the coordination of efforts during World War II and the immediate postwar period. In these documents approximately forty members' names were individually mentioned—none of whom were women. One document contained a list of past officers, editorial board member, and nominating committee members since 1935, names of people who were to be provided a questionnaire on "The Function of Government in the Postwar American Economy." One woman is mentioned on this list: Mabel Newcomer. As her biography makes clear, Newcomer was a professional economist. See Vassar Historian, "Mabel Newcomer," *Vassar Encyclopedia*, http://vcencyclopedia.vassar.edu/faculty/prominent-faculty/mabel-newcomer.html (accessed November 20, 2020).

25. Cynthia F. Epstein, "Encountering the Male Establishment: Sex-Status Limits on Women's Careers in the Professions," *American Journal of Sociology* 75, no. 6 (1970): 974.

26. See Robert W. Dimand, Geoffrey Black and Evelyn L. Forget, "Women's Participation in the ASSA meetings," *Oeconomia: History/ Methodology/ Philosophy* 1, no. 1 (2011): 9.

27. See Claire H. Hammond, "American Women and the Professionalization of Economics," *Review of Social Economy* 51, no. 3 (1993): 367.

28. See Bernstein, *A Perilous Progress,* 26.

29. See the tribute to Phyllis A. Wallace in Institute for Work and Employment Research, Tribute to Phyllis A. Wallace, MIT, https://iwer.mit.edu/about/iwer-pioneers/phyllis-a-wallace/ (accessed July 20, 2021).

30.   Francine Blau and Marianne Ferber, "Women's Earnings and Occupations," in *Women and Work: Industrial Relations Association Research Volume*, ed. Karen Koziara, Michael Moskow, and Lucretia D. Tanner (Washington, DC: Bureau of National Affairs, 1987), 51.

EPILOGUE

1.   The original resolution stated: "Resolved that the American Economic Association declares that economics is not a man's field." However, in the final version "not exclusively" was slipped in prior to the vote. For a full discussion, see Cleo Chassonery-Zkaigouche, Beatrice Cherrier, and John D. Singleton, "Economics is Not a Man's Field: CSWEP and the First Gender Reckoning in Economics (1971–1991)," *AEA/ASSA Conference* 2020, https://www.aeaweb.org/conference/2020/preliminary/1872.

2.   American Economic Association, "Minutes of the Annual Meeting, December 28, 1971, New Orleans, Louisiana," *American Economic Review* 62, no. 2 (1972): 470–74.

3.   The first CSWEP survey was sent to over 2,000 institutions in the United States. See American Economic Association, "Report of the Committee on the Status of Women in the Economics Profession," *American Economic Review* 63, no. 2 (1973): 508–11.

4.   American Economic Association, "Report of the Committee on the Status of Women," 510.

5.   See Hilary Herbold, "Never a Level Playing Field: Blacks and the GI Bill," *Journal of Blacks in Higher Education*, no. 6 (Winter 1994–95): 107, and Margaret Rossiter, *Women Scientists in America: Before Affirmative Action, 1940–1972* (Baltimore, MD: Johns Hopkins University Press, 1995), 31 and 34.

6.   History of Women Faculty in Economics, University of California–Berkeley. See https://www.econ.berkeley.edu/women-history (accessed July 19, 2021).

7.   See Evelyn L. Forget, "American Women and the Economics Profession in the Twentieth Century," *Oeconomia: History, Methodology, Philosophy* 1, no. 1 (2011): 25.

8.   Evelyn L. Forget, "American Women and the Economics Profession," 25.

9.   The names of people serving on the editorial board of the *AER* are found in the "Volume Matter," "Volume Information," and "Front Matter" of various issues of the *AER* from 1945 through 1970.

10.   See Sarah Thébaud and Maria Charles, "Segregation, Stereotypes, and STEM," *Social Sciences* 7, no. 111 (2018): 1–18.

11.   For differences in views between men and women that could influence research, see Ann Mari May, Mary G. McGarvey, and Robert Whaples, "Are Disagreements Among Male and Female Economists Marginal at Best?: A Survey of AEA Members and Their Views on Economics and Economic Policy," *Contemporary Economic Policy* 32, no. 1 (2014): 111–32, and Ann Mari May, Mary G. McGarvey, and David Kucera,

"Gender and European Economic Policy: A Survey of the Views of European Economists on Contemporary Economic Policy," *Kyklos* 71, no. 1 (2018): 162–83.

12.   Amanda Bayer and Cecilia Elena Rouse, "Diversity in the Economics Profession: A New Attack on an Old Problem," *Journal of Economic Perspectives* 30, no. 4 (2016): 221 and 223.

13.   The AEA Policy on Harassment and Discrimination is found at https://www.aeaweb .org/about-aea/aea-policy-harassment-discrimination. Information about the AEA ombudsperson is found at https://www.aeaweb.org/about-aea/aea-ombudsperson. All websites accessed March 30, 2021.

14.   See John M. McDowell, Larry D. Singell Jr., and James P. Ziliak, "Gender and Promotion in the Economics Profession," *IL Review* 54, no. 2 (2001): 24–244; Donna K. Ginther and Shulamit Kahn, "Women in Academic Economics: Have We Made Progress?," *AEA Papers and Proceedings* 111 (2021): 138–42; Shelly Lundberg and Jenna Stearns, "Women in Economics: Stalled Progress," *Journal of Economic Perspectives* 33, no. 1 (2019): 3–22.

15.   Tommaso Colussi, "Social Ties in Academia: A Friend Is a Treasure," *Review of Economics and Statistics* 100, no. 1 (2018): 45–50.

16.   Heather Sarsons, "Recognition for Group Work: Gender Differences in Academia," *American Economic Review* 107, no. 5 (2017): 141–45.

17.   See Karen E. Dynan and Cecilia Elena Rouse, "The Underrepresentation of Women in Economics: A Study of Undergraduate Economics Students," *Journal of Economic Education* 28, no. 4 (1997): 350–68, and Patrick J. McEwan, Sheridan Rogers, and Akila Weerapana, "Grade Sensitivity and the Economics Major at a Women's College," *AEA Papers and Proceedings* 111 (May 2021): 102–6.

18.   Gauri Kartini Shastry, Olga Shurchkov, and Lingjun Lotus Xia, "Luck or Skill: How Women and Men React to Noisy Feedback," *Journal of Behavioral and Experimental Economics* 88 (2020): 101592.

19.   Tatyana Avilova and Claudia Goldin, "What Can UWE Do for Economics?," *AEA Papers and Proceedings* 108 (2018): 186–90.

20.   Lillian MacNell, Adam Driscoll, and Andrea N. Hunt," What's in a Name: Exposing Gender Bias in Student Ratings of Teaching," *Innovative Higher Education* 40 (2015): 291–303.

BIBLIOGRAPHY

Aarim-Heriot, Najai. *Chinese Immigrants, African Americans, and Racial Anxiety in the United States, 1848–82.* Urbana: University of Illinois Press, 2006.

Abbott, Andrew. *The System of Professions: An Essay on the Division of Expert Labor.* Chicago: University of Chicago Press, 1988.

Akee, Randall. "The Race Problem in Economics." *Brookings,* January 22, 2020. https:// www.brookings.edu/blog/up-front/2020/01/22/the-race-problem-in-economics/.

Albisetti, James C. *Schooling German Girls and Women.* Princeton, NJ: Princeton University Press, 1988.

Alexander, Sadie Tanner Mossell (interviewee). "Sadie Tanner Mossell Alexander Oral History." Interview by Walter M. Phillips, October 20, 1976, Special Collections Oral Histories Repository, Temple University Libraries.

——. "Sadie Tanner Mossell Alexander Oral History." Interview by Walter M. Phillips, October 12, 1977, Special Collections Oral Histories Repository, Temple University Libraries.

American Economic Association. "The AEA Code of Professional Conduct." Adopted April 20, 2018. https://www.aeaweb.org/about-aea/code-of-conduct.

——. "AEA Ombudsperson." https://www.aeaweb.org/about-aea/aea-ombudsperson (accessed November 20, 2021).

——. "The AEA Policy on Harassment and Discrimination." https://www.aeaweb.org/about -aea/aea-policy-harassment-discrimination (accessed November 20, 2021).

——. "AEA Professional Climate Survey: Final Report." AEA, September 15, 2019. https:// www.aeaweb.org/resources/member-docs/final-climate-survey-results-sept-2019.

——. "American Economic Association." *Publications of the American Economic Association* 3, no. 1 (1902): 5–41.

——. "American Economic Association." *Publications of the American Economic Association* 5, no. 1 (1904): 1–37.

——. "Business Meetings at Washington D.C: December 27–30, 1911." *American Economic Review* 2, no. 1 (1912): 131–46.

——. "Exhibit II: List of Chairmen or Heads of Departments of Economics, Deans of Schools of Business, and Directors of Business Research Bureaus and Institutions in Selected Colleges and Universities." *American Economic Review* 39, no. 1 (1949): 333–36.

——. "Constitution By-Laws and Resolutions of the American Economic Association." *Publications of the American Economic Association* 1, no. 1 (1886): 35–46.

——. "Constitution, By-Laws, and Resolutions of the American Economic Association with List of Officers and Members." *Publications of the American Economic Association* 4, July Supplement (1889): 1–28.

——. "Exhibit IV: The Profession of Economist." *American Economic Review* 39, no. 1 (1949): 341–43.

——. "Foreword." *American Economic Review* 39, no. 1 (1949): iii.

——. "The Fourteenth Annual Meeting." *Publications of the American Economic Association* 3, no. 1 (1902): 42–58.

——. "Minutes of the Annual Meeting, December 28, 1971, New Orleans, Louisiana." *American Economic Review* 62, no. 2 (1972): 470–474.

——. "Proceedings of the Second Annual Meeting of the American Economic Association, Boston and Cambridge. May 21–25, 1887." *Publications of the American Economic Association* 3, no. 3 (1888): 43–86.

——. "Program of the Twenty-Seventh Annual Meeting." *American Economic Review* 5, no. 1 (1915): 1–2.

——. "Report of the Auditing Committee." *American Economic Review* 10, no. 1 (1920): 236–37.

——. "Report of the Auditing Committee." *American Economic Review* 11, no. 1 (1921): 188–89.

——. "Report of the Auditing Committee." *American Economic Review* 20, no. 1 (1930): 188–92.

——. "Report of the Committee on the Status of Women in the Economics Profession." *American Economic Review* 63, no. 2 (1973): 508–511.

——. "Report of the Finance Committee." *American Economic Review* 20, no. 1 (1930): 192–93.

——. "Report of the Membership Committee." *American Economic Review* 13, no. 1 (1923): 256.

——. "Report of the Secretary for the Year Ending December 15, 1913." *American Economic Review, Supplement* 4, no. 1 (1914): 201–3.

——. "Report of the Secretary for the Year Ending December 18, 1917." *American Economic Review* 8, no. 1 (1918): 300–301.

——. "Report of the Secretary for the Year Ending December 18, 1918." *American Economic Review* 9, no. 1 (1919): 354–58.

——. "Report of the Secretary for the Year Ending December 29, 1919." *American Economic Review* 10, no. 1 (1920): 230–34.

——. "Report of the Secretary for the Year Ending December 15, 1930." *American Economic Review* 21, no. 1 (1931): 271–75.

——. "Report of the Secretary for the Year Ending December 12, 1931." *American Economic Review* 22, no. 1 (1932): 279–82.

——. "Report of the Special Committee on Finance of the American Economic Association." *American Economic Review* 13, no. 1 (1923): 255–56.

——. "Report of the Treasurer." *Publications of the American Economic Association* 6, no. 1/2 (1891): 182–83.

——. "The Seventh Annual Meeting." *Publications of the American Economic Association* 10, no. 3 (1895): 39–50.

——. "The Sixth Annual Meeting." *Publications of the American Economic Association* 9, no. 1 (1894): 41–46.

——. "The Thirteenth Annual Meeting." *Publications of the American Economic Association* 2, no. 1 (1901): 43–54.

——. "The Twenty-Second Annual Meeting." *American Economic Association Quarterly* 11, no. 2 (1910): 49–79.

American Economic Association Records. Box 1, "AEA Histories, A. W. Coats, 1952–1963; Journal of Economic Literature, Mark Perlman, editor. Correspondence, [1968] 1970–1980." David M. Rubenstein Rare Book & Manuscript Library, Duke University.

——. Box 2, "Organization, [1885]; Minutes, 1886–1908; Membership 1890–1896; Accounts, 1889–1894; Annual Meetings, 1886–1905." David M. Rubenstein Rare Book & Manuscript Library, Duke University.

——. Box 3, "Annual Meetings, 1908–1924," David M Rubenstein Rare Book & Manuscript Library, Duke University.

——. Box 4, "Correspondence. Incoming, 1888 March–1896 February." David M. Rubenstein Rare Book & Manuscript Library, Duke University.

——. Box 12, "Correspondence of 1910–1911; Thomas N. Carver, Secretary-Treasurer." David M. Rubenstein Rare Book & Manuscript Library, Duke University.

——. Box 14, "Correspondence, including reports, 1914–1915. Allyn A. Young, Secretary-Treasurer." David M. Rubenstein Rare Book & Manuscript Library, Duke University.

——. Box 16, "Correspondence 1918–1919. Allyn A. Young, Secretary-Treasurer." David M. Rubenstein Rare Book & Manuscript Library, Duke University.

——. Box 59, "Correspondence: Committees, AEA, and Miscellaneous Business, 1940–1945 (1959) James Washington Bell, Secretary-Treasurer." David M. Rubenstein Rare Book & Manuscript Library, Duke University.

——. Box 60–61, "Correspondence: Committees, AEA, and Miscellaneous Business, 1946–1950 (1956), James Washington Bell, Secretary-Treasurer." David M. Rubenstein Rare Book & Manuscript Library, Duke University.

——. Box 62, "Correspondence of AEA re founding journal and special editorial correspondence, AER, 1910–1940, Davis R. Dewey, Managing Editor." David M. Rubenstein Rare Book & Manuscript Library, Duke University.

——. Box 64–69, "Correspondence of David R. Dewey with editors and authors of articles and communications, 1910–1917." David M. Rubenstein Rare Book & Manuscript Library, Duke University.

——. Box 70–71, "Correspondence of Davis R. Dewey with editors and authors of articles and communications, 1918–1919." David M. Rubenstein Rare Book & Manuscript Library, Duke University.

Attaway, Doris E., and Marjorie R. Barritt, eds. *Women's Voices: Early Years at the University of Michigan.* Ann Arbor, MI: Bentley Historical Library, 2000.

Avilova, Tatyana, and Claudia Goldin. "What Can UWE Do for Economics?" *AEA Papers and Proceedings* 108 (2018): 186–90.

Barker, Richard. "The Big Idea: No, Management Is Not a Profession." *Harvard Business Review* (July–August 2010): 52–60.

Bartlett, Robin L. "Katharine Coman." In *A Biographical Dictionary of Women Economists,* ed. Robert W. Dimand, Mary Ann Dimand, and Evelyn L. Forget, 115–17. Cheltenham, UK: Edward Elgar, 2000.

Bateman, Bradley W., and Ethan B. Kapstein. "Between God and the Market: The Religious Roots of the American Economic Association." *Journal of Economic Perspectives* 13, no. 4 (1999): 249–58.

Bayer, Amanda, and Cecilia Elena Rouse. "Diversity in the Economics Profession: A New Attack on an Old Problem." *Journal of Economic Perspectives* 30, no. 4 (2016): 221–42.

BBC News. "Cambridge University Anti-Women Students 'Confetti and Rockets' Digitized." BBC News, August 11, 2018. https://www.bbc.com/news/uk-england-cambridgeshire-45096690.

Becker, Gary S. *The Economics of Discrimination.* Chicago: University of Chicago Press, 1957.

——. *A Treatise on the Family.* Cambridge, MA: Harvard University Press, 1981.

Bell, Carolyn Shaw. "Report of the Committee on the Status of Women in the Economics Profession." *American Economic Review* 63, no. 2 (1973): 508–11.

Bernard, Jessie. *Academic Women.* University Park: Pennsylvania University Press, 1964.

Bernstein, Michael A. *A Perilous Progress: Economists and Public Purpose in Twentieth-Century America.* Princeton, NJ: Princeton University Press, 2001.

Blau, Francine, and Marianne Ferber. "Women's Earnings and Occupations." In *Women and Work: Industrial Relations Association Research Volume,* ed. Karen Koziara, Michael Moskow and Lucretia D. Tanner, 37–68. Washington, DC: Bureau of National Affairs, 1987.

Blau, Francine D., Marianne A. Ferber, and Anne E. Winkler. *The Economics of Women, Men, and Work.* Upper Saddle River, NJ: Pearson Prentice Hall, 2006.

Board of Regents, University of Wisconsin. *Annual Report for the Year Ending September 30, 1877.* Madison: University of Wisconsin Press, 1877.

Bordin, Ruth. *Women at Michigan: The "Dangerous Experiment," 1870s to the Present.* Ann Arbor: University of Michigan Press, 1999.

Boschini, Anne, and Anna Sjögren. "Is Team Formation Gender Neutral? Evidence from Coauthorship Patterns." *Journal of Labor Economics* 25, no. 2 (2007): 325–65.

Brady, Dorothy Stahl. *On the Solution of Homogeneous Linear Integral Equations*. PhD thesis. University of California, 1933.

Casselman, Ben, and Jim Tankersley. "Female Economists Push Their Field Toward a #MeToo Reckoning." *New York Times*, January 10, 2019.

Casselman, Ben, and Jim Tankersley. "Economics, Dominated by White Men, Is Roiled by Black Lives Matter." *New York Times*, June 10, 2020.

Casselman, Ben, Jim Tankersley, and Jeanna Smialek. "A Year After a #MeToo Reckoning, Economists Still Grapple With It." *New York Times*, January 7, 2020.

Ceplair, Larry. *Charlotte Perkins Gilman: A Nonfiction Reader*. New York: Columbia University Press, 1991.

Chassonnery-Zaigouche, Cleo, Beatrice Cherrier, and John D. Singleton. "Economics Is Not a Man's Field: CSWEP and the First Gender Reckoning in Economics (1971–1991)." AEA/ASSA Conference 2020. https://www.aeaweb.org/conference/2020/preliminary /1872.

Cherrier, Beatrice. "Classifying Economics: A History of the *JEL* Codes." *Journal of Economic Literature* 55, no. 2 (2017): 545–79.

Church, Robert L. "Economists as Experts: The Rise of an Academic Profession in the United States, 1870–1920." In *The University in Society*, vol. 2, ed. Lawrence Stone, 571–610. Princeton, NJ: Princeton University Press, 1974.

Clarke, Edward H. *Sex in Education, or, A Fair Chance for the Girls*. Boston: James R. Osgood, 1873.

Clarke, Kim. "Madelon's World." *Heritage Project*. University of Michigan. https://heritage .umich.edu/stories/madelons-world/ (accessed October 16, 2020).

Coats, A. W. "The American Economic Association and the Economics Profession." *Journal of Economic Literature* 23, no. 4 (1985): 1697–727.

——. "The American Economic Association's Publications: An Historical Perspective." *Journal of Economic Literature* 7, no. 1 (1969): 57–68.

——. "The First Two Decades of the American Economic Association." *American Economic Review* 50, no. 4 (1960): 556–74.

——. "Henry Carter Adams: A Case Study in the Emergence of the Social Sciences in the United States, 1850–1900." *Journal of American Studies* 2, no. 2 (1968): 177–97.

——. *The Sociology and Professionalization of Economics: British and American Economic Essays*. Vol. 2. London: Routledge, 1993.

Coghlan, Catherine L. "Please Don't Think of Me as a Sociologist: Sophonisba Preston Breckinridge and the Early Chicago School." *American Sociologist* 36, no. 1 (2005): 3–22.

Colander, David, and Joanna Wayland Woos. "Institutional Demand-Side Discrimination Against Women and the Human Capital Model." *Feminist Economics* 3, no. 1 (1997): 53–64.

Collier, Irwin. "Economics in the Rear-View Mirror: Archival Artifacts from the History of Economics." *Irwin Collier*, 2017. http://www.irwincollier.com/harvard-nine-radcliffe -graduate-students-petition-to-attend-economics-seminary-1926/.

Colussi, Tommaso. "Social Ties in Academia: A Friend Is a Treasure." *Review of Economics and Statistics* 100, no. 1 (2018), 45–50.

Comstock, Ada. "The Fourth R for Women." *Century Magazine* 117 (1929): 413.

Cornford, Daniel, ed. *Working People of California*. Berkeley: University of California Press, 1995.

Crane, Diana. "The Gatekeeper's of Science: Some Factors Affecting the Selection of Articles for Scientific Journals." *American Sociologist* 2, no. 4 (1967): 195–201.

Crees, Richard F. *CBA: The First 75 Years*. Self-published, 1994.

Cross, Ira B. "Co-operation in California." *American Economic Review* 1, no. 3 (1911): 535–44.

———. *A History of the Labor Movement in California*. Berkeley: University of California Press, 1935.

———. "Review of A History of California Labor Legislation by Lucile Eaves." American Economic Review 1, no. 1 (1911): 106–9.

———. "Workmen's Compensation in California." *American Economic Review* 4, no. 2 (1914): 454–60.

Cross, Ira B. (interviewee). "Portrait of an Economics Professor." Oral History Transcript. Regional Oral History Office. Bancroft Library, University of California, Berkeley, 1967.

Deegan, Mary Jo. *Women in Sociology: A Bio-Bibliographical Sourcebook*. New York: Greenwood Press, 1991.

Department of Economics, Stanford University. "Our Mission." https://economics.stanford .edu/about/our-mission (accessed November 20, 2021).

Department of Economics, University of Arizona. "Economics Faculty," Arizona Board of Regents, University of Arizona. https://archive.catalog.arizona.edu/faculty/984/econ .html (accessed November 9, 2020).

Dewey, Davis R. "History of California Labor Legislation." *American Economic Review* 2, no. 1 (1912): 115.

Dimand, Robert W. "The Neglect of Women's Contributions to Economics." In *Women of Value: Feminist Essays on the History of Women in Economics*, ed. Mary Ann Dimand, Robert W. Dimand, and Evelyn L. Forget, 1–24. Aldershot, UK: Edward Elgar, 1995.

———. "Women Economists in the 1890s: Journals, Books and the Old Palgrave." *Journal of the History of Economic Thought* 21, no. 3 (1999): 269–88.

Dimand, Robert W., and Geoffrey Black. "Clare de Graffenreid and the Art of Controversy: A Prizewinning Woman Economist in the First Decade of the American Economic Association." *Journal of the History of Economic Thought* 34, no. 3 (2012): 339–53.

Dimand, Robert W., Geoffrey Black, and Evelyn L. Forget. "Women's Participation in the ASSA Meetings." *Oeconomia: History/Methodology/Philosophy* 1, no. 1 (2011): 33–49.

Donnan, Elizabeth. "Reviewed Work(s): A Legacy of Wage-Earning Women: A Survey of Gainfully Employed Women of Brattleboro, Vermont and of Relief Which They have Received form the Thomas Thompson Trust by Lucile Eaves." *American Economic Review* 16, no. 2 (1926): 331–32.

Dulles, Eleanor Lansing. *Eleanor Lansing Dulles, Chances of a Lifetime: A Memoir*. Englewood Cliffs, NJ: Prentice Hall, 1980.

Dynan, Karen E., and Cecilia Elena Rouse. "The Underrepresentation of Women in Economics: A Study of Undergraduate Economics Students." *Journal of Economic Education* 28, no. 4 (1997): 350–68.

Dzuback, Mary Ann. "Gender, Professional Knowledge, and Institutional Power: Women Social Scientists and the Research University." In *The Woman Question' and Higher Education: Perspectives on Gender and Knowledge Production in America*, ed. Ann Mari May, 52–73. Cheltenham, UK: Edward Elgar, 2008.

——. "Women Economists in the Academy: Struggles and Strategies, 1900–1940." In *The Routledge Handbook of the History of Women's Economic Thought*, ed. Kirsten Madden and Robert W. Dimand, 211–28. London: Routledge, 2019.

Eaves, Lucile. "A Communication." *American Economic Review* 1, no. 3 (1911): 587–89.

——. "My Sociological Life History—1928," ed. Michael R. Hill. *Sociological Origins* 2, no. 2 (2000): 65–70. http://www.sociological-origins.com/files/1928-2000_Eaves_-_My_Sociological_Life_History.pdf.

——. "Social Politics in California." *American Economic Review* 4, no. 2 (1914): 450–54.

The Economist. "Barriers to Entry." May 10, 2018.

——. "A Dispiriting Survey of Women's Lot in University Economics." March 23, 2019.

——. "Economics Is Uncovering Its Gender Problem." March 21, 2019.

Eells, Walter Crosby. "Earned Doctorates for Women in the Nineteenth Century." *AAUP Bulletin* 42, no. 4 (1956): 644–51.

Eisenmann, Linda. "Women, Higher Education, and Professionalization." *Harvard Educational Review* (Winter 1996).

Eliot, Charles. "Remarks of President Eliot of Harvard College before the Trustees of the Johns Hopkins University." In binder labeled "Johns Hopkins University 1874," 50–53. Special Collections Holdings, Ferdinand Hamburger Jr. Archives, Johns Hopkins University, 1874.

Elliott, Diana B., Kristy Krivickas, Matthew W. Brault, and Rose M. Kreider. "Historical Marriage Trends from 1890–2010: A Focus on Race Differences." Census Working Paper Number SEHSD-WP2012-12, U.S. Census Bureau (2012). https://www.census.gov/library/working-papers/2012/demo/SEHSD-WP2012-12.html.

Ely, Richard T. "The American Economic Association 1885–1909." *American Economic Association Quarterly* 11, no. 1 (1910): 47–111.

——. "Constitution By-Laws and Resolutions of the American Economic Association." *Publications of the American Economic Association* 1, no. 1 (1886): 35–46.

——. "Proceedings of the Second Annual Meeting of the American Economic Association, Boston and Cambridge. May 21–25, 1887." *Publications of the American Economic Association* 3, no. 3 (1888): 43–86.

England, Minnie Throop. *Church Government and Church Control*. PhD thesis. University of Nebraska, 1906.

Epstein, Cynthia F. "Encountering the Male Establishment: Sex-Status Limits on Women's Careers in the Professions." *American Journal of Sociology* 75, no. 6 (1970): 965–82.

Feagin, Joe R., and Clairece Booher Feagin. *Discrimination American Style: Institutional Racism and Sexism*. Upper Saddle River, NJ: Prentice Hall, 1978.

Feminist Majority Foundation. "Founding Feminists: September 25, 1932." https://feminist.org/news/founding-feminists-september-25-1932 (accessed November 16, 2020).

Ferber, Marianne, and Michelle Teiman. "Are Women Economists at a Disadvantage in Publishing Journal Articles?" *Eastern Economic Journal* 9, no. 3/4 (1980): 189–93.

Feyerabend, Paul. *Against Method: Outline of an Anarchistic Theory of Knowledge*. Atlantic Highlands, NJ: Humanities Press, 1975.

Fitzpatrick, Ellen. *Endless Crusade: Women Social Scientists and Progressive Reform*. Oxford: Oxford University Press, 1990.

——. "For the 'Women of the University,' Marion Talbot, 1858–1948." In *Lone Voyagers: Academic Women in Coeducational Institutions, 1870–1937*, ed. Geraldine Jonçich Clifford, 87–97. New York: Feminist Press, 1989.

Flexner, Abraham, "The Problem of College Pedagogy." *Atlantic Monthly* 103 (1909): 838–44.

Folbre, Nancy. *Greed, Lust, and Gender: A History of Economic Ideas*. Oxford: Oxford University Press, 2009.

Forget, Evelyn L. "American Women and the Economics Profession in the Twentieth Century." *Oeconomia: History, Methodology, Philosophy* 1, no. 1 (2011): 19–31.

Fourcade, Marion. *Economists and Societies: Discipline and Profession in the United States, Britain, and France, 1890s to 1990s*. Princeton, NJ: Princeton University Press, 2009.

Franklin, Jonathan S. *A History of Professional Economists and Policymaking in the United States: Irrelevant Genius*. New York: Routledge, 2016.

Freeman, Jo. "Women on the Social Science Faculties Since 1892." Paper delivered at the Political Science Association Conference, Winter 1969. https://eric.ed.gov/?q=%22male+chauvinism%22&id=ED041567.

Freidson, Eliot. *Profession of Medicine: A Study of the Sociology of Applied Knowledge*. Chicago: University of Chicago Press, 1988.

Furner, Mary O. *Advocacy and Objectivity: A Crisis in the Professionalization of American Social Science, 1865–1905*. Lexington: University of Kentucky Press, 1973.

Gilman, Charlotte Perkins. *The Living of Charlotte Perkins Gilman: An Autobiography*. New York: D. Appleton-Century, 1935.

——. *Women and Economics: A Study of the Economic Relation Between Men and Women as a Factor in Social Evolution*. Boston: Small, Maynard, 1898.

Gilman, Charlotte Perkins, and Francis H. McLean. "Child Labor in the United States: Discussion." *Publications of the American Economic Association* 3rd series, 8, no. 1 (1907): 260–67.

Ginther, Donna K., and Shulamit Kahn. "Academic Women's Careers in the Social Sciences: Progress, Pitfalls, and Plateaus." In *The Economics of Economists: Institutional Setting, Individual Incentives, and Future Prospects*, ed. Alessandro Lanteri and Jack Vromen, 285–315. Cambridge: Cambridge University Press, 2014.

——. "Women in Academic Economics: Have We Made Progress?" *AEA Papers and Proceedings* 111 (2021): 138–42.

——. "Women in Economics: Moving Up or Falling Off the Academic Career Ladder?" *Journal of Economic Perspectives* 18, no. 3 (2004): 193–214.

Goellnicht, Donald. "From Novitiate Culture to Market Economy: The Professionalization of Graduate Students." *English Studies in Canada* 19, no. 4 (1993): 471–84.

Goldin, Claudia. "The Meaning of College in the Lives of American Women: The Past One-Hundred Years." Working Paper No. 4099, National Bureau of Economic Research (1992).

———. *Understanding the Gender Gap: An Economic History of American Women*. Oxford: Oxford University Press, 1990.

Goldin, Claudia, and Lawrence F. Katz. "Putting the 'Co' in Education: Timing, Reasons, and Consequences of College Coeducation from 1835 to the Present." *Journal of Human Capital* 5, no. 4 (2011): 377–417.

Goldin, Claudia, Lawrence F. Katz, and Ilyana Kuziemko. "The Homecoming of American College Women: The Reversal of the College Gender Gap." *Journal of Economic Perspectives* 20, no. 4 (2006): 133–56.

Goodspeed, Thomas Wakefield. *A History of The University of Chicago: The First Quarter Century*. Chicago: University of Chicago Press, 1916.

Gordon, Lynn D. *Gender and Higher Education in the Progressive Era*. New Haven, CT: Yale University Press, 1990.

Graham, Patricia Albjerg. "Expansion and Exclusion: A History of Women in American Higher Education." *Signs* 3, no. 4 (1978): 759–73.

Hall, Vance M. D. "The Contribution of the Physiologist, William Benjamin Carpenter (1813–1885), to the Development of the Principles of the Correlation of Forces and the Conservation of Energy." *Medical History* 23, no. 2 (1979): 129–55.

Hammond, Claire H. "American Women and the Professionalization of Economics." *Review of Social Economy* 51, no. 3 (1993): 347–70.

Harding, Sandra. "Rethinking Standpoint Epistemology: What Is 'Strong Objectivity?'" In *Feminist Epistemologies*, edited by Linda Alcoff and Elizabeth Potter, 49–83. London: Routledge, 1993.

———. *The Science Question in Feminism*. Ithaca, NY: Cornell University Press, 1986.

———. *Whose Science? Whose Knowledge? Thinking from Women's Lives*. Ithaca, NY: Cornell University Press, 1991.

Harrison, David. "Female Economists, in Survey, Cite Gender Discrimination." *Wall Street Journal*, March 18, 2019.

Harvard University Archives. *Department of Economics, Correspondence and Papers (1902–1950)*. Box 25, Folder "Economics Seminary 1925–33."

Herbold, Hilary. "Never a Level Playing Field: Blacks and the GI Bill." *Journal of Blacks in Higher Education Winter*, no. 6 (Winter 1994–95): 104–8.

Hengel, Erin. "Publishing While Female: Are Women Held to Higher Standards? Evidence from Peer Review." Cambridge Working Papers in Economics 1753, University of Cambridge (2017).

Hill, Joseph A. *Women in Gainful Occupations, 1870 to 1920: A Study of the Trend of Recent Changes in the Numbers, Occupational Distribution, and Family Relationship of Women Reported in the Census as Following a Gainful Occupation*. Census Monograph 9. Washington, DC: U.S. Government Printing Office, 1929.

Hills, William H. *The Writer: A Monthly Magazine for Literary Workers*. Vol. 10. Boston: Writer Publishing Company, 1897.

Hofstadter, Richard. *Anti-Intellectualism in American Life.* New York: Vintage Books, 1963.

Hofstadter, Richard, and Walter P. Metzger. *The Development of Academic Freedom in the United States.* New York: Columbia University Press, 1955.

Hooks, Janet M. "Women's Occupations Through Seven Decade." *Women's Bureau Bulletin* 218 (1947).

Horowitz, Helen Lefkowitz. *Alma Mater: Design and Experience in the Women's Colleges from their Nineteenth-Century Beginnings to the 1930s.* Amherst, MA: University of Massachusetts Press, 1984.

——. *The Power and Passion of M. Carey Thomas.* Urbana: University of Illinois Press, 1999.

Hurlbert, Jeanne S., and Rachel A. Rosenfield. "Getting a Good Job: Rank and Institutional Prestige in Academic Psychologists' Careers." *Sociology of Education* 65, no. 3 (1992): 188–207.

Hutcheon, Linda. "Rhetoric and Competition: Academic Agonistics." *Common Knowledge* 9, no. 1 (2003): 42–49.

Institute for Work and Employment Research. "Phyllis A. Wallace: A Tribute." MIT. https://iwer.mit.edu/about/iwer-pioneers/phyllis-a-wallace/ (accessed July 20, 2021).

Johnson, Alvin S. "Book Reviews: *Value and Distribution* by Herbert Joseph Davenport." *Journal of Political Economy* 16, no. 6 (1908): 380–85.

Johnson, Elton L. "Misconceptions About the Early Land-Grant Colleges." *Journal of Higher Education* 52, no. 4 (1981): 333–51.

Johnson, Joan Marie. *Southern Women at the Seven Sister Colleges: Feminist Values and Social Activism 1875–1915.* Athens: University of Georgia Press, 2008.

Judd, M. Ann. "The Yale Economics Department: Memories and Musings of Past Leaders." 1999. https://web.archive.org/web/20000816052151/www.econ.yale.edu/depthistory.html.

Kaestle, Carl F., and Janice A. Radway. "Introduction." In *A History of the Book in America,* vol. 4, ed. Carl F. Kaestle and Janice A. Radway, 49–55. Chapel Hill: University of North Carolina Press, 2009.

Kahn, Shulamit B. "Women in the Economics Profession." *Journal of Economic Perspectives* 9, no. 4 (1995): 193–206.

Kanter, Rosabeth Moss. *Men and Women of the Corporation.* New York: Basic Books, 1977.

Kaufman, Debra Renee. "Association Ties in Academe: Some Male and Female Differences." *Sex Roles* 4, no. 1 (1978): 9–21.

Kazin, Michael. "The Great Exception Revisited: Organized Labor and Politics in San Francisco and Los Angeles, 1870–1940." *Pacific Historical Review* 55, no. 3 (1986): 371–402.

Kiddle, Henry, and Alexander J. Schem, eds. *The Yearbook of Education for 1878.* New York: E. Steiger, 1878.

Kingsbury, Susan Myra. *An Introduction to the Records of the Virginia Company of London.* Washington, DC: U.S. Government Printing Office, 1905.

Knowles, Jane. "Harvard's Invisible Faculty: Four Portraits." In *Yards and Gates: Gender in Harvard and Radcliffe History,* ed. Laurel Thatcher Ulrich, 187–94. New York: Palgrave Macmillan, 2004.

Konrad, Alison M., and Jeffrey Pfeffer. "Understanding the Hiring of Women and Minorities in Educational Institutions." *Sociology of Education* 64, no. 3 (1991): 141–57.

Kuhn, Thomas. *The Structure of Scientific Revolutions.* Chicago: University of Chicago Press, 1962.

Kulis, Stephen. "Gender Segregation Among College and University Employees." *Sociology of Education* 70, no. 2 (1997): 151–73.

Kyrk, Hazel. *Economic Problems of the Family.* New York: Harper & Brothers, 1933.

Langan, Andrew. "Female Managers and Gender Disparities: The Case of Academic Department Chairs." Working Papers. Princeton University. https://scholar.princeton .edu/alangan/publications/female-managers-and-gender-disparities-case-academic -department-chairs (accessed November 24, 2020).

Larson, Magali Sarfatti. *The Rise of Professionalism: Monopolies of Competence and Sheltered Markets.* New Jersey: Transaction Publishers, 2013.

Libby, Barbara. "Statistical Analysis of Women in the Economics Profession." *Essays in Economic and Business History* 5 (1987): 179–201.

——. "Women in Economics Before 1940." *Essays in Economic and Business History* 3 (1984): 273–90.

——. "Women in the Economics Profession 1900–1940: Factors in Declining Visibility." *Essays in Economic and Business History* 8 (1990): 121–30.

Long, Clarence D. *Wage and Earnings in the United States, 1860–1890.* Princeton, NJ: Princeton University Press, 1960.

Long, Heather. "Female Economists Report Widespread Discrimination and Sexual Assault, Prompting Calls for Major Change." *Washington Post,* March 18, 2019.

——. "'Please, Listen to Us': What It's Like Being Female at America's Biggest Economic Conference." *Washington Post,* January 18, 2019.

Long, J. Scott, Paul D. Allison, and Robert McGinnis. "Rank Advancement in Academic Careers: Sex Differences and the Effects of Productivity." *American Sociological Review* 58, no. 5 (1993): 703–22.

Longawa, Vicky M. "Episodes in the History of the Journal of Political Economy." *Journal of Political Economy* 100, no. 6 (1992): 1087–91.

Longino, Helen. *Science as Social Knowledge: Values and Objectivity in Scientific Inquiry.* Princeton, NJ: Princeton University Press, 1990.

Lowell, A. Lawrence. "The Profession of Business." *Harvard Business Review* (January 1923): 129–31.

Lundberg, Shelly. "Report: Committee on the Status of Women in the Economics Profession (CSWEP)." *AEA Papers and Proceedings* 108 (2018): 704–21.

Lundberg, Shelly, and Jenna Stearns. "Women in Economics: Stalled Progress." *Journal of Economic Perspectives* 33, no. 1 (2019): 3–22.

Maclay, Kathleen. "Berkeley Economist Leads Petition Drive to Fight Pervasive Misogyny." *Berkeley News,* October 31, 2017.

MacNell, Lillian, Adam Driscoll, and Andrea N. Hunt. "What's in a Name: Exposing Gender Bias in Student Ratings of Teaching." *Innovative Higher Education* 40 (2015): 291–303.

Madden, Kirsten K., Janet A. Seiz, and Michèle Pujol. *A Bibliography of Female Economic Thought up to 1940.* London: Routledge, 2004.

Malveaux, Julianne. "Tilting Against the Wind: Reflections on the life and work of Dr. Phyllis Ann Wallace." *American Economic Review* 84, no. 2 (1994): 93–97.

Mancini, Olivia. "Passing as White: Anita Hemmings 1897." *Vassar: The Alumni Quarterly* 98, no. 1 (2001). https://vq.vassar.edu/issues/2002/01/features/passing-as-white.html.

Martinez, Pila. "Retired Professor Leahmae McCoy; Broke Barriers at UA Economics Dept." *Arizona Daily Star*, January 1, 1999.

May, Ann Mari, and Robert W. Dimand. "Trouble in the Inaugural Issue of the American Economic Review: The Cross/Eaves Controversy." *Journal of Economic Perspectives* 23, no. 3 (2009): 189–204.

——. "Women in the Early Years of the American Economic Association: A Membership Beyond the Professoriate Per Se." *History of Political Economy* 51, no. 4 (2019): 671–702.

May, Ann Mari, Mary G. McGarvey, and David Kucera. "Gender and European Economic Policy: A Survey of the Views of European Economists on Contemporary Economic Policy." *Kyklos* 71, no. 1 (2018): 162–83.

May, Ann Mari, Mary G. McGarvey, and Robert Whaples. "Are Disagreements Among Male and Female Economists Marginal at Best?: A Survey of AEA Members and Their Views on Economics and Economic Policy." *Contemporary Economic Policy* 32, no. 1 (2014): 111–32.

Mazón, Patricia M. *Gender and the Modern Research University: The Admission of Women to German Higher Education, 1865–1914*. Palo Alto, CA: Stanford University Press, 2003.

McCullough, Rachel. "Interview with Anne Carter." Newsletter of the Committee on the Status of Women in the Economics Profession (CSWEP) (Spring 2009).

McDowell, John M., Larry D. Singell Jr., and James P. Ziliak. "Gender and Promotion in the Economics Profession." *IL Review* 54, no. 2 (2001): 224–44.

McDowell, John M., and Janet Kiholm Smith. "The Effect of Gender-Sorting on Propensity to Co-Author: Implications for Academic Promotion." *Economic Inquiry* 30, no. 1 (1992): 68–82.

McEwan, Patrick J., Sheridan Rogers, and Akila Weerapana. "Grade Sensitivity and the Economics Major at a Women's College." *AEA Papers and Proceedings* 111 (May 2021): 102–6.

McGuire, John Thomas. "'The Most Unjust Piece of Legislation': Section 213 of the Economy Act of 1932 and Feminism During the New Deal." *Journal of Policy History* 20, no. 4 (2008): 516–41.

McNeill, Leila. "The Statistician Who Debunked Sexist Myths about Skull Size and Intelligence." *Smithsonian Magazine*, January 14, 2019.

Mims, Edwin. *History of Vanderbilt University*. Nashville, TN: Vanderbilt University Press, 1946.

Mincer, Jacob. "Labor Force Participation of Married Women: A Study of Labor Supply." In *Aspects of Labor Economics*, ed. H. Gregg Lewis, 63–106. Princeton, NJ: Princeton University Press, 1962.

Nagowski, Matthew P. "Inopportunity of Gender: The G. I. Bill and the Higher Education of the American Female, 1939–1954." DigitalCommons@ILR, 2005. https://digitalcommons.ilr.cornell.edu/student/97.

National Center for Educational Statistics. *120 Years of American Education: A Statistical Portrait*. Ed. Thomas D. Snyder. Washington, DC: U.S. Department of Education, 1993.

National Roster of Scientific and Specialized Personnel. *Report of the National Roster of Scientific and Specialized Personnel to the National Resources Planning Board*. Washington, DC: U.S. Government Printing Office, 1942.

National Science Foundation, Division of Science Resources Statistics. *U.S. Doctorates in the 20th Century. NSF 06-319*. Lori Thurgood, Mary J. Golladay, and Susan T. Hill. Arlington, VA: NSF, 2006.

National Science Foundation, National Center for Science and Engineering Statistics. "Doctorate Recipients from U.S. Universities: 2018." Special Report NSF 20-301. NSF (2019). https://ncses.nsf.gov/pubs/nsf20301/.

Nebraska History Museum. "University of Nebraska, 1878." https://history.nebraska.gov /publications/university-nebraska-1878 (accessed July 15, 2020).

Nyswander, Rachel Fesler, and Janet M. Hooks. "Employment of Women in the Federal Government 1923–1939." *Bulletin of the Women's Bureau* 182 (1941).

Page, Scott E. *The Difference: How the Power of Diversity Creates Better Groups, Firms, Schools, and Societies*. Princeton, NJ: Princeton University Press, 2007.

Palmieri, Patricia Ann. *In Adamless Eden: The Community of Women Faculty at Wellesley*. New Haven, CT: Yale University Press, 1995.

Parrish, John B. "Rise of Economics as an Academic Discipline: The Formative Years to 1900." *Southern Economic Journal* 34, no. 1 (1967): 1–16.

Perkins, Linda M. "The History of Black Women Graduate Students, 1921–1948." In *The SAGE Handbook of African American Education*, ed. Linda C. Tillman, 52–65. Los Angeles: Sage, 2009.

——. "The Impact of the 'Cult of True Womanhood' on the Education of Black Women." Journal of Social Issues 39, no. 3 (1983): 17–28.

——. "The Racial Integration of the Seven Sister Colleges." *Journal of Blacks in Higher Education* 19 (Spring 1998): 104–8.

Peixotto, Jessica Blanche. *The French Revolution and Modern French Socialism*. New York: Thomas Y. Crowell, 1901.

Phillips, Katherine W., Sun Young Kim-Jun, and So-Hyeon Shim. "The Value of Diversity in Organizations: A Social Psychological Perspective." In *Social Psychology and Organizations*, ed. David De Cremer, Rolf van Dick, and J. Keith Murnighan, 253–72. London: Routledge, 2011.

Pidgeon, Mary Elizabeth. *Changes in Women's Occupations 1940–1950*. Women's Bureau Bulletin 253 (1954).

Pleck, Elizabeth. "The Unfulfilled Promise: Women and Academe." *Sociological Forum* 5, no. 3 (1990): 517–24.

Preston, Jo Anne. "Negotiating Work and Family: Aspirations of Early Radcliffe Graduates." In *Yards and Gates: Gender in Harvard and Radcliffe History*, ed. Laurel Thatcher Ulrich, 173–74. New York: Palgrave Macmillan, 2004.

Pujol, Michèle A. *Feminism and Anti-Feminism in Early Economic Thought*. Aldershot, UK: Edward Elgar, 1992.

Pusey, Grace. "Enid Cook, 1927–1931: Bryn Mawr's First Black Graduate." *Black at Bryn Mawr*, February 8, 2015. https://blackatbrynmawr.blogs.brynmawr.edu/2015/02/09/enid-cook-first-black-graduate/.

Radke-Moss, Andrea G. *Bright Epoch: Women and Coeducation in the American West.* Lincoln: University of Nebraska Press, 2008.

Regional Oral History Office. "Elizabeth, Paschel Pioneering Career Woman: New Deal Labor Economist, Social Security Administration Program Chief, Ford Foundation Executive." Bancroft Library, University of California, Berkeley. https://ohc-search.lib.berkeley.edu/catalog?sort=score+desc,+pub_date_sort+desc,+title_sort+asc&commit=Search&search_field=advanced&op=OR&interviewees=Elizabeth+paschal (accessed November 20, 2021).

Reid, Margaret G. *Economics of Household Production.* New York: Wiley, 1934.

Rennie, Drummond. "Editorial Peer Review: Its Development and Rationale." In *Peer Review in Health Sciences*, ed. Fiona Godlee and Tom Jefferson, 1–13. London: BJM Books, 1999.

Reskin, Barbara F. "Sex Differentiation and the Social Organization of Science." *Sociological Inquiry* 48, no. 3–4 (1978): 6–37.

Reskin, Barbara F., and Denise D. Bielby. "A Sociological Perspective on Gender and Career Outcomes." *Journal of Economic Perspectives* 19, no. 1 (2005): 71–86.

Robbins, Lionel. *An Essay on the Nature and Significance of Economic Science.* London: Macmillan, 1932.

Roebuck, Julian B., and Komanduri S. Murty. *Historically Black Colleges and Universities: Their Places in American Higher Education.* Westport, CT: Praeger, 1993.

Romer, Paul M. "Mathiness in the Theory of Economic Growth." *American Economic Review* 105, no. 5 (2015): 89–93.

Rose, Evan K. "The Rise and Fall of Female Labor Force Participation During WWII in the United States." *Journal of Economic History* 78, no. 3 (2018): 1–39.

Rosenberg, Rosalind. "The Limits of Access: The History of Coeducation in America." In *Women and Higher Education in American History*, ed. John M. Faragher and Florence Howe, 107–29. New York: Norton, 1988.

Rosenberg, Rosalind. *Changing the Subject: How Women of Columbia Shaped the Way We Think About Sex and Politics.* New York: Columbia University Press, 2004.

Ross, Dorothy. *The Origins of American Social Science.* Cambridge: Cambridge University Press, 1991.

Rossiter, Margaret W. "Doctorates for American Women, 1868–1907." *History of Education Quarterly* 22, no. 2 (1982): 159–83.

Rossiter, Margaret W. *Women Scientists in America: Before Affirmative Action, 1940–1972.* Baltimore, MD: Johns Hopkins University Press, 1995.

——. *Women Scientists in America: Struggles and Strategies to 1940.* Baltimore, MD: Johns Hopkins University Press, 1982.

Rothstein, Donna S. "Do Female Faculty Influence Female Students' Educational and Labor Market Attainments?" *IL Review* 48, no. 3 (1995): 515–30.

Rudman, Laurie A., Corinne A. Moss-Racusin, Julie E. Phelan, and Sanne Nauts. "Status Incongruity and Backlash Effects: Defending the Gender Hierarchy Motivates Prejudice Against Female Leaders." *Journal of Experimental Social Psychology* 48, no. 1 (2012): 165–79.

Rudolph, Frederick. *The American College and University: A History.* New York: Knopf, 1962.

Saint Paul Daily Globe. "The Woman's Conference." March 9, 1889, 7.

Sandilands, Roger. "New Evidence on Allyn Young's Style and Influence as a Teacher." *Journal of Economic Studies* 26, no. 6 (1999): 453–79.

Sarsons, Heather. "Recognition for Group Work: Gender Differences in Academia." *American Economic Review* 107, no. 5 (2017): 141–45.

Saxton, Alexander. *The Indispensable Enemy: Labor and the Anti-Chinese Movement in California.* Berkeley: University of California Press, 1971.

Scharf, Lois. *To Work and to Wed: Female Employment, Feminism, and the Great Depression.* Westport, CT: Greenwood Press, 1980.

Schiebinger, Londa. *Has Feminism Changed Science?* Cambridge, MA: Harvard University Press, 1999.

——. "Skeletons in the Closet: The First Illustrations of the Female Skeleton in Eighteenth-Century Anatomy." *Representations* 14 (Spring 1986): 42–82.

Schwartz, Robert A. "How Deans of Women Became Men." *Review of Higher Education* 20, no. 4 (1997): 419–36.

Scott, Anne Firor. "The Ever Widening Circle: The Diffusion of Feminist Values from the Troy Female Seminary, 1822–1872." *History of Education Quarterly* 19, no. 1 (1979): 3–25.

Shastry, Gauri Kartini, Olga Shurchkov, and Lingjun Lotus Xia. "Luck or Skill: How Women and Men React to Noisy Feedback." *Journal of Behavioral and Experimental Economics* 88 (2020): 101592.

Silverberg, Helene. *Gender and American Social Science: The Formative Years.* Princeton, NJ: Princeton University Press, 1998.

Sinclair, Andrew. *The Better Half: The Emancipation of the American Woman.* New York: Harper and Row, 1965.

——. *The Emancipation of American Women.* New York: Harper & Row, 1966.

Slater, Robert Bruce. "The First Black Graduates of the Nation's 50 Flagship State Universities." *Journal of Blacks in Higher Education* 13 (Autumn 1996): 72–85.

Smart, John C. "Gender Equity in Academic Rank and Salary." *Review of Higher Education* 14, no. 4 (1991): 511–26.

Smith College Archives. "Smith College Ivy Day 1895." Smith College. https://www.smith.edu/libraries/libs/archives/gallery/images/womenseducation/sc_ivy.JP G (accessed October 16, 2020).

Smith College Archives. "Mabel Milham Roys and Otelia Cromwell in the Ivy Day Procession at Smith College, 1900." Class of 1900 Records, Smith College. https://libex.smith.edu/omeka/exhibits/show/black-students-alliance/item/414 (accessed October 16, 2020).

Smith, Noah. "Economics Starts Reckoning with Its Gender Bias Problem." *Bloomberg Opinion,* January 10, 2018.

Solomon, Barbara Miller. *In the Company of Educated Women: A History of Women and Higher Education in America*. New Haven, CT: Yale University Press, 1985.

Solomon, Barbara Miller, and Patricia M. Nolan. "Education, Work, Family, and Public Commitment in the Lives of Radcliffe Alumnae, 1883–1928." In *Changing Education: Women as Radicals and Conservators*, ed. Joyce Antler and Sari Knopp Biklin, 139–55. Albany: State University of New York Press, 1990.

Spencer, Herbert. "Psychology of the Sexes." *Popular Science Monthly* 14 (November 1873): 30–38.

——. *Social Statics; or, the Conditions Essential to Human Happiness*. London: John Chapman, 1851.

Spencer, Herbert. *The Study of Sociology*. London: Henry S. King, 1873.

Stage, Sarah. "Home Economics: What's in a Name?" In *Rethinking Home Economics: Women and the History of a Profession*, ed. Sarah Stage and Virginia B. Vincenti, 1–14. Ithaca, NY: Cornell University Press, 1997.

Storrs, Landon R. Y. *The Second Red Scare and the Unmaking of the New Deal Left*. Princeton, NJ: Princeton University Press, 2013.

Strassmann, Diana. "Not a Free Market: The Rhetoric and Disciplinary Authority in Economics." In *Beyond Economic Man: Feminist Theory and Economics*, ed. Marianne A. Ferber and Julie A. Nelson, 54–68. Chicago: University of Chicago Press, 1993.

Strober, Myra H. *Interdisciplinary Conversations: Changing Habits of Thought*. Palo Alto, CA: Stanford University Press, 2011.

Swarthmore College Archives. "Emily Greene Balch Papers." Swarthmore College Peace Collection, Swarthmore College.

Thébaud, Sarah and Maria Charles. "Segregation, Stereotypes, and STEM." *Social Sciences* 7, no. 7 (2018): 1–18.

Thompson, Patricia J. "Beyond Gender: Equity Issues for Home Economics Education." *Theory Into Practice* 25, no. 4 (1986): 276–83.

Thurgood, Lori, Mary J. Golladay, and Susan T. Hill. *U.S. Doctorates in the 20th Century*, NSF 06-319. Arlington, VA: National Science Foundation, Division of Science Resources Statistics, 2006.

Tobin, James. "The First Women." *Heritage Project*. University of Michigan https://heritage.umich.edu/stories/the-first-women/ (accessed October 16, 2020).

Tolbert, Pamela S., and Alice A. Oberfield. "Sources of Organizational Demography: Faculty Sex Ratios in Colleges and Universities." *Sociology of Education* 64, no. 4: 305–14.

Tomaskovic-Devey, Donald. *Gender and Racial Inequality at Work: The Sources and Consequences of Job Segregation*. Ithaca, NY: Cornell University Press, 1993.

Torgler, Benno, and Marco Piatti. *A Century of American Economic Review: Insights on Critical Factors in Journal Publishing*. New York: Palgrave Pivot, 2013.

Trachtenberg, Alan. *The Incorporation of America: Culture and Society in the Gilded Age*. New York: Hill and Wang, 1982.

Tullberg, Rita McWilliams. *Women at Cambridge*. Cambridge: Cambridge University Press, 1998.

University of California–Berkeley. *History of Women Faculty in Economics.* https://www
.econ.berkeley.edu/women-history (accessed July 19, 2021).

U.S. Bureau of the Census. *Thirteenth Census of the United States: 1910,* Population, vol. 4,
Occupations. Washington, DC: U.S. Government Printing Office, 1911.

——. *Fifteenth Census of the United States: 1930, Population,* vol. 5, *Occupations.* Washington, DC: U.S. Government Printing Office, 1933.

——. *Fifteenth Census of the United States, 1930. Population,* vol. 5, *General Report on Occupations.* Washington, DC: U.S. Government Printing Office, 1930.

——. *Historical Statistics of the United States, Colonial Times to 1970.* Bicentennial ed., part 1
and Part 2. Washington, DC: U.S. Printing Office, 1975.

——. *Occupation Statistics, 1910.* Washington, DC: U.S. Government Printing Office, 1914.
https://www.census.gov/library/publications/1914/dec/vol-4-occupations.html.

Valian, Virginia. *Why So Slow? The Advancement of Women.* Cambridge, MA: MIT Press,
1998.

Vassar Encyclopedia. "Mabel Newcomer." http://vcencyclopedia.vassar.edu/faculty/promi
nent-faculty/mabel-newcomer.html (accessed November 20, 2020).

Veblen, Thorstein. *The Theory of the Leisure Class.* New York: Prometheus Books, [1899]
1998.

Vertinsky, Patricia. "Exercise, Physical Capability, and the Eternally Wounded Woman in
Late Nineteenth Century North America." *Journal of Sport History* 14, no. 1 (1987): 7–27.

Walsh, Mary Roth. *Doctors Wanted, No Women Need Apply: Sexual Barriers in the Medical
Profession, 1835–1975.* New Haven, CT: Yale University Press, 1977.

Wayne, Tiffany K. "Education and the Professions." In *Women's Roles in Nineteenth-
Century America,* ed. Tiffany K. Wayne, 79–87. Westport, CT: Greenwood, 2007.

Weeden, Kim A., Sarah Thébaud, and Dafna Gelbgiser. "Degrees of Difference: Gender Segregation of U.S. Doctorates by Field and Program Prestige." *Sociological Science* 4,
(2017): 123–50.

West, James L. W., III. "The Expansion of the National Book Trade." In *A History of the
Book in America,* vol. 4, ed. Carl F. Kaestle and Janice A. Radway, 78–89. Chapel Hill:
University of North Carolina Press, 2009.

Williams, Heather Andrea. *American Slavery: A Very Short Introduction.* Oxford: Oxford
University Press, 2014.

Wilson, Ann. "Settlement Work in a Union Town: Lucile Eaves, The San Francisco Settlement
Association, and Organized Labor, 1894–1906." *Ex Post Facto* 11 (Spring 2002): 79–98.

Wolfers, Justin. "Evidence of a Toxic Environment for Women in Economics." *New York
Times,* August 18, 2017.

Woodson, Carter G. *The Education of the Negro Prior to 1861.* Washington, DC: Associated
Publishers, 1919.

Wooldridge, Jeffrey M. *Introductory Econometrics: A Modern Approach.* Mason, OH:
South-Western Cengage Learning, 2009.

Woolf, Virginia. *Mrs. Dalloway.* London: Hogarth Press, 1925.

Wu, Alice H. "Gender Bias Among Professionals: An Identity-Based Interpretation."
Review of Economics and Statistics 102, no. 5 (2020): 867–80.

——. "Gendered Language on the Economics Job Market Rumors Forum." *American Economic Association Papers and Proceedings* 108 (2018): 175–79.

——. "Gender Stereotyping in Academe: Evidence from Economics Job Market Rumors Forum." Undergraduate thesis. University of California, Berkeley, 2017. https://scholar.harvard.edu/alicewu/publications/gender-stereotyping-academia-evidence-economics-job-market-rumors-forum.

Yale University. *Obituary Record of Yale Graduates, 1922–1923.* New Haven, CT: Yale University, 1923.

Zschoche, Sue. "Dr. Clarke Revisited: Science, True Womanhood, and Female Collegiate Education." *History of Education Quarterly* 29, no. 4 (1989): 545–69.

INDEX

Page locators in italics refer to figures and tables.

Crane, Diane, 138
craniometry and brain weight, 20–21
Cromwell, Otelia, 16, 35
Cross, Ira Brown, 103–13, 115–18, 199n12; at
University of California, 117–18
cultural stereotypes, and occupational
segregation, 6–7, 169
Cunningham, Theodora B., 78

Darwin, Charles, 22
*Das Studium und die Ausübung der
Medizin durch Frauen* (Bischoff), 20, 21
Davenport, Herbert Joseph, 113–16
Davis, Katharine Bement, 78
dean of women, 152, 153
Deibler, F. S. (Frederick Shipp), 65, 67
department chairs, 141
de Vries, Margaret Garritsen, 154
Dewey, Davis Rich, 4, 38, 59–60, 64, 78–79;
and Cross/Eaves controversy, 104–13, 115;
as editor of *AER*, 4, 38, 78–79, 103, 115,
123; organizational format developed by,
157–58; on state of book reviewing, 114
Dewey, John, 123
Dickens, Helen, 32–33
Dimand, Robert W., 164
discourse, professional, 7
discrimination: and free market, 12, 25–28,
143–44, 165; principles adopted by AEA,
4–5, 166, 211n1; theory of, 5–6
disinterestedness, ethics of, 11
dissertations, 37, 60, 86, 169
Distinguished Daughters of Pennsylvania,
33
diversity, and public policy, 8–10
Dixon, Frank H., 58–59, 77
doctorates: and coauthorship, 91–94,
204n27, 204n28; early accomplishments
of women, 30–33; earned by Black women,
31, 43–44, 164–65; earned by men, 38–39,
41, 81, 124; in economics, earned by
women, 2, 37–39, 70–73, 72, 75–76, 76, 88,
145–51; and faculty appointments, 43;

gender difference in economics, 2, 39–42;
in home economics, 152–53; honorary,
118, 120–21; and likelihood of monograph
publication, 87–88, 90–93; mathematics
degrees, 51–52; in other than economic
fields, 27–28, 51, 72, 80, 92–93, 95–98,
124–25, 130–31, 134, 136–38, 204n27;
"Radcliffe-Harvard," 34, 46, 119; and
social status, 27–28, 82; and
specialization, 80; as symbol of
expertise, 120; and tiers of institutions,
40–41; in twenty-first century, 169–70;
women economists characterized as
sociologists, 26–27, 81–82. *See also*
education for women; employment after
doctorate, women's; graduate training
dogma, disciplinary, 6–7
domestic code (cult of womanhood), 19
domestic studies (home economics), 24–25,
70, 78, 151, 152–53
Douglas, Dorothy Wolff, 126–27, 128, 129
Driscoll, Adam, 171
Du Bois, W. E. B., 17
Dulles, Eleanor Lansing, 4, 119–20
Dunbar, Charles F., 38–39, 124–25
Dzuback, Mary Ann, 127

Eaves, Lucile, 101–13, 116–18, 184n1, 199n12,
199n16
Economic Bulletin, 103, 115; books listed in,
86–87, 91, 97, 98, 124
Economic Problems of the Family (Kyrk),
152
economics: classification of economists,
157–63; competition as disciplinary
dogma of, 6–7; doctorates in earned by
women, 37–38, 71–73, 72, 75–76, 76, 88,
145–51; explanations for lack of women
in, 5–9; gender problem in, 2–5;
marginalization of women in, 9, 13, 18,
155, 163–65, 183n61; "mathiness" of, 82,
196n24; and meritocratic mindset, 138;
profession of economist, 161–63;

Hull, Charles H., 57
Hull House, 71
human capital theories, 5
Hunt, Andrea, 171
Hutcheon, Linda, 7
Hypps, Irene Malvan, 164–65

Idaho Industrial Institute, 71
identity, academic, 14, 38, 157–58
individual traits, and cultural gender
  stereotypes, 6–7
institutional affiliation, 14, 78, 83, 99–100,
  186n24; instability of for women, 128; and
  journal positions, 123; and likelihood of
  publication, 129–38, 204n27, 204n28;
  negative effect on likelihood of multiple
  publications, 131–32, 135, 137, 204n27;
  positive effect on likelihood of multiple
  publications, 134–35
institutional discrimination theory, 5–6
Iowa State University, 168
Ivy Day (Smith College), 16
Ivy League schools, 146

Jewish men in publishing, 85
job market rumors graduate student
  forum, 8, 176n32
Johnson, Alvin S., 113–16
Journal of Political Economy (JPE), 86,
  113–16, 122, 202n14
journals, 10, 13; association, 122–23, 133;
  coauthorship of articles, 132–33; "high
  achievers" in, 126–29; multiple articles
  by men in, 130–38; multiple articles by
  women in, 126–29, 132–33, 136; new books
  listed in, 86–87, 90–91, 97–98, 105; no
  doctorate and likelihood of publication,
  131, 133–34, 204n27; and non-AEA
  members, 124–26, 130–32, 135, 137; as
  options for women's participation, 116;
  peer review, 3, 122, 139; in perspective,
  138–39; scholarly, rise of, 120–23;
  sociological, 118; university, 122–23;

women as article subjects, 128–29. *See
  also* old boy network
jurisdictional disputes, 13, 50, 79–82, 156,
  158

Katz, Lawrence, 5
Kelley, Florence, 71
Kemmerer, Edwin W., 103, 115
Kies, Marietta, 71
Kingsbury, Susan, 51, 60, 77
knowledge: consumers vs. producers, 14,
  165; "feminine" and "unfeminine,"
  183n61; gender politics of, 29; unequal
  distribution of, 11
knowledge production, 86, 165; accountable
  to external institutions, 50; faculty's
  emerging role in, 13–14, 121; as social
  process, 28–29; women as active in, 99.
  See also monographs
Kuziemko, Ilyana, 5
Kyrk, Hazel, 152, 207n33

labor market: categories of employment for
  persisters, 73–75, *74–75*; cultural
  stereotypes and occupational
  segregation, 6–7, 169; government
  positions, 67–68, 143–47; and
  institutional connections, 43; and
  marriage, 26, 44–45, 142–43, 149–50;
  segregated, 6, 19, 26, 167; women as
  threat in, 18–19; for women of color, 31;
  and women's likelihood of joining AEA,
  42; women's participation rates, 26;
  during World War II era, 153–54. *See also*
  employment after doctorate, women's;
  free market rhetoric
labor movement, 102; in California, 106, 117,
  201n36
land-grant colleges and universities, 17–18,
  179n12; vocational education, 24–25;
  women as essential to, 18
Lange, Helene, 19–20
Larson, Magali Sarfatti, 11–12

social differentiation, 138
social sciences, 2, 14, 28–29, 80, 82
Social Statics (Spencer), 22
social status, 12–13, 49; and preservation of
    male domination, 23–24, 181n39; sex as
    "master status," 138; women as threat to,
    18–19, 79–82. *See also* competition
sociologists, 13, 51, 81; women with
    doctorates in economics characterized
    as, 26–27, 81–82
sociology, 13–14, 27–28, 80–82, 117, 118, 160;
    women said to be natural constituency
    for, 14, 80, 82
sociology of knowledge tradition, 28–29
Solomon, Barbara, 142
Southern United States, 44–45
South Park Settlement (San Francisco), 102,
    198n4
specialization, 80
Spencer, Herbert, 21–22, 181n33
standards, 6, 11–12, 29, 118, 121–22, 156–57,
    163
Stanford, Jane, 50, 102
Stanford University, 23, 50, 101–3;
    Department of Economics and
    Sociology, 103
state universities: and Black students, 16–17,
    44; coeducational, 17–19; dean of women
    role, 152, 153; in South, 16–17; women's
    employment in, 14, 146
status groups, 5–6
Stebbins, Lucy Ward, 152
Stecker, Margaret Loomis, 126–27, 203n24
STEM fields, 2, 6, 93
Stockwell, Madelon, 18
Strober, Myra, 5, 207n33
Study of Sociology, The (Spencer), 23
suffrage movement, 71
Syracuse University, 27, 39, 70

Talbot, Marion, 152, 207n31
Taussig, Frank W., 124–25, 159
Taylor, James Monroe, 36

teams, diversity in, 8–10
tenacious persisters, as category of women
    economists, 71–76, 72, 74–75, 76, 83
tenure, 3, 170–71, 184n1
Thayer, John Eliot, 124
Thébaud, Sarah, 2, 6, 169
Theory of the Leisure Class, The (Veblen),
    23–24, 25
Thomas, M. Carey, 35–36
Timlin, Mabel Frances, 168
Trinity College (Dublin), 20
Troy Female Seminary, 19
tuition, for women only, 25

undergraduate training and degrees, 16–17,
    27, 34–36, 39–42
Undergraduate Women in Economics
    project, 171
universities. *See* colleges and universities
University of Arizona, 140–41, 205n2
University of California–Berkeley, 40, 41,
    102, 167
University of Chicago, 13–14, 23, 25, 27, 101;
    Department of Household
    Administration, 152; doctorates awarded
    to women, 40, 168; *Journal of Political
    Economy* (*JPE*), 86, 113–16, 122, 202n14;
    journals, 122
University of Illinois, 41
University of Illinois at Urbana-
    Champaign, 168
University of Iowa, 41
University of Maryland, 44
University of Michigan, 18, 41
University of Minnesota, *AER* editors
    from, 123
University of Nebraska, 23, 25, 102, 181n39
University of Pennsylvania, 31–32;
    doctorates awarded to women, 31, 40, 41
University of Virginia, 23
University of Wisconsin, 18, 22–23, 35, 37,
    45, 123; *AER* editors from, 123; doctorates
    awarded to women, 40, 124